Eros
and
Vision

Jean H. Hagstrum

Eros and Vision: The Restoration to Romanticism

Northwestern University Press
Evanston, IL

Northwestern University Press
Evanston, IL 60201

Printed in the United States of America

Library of Congress Cataloging-in-Publication Data

Hagstrum, Jean H.
    Eros and vision : the restoration to romanticism / Jean H.
Hagstrum.
        p.   cm.
    Bibliography: p.
    Includes index.
    ISBN 0-8101-0828-3. — ISBN 0-8101-0829-1 (pbk.)
    1. English literature—18th century—History and criticism.
2. English literature—Early modern, 1500-1700—History and
criticism. 3. English literature—19th century—History and
criticism. I. Title.
PR442.H34 1989
820'.9—dc19   88-36852
                                                                        CIP

*For my
lifelong friend
and
dearest reader,
Moody Prior*

Contents

List of Illustrations

Preface

The twelve essays that constitute this book were written from about 1972 almost to the present. They represent, I believe, my latest and best thinking about the period—from the Restoration to Romanticism—with which my scholarly career has been mostly concerned. I use the word *period* in the singular because in my view of art and literature from 1660 to 1827 (the year Blake died) I see an inescapable continuity despite wrenching revolutions in politics, religion, philosophy, and artistic taste. I have just said *despite,* but it may be the wrong word. For the continuity I have in mind is itself *made up* of contrast and conflict, often of an invigorating, intense, and altogether fruitful variety. I am therefore confident that I am true to my historical materials when I juxtapose prominently within the compass of a single volume such energetic contrarieties as Samuel Johnson and William Blake and compress within the tight boundaries of a short title two such potentially tendentious and volatile words as *eros* and *vision,* which could easily fly apart. I do so for both Johnsonian and Blakean reasons. Johnson believed that without the spicy friction of dissimilitude there could be neither art nor love, criticism nor friendship; Blake believed that without the intellectual battle of contraries there could be no progression whatever—anywhere, at any time. "Opposition is true Friendship," wrote Blake, and he might have added, "true Art" as well.

The entire period that concerns me here, beginning in a Restoration after a bloody civil war and ending in powerful reactions to revolutions on two continents, did, in my considered judgment, achieve this kind of complex unity and troubled integrity—a perception which I think is strongly supported by the essays that follow. Such persistent though always threatened continuity is necessarily revealed best in the latter end of a period. Blake, Byron, Shelley, and Jane Austen (the later authors I discuss more fully here) show that they are absorbing a heritage even when—perhaps especially when—they are revising their predecessors and inverting previously used terms of creation and discourse. This kind of argument I have made at length about other Romantics in *The Romantic Body* (1985): here I need only repeat my conviction that most early nineteenth-century creators come into the sharpest focus for the critic or historian who knows and senses along with them their inheritance from those earlier authors who are also the subject of my inquiries here. Thus I hope the reader will find it illuminating and invigorating to ignore conventional curricular and textbookish separations of the Romantic from the so-called Neoclassic and Augustan (both inadequate and outdated words!), while at the same time he confronts within each author discussed and each topic explored the inherent polarities and also a consuming drive toward wholeness.

The quest by literary leaders for integrity within themselves and their culture is, I believe, the underlying though sometimes unstated preoccupation of the period and also of the essays in this book. Self-fashioning in and for the secular world did not go out with the Renaissance; and baroque religion and art on the post-Tridentine Continent and intense dissenting piety in England were not ultimately able to redirect the Western gaze from this world to the next. The searchings and climbings of my period were made in a world of radically changing values and opening possibilities, and when the individual achieved intellectual integrity it was by absorbing history, by locating oneself in relation to a challenged tradition, by creating a canon of work that at once reflects and changes culture. It is not by chance that chronologically the earliest writer I analyze, Dryden, I present as a young dramatist coming into his own in that eventful postwar and Restoration decade, the 1660s. His struggle toward synthesis and individuality is in large measure that of the eighteenth century he so significantly helped to create. Samuel Johnson stressed his urbanity, naturalness, and clarity, praising him for having found literary England brick and leaving it marble. But in order to bring out the conflict that is almost always the matrix of achievement, I have privileged what has too often been ne-

glected, the antithetical underdog in Dryden's binary thought-struc-
tures—the devil, animals, darkness—in short, the grotesque. And in
the last essay of the volume I portray a Blake in tortured struggle
ultimately fashioning an independent, fiery, and productive personality,
not indeed against a literary ancestor but more deeply against a religious ancestor, God, whom in the end he transforms into a psychologically nuanced, humanly plausible, and artistically compelling father.

What I have just said about psychic integrity leads me directly to
the first important meaning I wish the reader to derive from my title
word, *vision*. In its largest sense it refers to global interior seeing and
hence invokes religion, directly or indirectly, even though that invo-
cation may at first seem paradoxical in an increasingly secular ambience. For me some personal ironies reside in my last sentence. As I
recall it now, my earliest experience of the eighteenth century centered
in Voltaire and Enlightened France; and I am certain I then hoped that
in my investigations I would escape religion or at least find articulate
allies as I set out to *épater les fidèles*. But the eighteenth-century fledg-
ling had not counted on finding a manuscript sermon by Johnson in
the Sterling Library at Yale, which he felt he must exploit and which
made him confront directly the religious thought of that great "ratio-
nalist." Nor was he prepared for the discovery that among the wittiest
and seemingly most irreverent satirists Dryden was a Christian polemicist, Pope a Roman Catholic, and Swift and Sterne Anglican divines.
And he soon learned that Blake for all his blazingly irreverent antino-
mianism and religious revisionism publicly identified himself as a soldier of Christ.

I do not know that many beginning scholars today share my own
early expectations of a largely secular milieu, but the present collection
demonstrates to me once more and many years later that these were
egregiously wrong. My longest essay, the first, is concerned with a key
eighteenth-century and Romantic term, *conscious*. Almost every student of English literature has heard of Steele's once famous and influential play, *The Conscious Lovers*. But how many, even among specialists
in the period, know what its title adjective means? Or are aware that
it can mean both *innocent* and *guilty*, that it introduces a pre-Freudian
version of the unconscious, that it is related to the philosophical search

for the self, that it could be an important critical term in disclosing the dynamics of a Jane Austen novel, or that it inevitably brings in *conscience*—and religion of both a legalistic and charismatic variety? Many of the essays on individual writers reveal a deep and complicated engagement with faith and morals, and it may not therefore be inappropriate that the book should end with essays on Blake's Christ and Blake's God.

But if *vision* invokes the religious, it inevitably, for me at least, invokes the visual as well—the imagistic, the pictorial. In an earlier book, *The Sister Arts* (1958), I considered the two arts of poetry and painting together, in close and mutual relationship, and investigated that hardy perennial of criticism and aesthetics, *ut pictura poesis* (as a picture, so a poem), stressing the analogy of the arts. Other scholars have since then studied the coincidence of the visual and the verbal with exciting results that show that the sisters often quarrel and that their opposition no less than their harmony has fructified our culture, past and present. But neither binary oppositions nor analogous relationships intended to produce a *tertium quid* (the illuminated book, *ekphrasis,* the emblem, film, TV scripts, videos) are my concern in this volume. Some of this pictorialist legacy from my own past does, to be sure, guide me in trying to establish a relationship between the arts of verbal and visual satire when I discuss masterpieces by Dryden, Pope, and Swift, and I consciously try to enrich the vocabulary for satire-criticism by introducing such concepts as "emblematic caricature" and "portrait caricature," which suggest that terms from either one art or the other are, alone and separate, truly inadequate for a complex critical task (see pp. 33–48).

In this volume, however, I am less concerned with the aesthetic ligature of two radically diverse modes of expression than with the older, mutually illustrative role of the two arts together, though I hope I dig more deeply than did my own predecessors of a generation or so ago. Here I find it useful to consider the verbal and the visual as parallel routes into and out of the imagination, as parallel revealers of *Zeitgeist,* as mutually illuminating definers of terms, movements, and meanings. Thus the illustrations of the Eros-Psyche legend (see pp. 72–83 and figs. 2–7) are intended to help the verbal texts define that important but extremely elusive concept, *delicacy,* while at the same time revealing a century-long feminization of culture in an increasing emphasis on similitude and equality in sexual relationships. Another way of putting all this is that my old interest in the sister arts is now allied with my newer interest in psychology—with the complex but fructifying interpenetration of artistic and personal emotion. Thus to explain the spell that Ann Radcliffe's extremely influential novel, *The Mysteries of Udolpho,* wove and weaves (see pp. 172–75), I have created a new term, the *psychological picturesque,* which unites the literary rendition of sublime and picturesque landscape with erotic desire, disclosing in the verbally sensuous the humanly sensual.

I have said that I was confronted early in my career by the religious in the eighteenth century and Romanticism. I came to the erotic late—and that under the tutelage of Jane Austen, strange though this may seem. When, as has been my wont with words that wear a patina of unfamiliarity, I tried to define *sensibility* and help my students understand what Austen and her predecessors meant by that term, I came to see that it possessed a distinctly erotic coloration and that it had had a long and complex history; and in a loving parody of a favorite author I applied the phrase *sex and sensibility* to a transforming cultural force that fermented from the Restoration to Romanticism (see *Sex and Sensibility: Ideal and Erotic Love from Milton to Mozart,* 1980). I have come to agree fully with Lawrence Stone that from 1660 to well past 1800 "individualism" was in fact "*affective.*" It should surprise no one who is familiar with my last two books (see also *The Romantic Body: Love and Sexuality in Keats, Wordsworth, and Blake,* 1985) or knows something of my ongoing project of tracing love and sexuality from antiquity to the Renaissance that I have become incapable of defining the sensibility of authors like Gray and Byron without trying to find out as much as I can about their particular sexual orientations (see pp. 156–67 and 177–79). Although a few years have now passed since I first lectured on Gray or wrote on Byron, I still strongly believe that the sensibility that lay behind the *Elegy Written in a Country Churchyard* was homoerotic and that the Thyrza lyrics were addressed to a young man for whom Byron felt sexual passion. And I hold these convictions without forfeiting a scintilla of sympathy for either author!

My long absorption in the art and mythology of Blake has shown me that sexual energy was omnipresent, flowing from word to design, design to word, and from one state of the human soul to another, being present with conscious and corrupt perversity in Experience as well as being delicately and perhaps unconsciously present in Innocence. It is also demonstrably present—vitally and centrally—even in the poet-painter's religion, as the illustration on Plate 21 of his *Milton* clearly shows (see my fig. 20, facing p. 217). Blake daringly gives powerful erotic implications to the scene in which Los, Blake's poet-figure, self-surrogate, and Christ-analogue, "kissed me and wish'd me health, / And I became One Man with him arising in my strength." The head of the kneeling Blake is thrust in an upward flamelike surge of the greatest intensity between the open legs of Los-Christ, the poet's eyes, nose, and mouth close to the standing figure's male member. An intense feeling of sexual identification seems inescapably present in one of Blake's most memorable visions.* I cannot always illustrate quite so vividly the overlapping of my categories as in this stunning union of agape and eros, nor do I wish to suggest that Blake's total orientation was homo-erotic. But I cannot escape the view that human sexuality—quite apart from any temporary or permanent orientation that it may take—has not left the literature of our period untouched, even in its more rational and controlled expressions.

The erotic in literature tends to shift the center of gravity to the author and to privilege biography, a fact that makes many queasy. I recognize the risks but have always been willing to take them. As one who even in the days of the New Criticism tended to write contextually, extratextually, supratextually, and more recently even subtextually, I do not understand why the author's psyche should be placed out of critical bounds any more than society, politics, religion, the related arts, or antecedent literature. When we seek to discover the historical and personal moment—or the desire to evade or alter it—as the motive

---

*This union of the religious and the erotic I had noticed some years ago, but I was disinclined to let it appear in a *Festschrift* honoring Geoffrey Keynes, where this essay first appeared. Some may find it amusing—or perhaps pathetic—that I should worry about offending Sir Geoffrey but not about a possible offense to Christ.

or matrix of expression, we may of course dirty the imaginative process with messy reality or complicate it with our own contemporary concerns. I make no secret of my interest in feminist criticism and in the thought of minority sexualities, which exert constant pressure on me in preparing my future study of the couple in earlier cultures. In *Sex and Sensibility* I found a feminist subtext in the conventional Nicholas Rowe's *The Fair Penitent* and a ringing indictment of society and a cry for freedom in the bourgeois George Lillo's prostitute Millwood of *The London Merchant.* At least one of my readers has found a touch of New Historicism in my treatment of the society Blake attacked, where "centuries of false seeing [had] been reified into institutions and cultural forms" (see later, p. 242). Some critics have detected Freud in my analyses of Goethe, Rousseau, and Thomas Gray in the pages that follow (see pp. 63, 65–66, 160–61). And although my conscious purpose in addressing Deconstruction and its allies in the lecture I here reprint (pp. 139–51) was to praise Samuel Johnson, on the bicentenary of his death, for his largely unsung critical sympathy and flexibility and to use his wit to expose verbal strutting and mental obfuscation, a few have found *me* excessively tolerant of my avant-garde colleagues.

To all this I must plead guilty, for I have found much challenge and stimulation in the current atmosphere. But in certain respects I have always kept my distance. Although impressed as much, I would suppose, as anyone by the ambiguities and paradoxes of literature, I have never shared the present taste for indeterminacy and radical undecidability; and the reader will find me quite unashamedly pushing toward positive and resolving interpretations whenever I think the evidence (available to any trained literary critic and student of culture) warrants taking a stand or tipping the scales. Nor have I been converted by the recent adherence to fatalism in language, whose prisoners we are alleged to be, although now and then we are allowed to rattle our chains. I do not believe that critical namings or analytical taxonomies create per se literary or philosophical being or value—though they may baptize, so to speak, bringing works of art into a new critical and scholarly fellowship. And not only works of art but scholars as well, for skill in the sister arts—to take an example close to my scholarly heart—has brought about several joint appointments to literary and art historical departments and also several new interdisciplinary groupings in the world of humanistic learning. In any event I regard the modest additions to or revisions of critical vocabulary that I have made in my earlier writings and that I propose in some of the pieces printed here not as determinative reifications but as suggestions that could affect perception and even subsequent behavior if persuasion has indeed taken place.

If I break with the dogma that language and its structures constitute a kind of fatality for writer and critic alike, I must also confess discomfort with the view that antecedent literary achievements and forms are uniquely or primarily influential in giving the poet his voice and his mode. This disagreement appears most clearly in my last essay, where I differ with Harold Bloom about the nature of Blake's *agon.*

In summary, I resist the view that an author is essentially a structural persona, a created and conventional stereotype, a linguistic-literary construct, or a belated comer produced by rhetoric, grammar, or antecedent artistic achievement.

I said in opening this preface that a portrayal of the self struggling to achieve identity in relation to culture is the central and unifying preoccupation of these essays and of the historical time-span they cover. In that quest for a communicating individuality, a quest often characterized by great personal and literary intensity, the psychic, the social, and the artistic "interinanimate." In such an ambience eros and vision are magnetic to one another; and when pried apart but held not too far from each other, they create a field of force. From that field the energies of *belles lettres* arise. Art exhilarates, then, not primarily by expressing ideas and doctrines, not by recalling other art, not by reflecting the structures inherent in language, although it may do all these—but by pulsing with the very rhythms of social and individual, intellectual and emotional life.

For me to pay all the debts I have incurred in the eighteenth-century and Romantic research that produced this book would plunge me into total bankruptcy. I hope some of them are at least acknowledged if not fully liquidated in my notes. In connection with these essays and this publication I should like to thank the staff of the Northwestern University Press, its director, Jonathan Brent, its Managing Editor, Susan Harris, and its anonymous consultants. I remain indebted to the Northwestern University Library for its many courtesies, especially to Rolf Erickson and Russell Maylone. The following—a few of whom have read all the chapters, others some, still others one only—also deserve my formal thanksgiving but also absolution from responsibility for errors and infelicities that remain: Marshall Brown, John J. Burke, Jr., James Downey, James Engell, Christopher Fox, Donald Greene, Emily Grosholz, Wendell Harris, Robert D. Hume, J. Paul Hunter, Paul J. Korshin, Jerome McGann, Earl Miner, Morton D. Paley, Arthur Sherbo, the late H. T. Swedenberg, Jr., Aileen Ward, René Wellek. As always, I have learned from and been encouraged by my Northwestern colleagues, Lawrence Lipking and Richard Wendorf. I wish to thank Martin Mueller, Chair of the English Department at Northwestern, for his constant support and also the courteous and efficient departmental staff, especially Kathleen Daniels for skillful typing and Kirstie Felland and Jamie O'Connor for their help in computer-related operations.

The dedication is made in loving gratitude, but I cannot believe it is an overestimation. Moody Prior has, through the many, many years of our friendship and academic association, read and commented on, intelligently, independently, and lengthily, everything I have ever written—except for a sermon in Swedish and a few other *jeux d'ésprit* which I published in my predoctoral days.

I thank the following for permission to reprint, with very few changes, materials first published by them:

AMS Press for "Toward a Profile..." (my chap. 1), originally in *Psychology and Literature in the Eighteenth Century,* ed. Christopher Fox (1987).

University of California Press for "Verbal and Visual Caricature..." (my chap. 2), originally in *England in the Restoration and Early Eighteenth Century,* ed. H. T. Swedenberg, Jr. (1972).

William Andrews Clark Memorial Library for "Such, Such..." (my chap. 3), originally in *Changing Taste in Eighteenth-Century Art and Literature,* ed. Earl Miner (1972).

University of Chicago Press for "Eros and Psyche" (my chap. 4), originally in *Critical Inquiry,* Spring 1977.

Unwin Hyman Limited for "Dryden's Grotesque" (my chap. 5), originally in *Writers and their Background: John Dryden,* ed. Earl Miner.

University of Wisconsin Press for "Samuel Johnson and the *Concordia Discors . . .*" (my chap. 6), originally in *The Unknown Samuel Johnson,* ed. John J. Burke, Jr., and Donald Kay (1983).

The Georgia Review for "Samuel Johnson among the Deconstructionists" (my chap. 7), originally pub. Fall 1985.

McGill-Queen's University Press for "Gray's Sensibility" (my chap. 8), originally in *Fearful Joy,* ed. James Downey and Ben Jones (1974).

University Press of Virginia for "Pictures to the Heart" (my chap. 9), originally in *Greene Centennial Studies,* ed. Paul J. Korshin and Robert R. Allen (1984).

Oxford University Press for "Byron's Songs of Innocence" (my chap. 10), originally in *Evidence in Literary Scholarship,* ed. René Wellek and Alvaro Ribeiro (1979).

Oxford University Press for "Christ's Body" (my chap. 11), originally in *William Blake: Essays in Honour of Sir Geoffrey Keynes,* ed. Morton D. Paley and Michael Phillips (1973).

Department of English and American Literature and Language, Harvard University, for " 'What Seems to Be: Is' " (my chap. 12), originally in *Johnson and his Age,* ed. James Engell (Harvard English Studies 12).

Part

I

1
Toward a Profile of
Conscious—*and* Unconscious—
in Eighteenth-Century
Literature

*F*rom one view *conscious* appears to be an empty word, requiring a phrasal neighborhood to give it content. When we encounter it standing alone we are impelled to ask, "conscious of what?" or "conscious to what?" The dative complement is unfamiliar today, but the genitive is fully familiar—as familiar as a noun clause following the word as its object: "I am conscious that my subject is complex." In such constructions as these the word reveals its dependence. But it does possess viability even when it is deponent (or cut off and truncated), and it can stand alone when it has uncoupled its phrasal or clausal followers. In modern speech we are all too familiar with such verbal detachments, and we speak of people who are, *tout simplement,* committed, detached, disinterested, convinced; and we praise—vulgarly and sentimentally, I am afraid—the "aware, caring person" without inquiring too precisely what it is that he is aware of or cares about. In eighteenth-century usage the word *conscious,* like the word *sensible* without its *of,* should give us pause when it remains an unattended adjective, modifying, to be sure, but itself unmodified. Do we know immediately or precisely what a conscious moon is, a conscious night, a conscious heart, or why in Wordsworth the Parcae are conscious?[1] We reach for meaning when in Dryden "the conscious

Priest . . . / Stood ready," when Pope says that "secret Transports touch'd the conscious Swain," when in *Clarissa* Lovelace makes a "conscious girl," who had just been described as *"sensible all over,"* blush again, or when in *Northanger Abbey* Henry Tilney is introduced to Mrs. Morland by her "conscious daughter."[2] Such adjectives, especially when modifying a real person and not a personified entity, are teasing or striking, perhaps even a bit upsetting. Even more so is the independent predicate nominative used by William Cowper as he ruminates before a fire: "I am conscious, and confess, / Fearless, a soul that does not always think."[3]

The reason such passages produce at least a brief pause of wonder is not simply that the meanings have changed since the seventeenth and eighteenth centuries but that an essentially parasitical word has been removed from its vine and allowed to stand unsupported, with the result that we must supply content, meaning, value, association.

It is today a fashionable practice—but also a very sound instinct—that leads us to etymology, and in this case the Latin supplies meanings that are simple and literal but also complex and even paradoxical. Such range and richness of meaning will be best served if I summarize this linguistic heritage by using a series of contrasts. *Conscious* refers to joint knowledge with another person, the prefix *con* being of importance; but it also refers to solitary knowledge, to knowledge of and by itself. Both the sacred and the individual knowledge can be guilty: a secret shared is often only a titillating delight but in other circumstances it may be criminal or conspiratorial; possessed alone, it can be self-accusatory but it can alternatively be innocent, self-fortifying, or capable of strengthening the bond of friendship. *Conscious* was not only used of human beings but of animals, plants, inanimate natural objects, and literary personifications; and it suggests complex relations within people, among people, between man and his environment, man and his intellectual products. Perhaps the deepest-lying, at once the most disturbing and fructifying of these contrasts, is the one between guilt and goodness—if not moral goodness, then at least some kind of good for the individual concerned.

This last contrast can be best illustrated from the *Aeneid,* the ancient literary work that most influenced the English uses of *conscious.*

5

Toward a Profile of Conscious

In its fourth book Dido and Aeneas meet in a cave and consummate their love. Though divinely arranged and even divinely sanctioned, this event Virgil indubitably regarded as evil—as a cause of death and woe; and Dido was as seriously deluded to think that it was love-inspired as she was sinful to veil it with the sacred name of marriage. To this union, pregnant with future suffering and peril, there are uncomfortable and disquieting witnesses: "fulsere ignes [lightnings flashed], "ulularunt . . . Nymphae" [nymphs howled], and "*conscius* Aether / conubiis" [literally, the air was knowledgeable with the "bridal" couple], the air and the lovers sharing a mischievous secret.[4] The use of the term is brilliant: the *con-* extends the guilty *-scius* to the natural surroundings, making an erring woman and man form with nature itself an ominous and menacing trio.

Book XII brings to a tragic end the heroic life of the third great character of the epic, the raging, warlike, but essentially courageous and noble Turnus. Not long before his grim death at the hands of Aeneas, Virgil describes his divided, tortured, but heroic mind in a subjectively directed passage highly congenial to the term *conscius:*

> Stupid he sate, his eyes on earth declin'd,
> And various cares revolving in his mind:
> Rage, boiling from the bottom of his breast,
> And sorrow mix'd with shame, his soul oppress'd;
> And conscious worth lay lab'ring in his thought,
> And love by jealousy to madness wrought.[5]

Dryden's "conscious worth" is Virgil's famous and influential "conscia virtus," which could also be conscious valor, might, or moral goodness. In any case, the phrase personifies a human quality, and transfers consciousness from the person to the personification, directing attention not to nature outside, as *Aether* does, but to the inner man.

Aeneas's decisive encounters with both Dido and Turnus have evoked the word *conscious,* the first to mean a guilty knowledge which the lovers share with nature and the other inner knowledge arising from a caldron of conflicting and agitated emotions to help nerve the hero's final foe to action. Both uses accompany eminently human conditions and are instinct with Virgil's legendary pathos. Together, the two constitute a paradox or a potential ambivalence. *Conscious* means guilty or innocent, referring either to a shared secret that chooses the dark over the light or to an inner awareness that drives outward from the recesses of the heart to daylight action and accomplishment, heroic though doomed.

The Guilty *Conscious*

I shall in this chapter be much concerned with these polarities of guilt and innocence in the English word *conscious* and also with the possible meeting, or the mutual canceling out, of these and other extremes. I do not of course wish to ignore what is less frequent and certainly less dramatic in English, the etymological meaning that the Oxford English Dictionary gives first: "Knowing, or sharing the knowledge of anything, together with another; . . ." That usage can be illustrated in Swift, who keeps it poetically secret whether Vanessa meets any success whatever in wooing Cadenus but who does give several alternative possibilities. These "Must never to Mankind be told, / Nor shall the conscious Muse unfold" (lines 826–27), where I take it that the Muse, quite without guilt or censure, though not without some coyness, "knows with" the couple, whose secret she keeps.

Such plain, untortured meaning our word might have had more frequently had not that powerful Christian word *conscience* (etymologically synonymous with *consciousness*) entered Western culture with a panoply of divine sanction. A "conscious" person who is also a believer will not only recall and so witness his own actions and secrets, shared or unshared; he will judge them. C. S. Lewis has neatly summarized the word's history: *conscience* "passed from the witness-box to the bench and even to the legislator's throne."[6] So deeply did self-examination become involved with self-evaluation that the two cannot easily be separated—nor can reason and the emotions, which it would seem inevitably unite under the pressures and complexities of the Christian moral life. As a medieval scholar has said of the period of his specialization, "Logically, there is a transition from being witness to being judge but, psychologically, recall and judgment are often simultaneous."[7] That simultaneity continued long after the Middle Ages and well into the eighteenth century, as the example of the tender-conscienced Samuel Johnson abundantly proves. For him merely to recall in solitude his inner state, present or past, was inevitably to judge it. Conscience in our culture simply cannot be divorced from conscious.

Believing this as I do, and have, it should not have been necessary to remind me that *conscious* is inevitably implicated with guilt, and I take this occasion to thank Arthur Sherbo for having brought back to my own consciousness the dark side of *conscious.*[8] Certainly the pre-Johnson dictionaries from 1662 on, where the word primarily and regularly means "inwardly guilty," "culpable," "self-convicted," bear him out.[9] Since the verbal inheritance from the Latin permitted *conscious* to refer equally to self-indictment or to self-exculpation, the prominence of guilt-meanings in modern times seems eloquent tribute to the √ continuing hold of Christian guilt-feelings. Surely the emphasis upon original and all-penetrating sin bears out Donald Greene's belief that Augustinianism remained powerful in the eighteenth century,[10] and explains—much more satisfactorily than the classical context of poetic diction that Sherbo brings forward—the persisting fact that an originally neutral word like "knowing with" should be so deeply drenched in mischief. Those marvelously revealing letters of the religious and scrupulous Clarissa display the Christian's dilemma: God is "the first gracious Planter," and so when the girl looks within she finds guiding principles already "implanted" which she should be able to follow. But at the same time God is "the all-gracious Inflicter," who must chasten us because we vaunt our "good inclinations" and are strangely drawn to sinning even "in our best performances."[11] *Conscious* being an inward-tending term, Clarissa as the most subjectively oriented of the great heroines of English literature may be one of our best guides to its meanings and implications even when she does not use it.

Arthos's list of the vocabulary of stock diction shows that most of the poetic uses of *conscious* from the seventeenth century on make guilty meanings predominate, as do Sherbo's more extensive word-surveys.[12] From Milton to Jane Austen the word often evokes some degree of guilt, and I do not need now to multiply examples. But because previous scholars have tended to concentrate on *conscious* as an instance of Latinate poetic diction, which often smells a bit of the lamp,

I do need to assert that English writers often used the term with solemn moral purpose in prose and poetry, in Latin and English. In Milton's *In Quintum Novembris* (line 150) the *tellus* is *conscia* because it is stained with crime and vengeance; in *Paradise Lost* (6:521) Night is "conscious" because it witnesses and is privy to the secret and abominable manufacture of the first artillery. In Dryden's translations of Ovid's epistles, the nurse in "Canace to Macareus" (line 56) is "conscious" because she sees and collaborates in the crime of incest, and in "Helen to Paris" Helen has "fearful conscious eyes" (line 143) because of her sin.

Some of these examples point to a peculiarly close association between the word *conscious* and sexual sin—an association forged because sinful lovers inevitably come in pairs and share guilty secrets, making the prefix of association (*con*) as apposite as the suffix of knowledge. Milton is quite explicit about this: because the night was made for love and associated with sexual activity, he encumbers the postlapsarian dreams of the first pair "with conscious [that is, guilty] dreams" (*Paradise Lost,* 9:1050). Pope's use of the term echoes Milton's brilliantly: he transfers to the night the guilt of Eloisa's and Abelard's love, enriching and deepening the term by associating it with several oxymorons like "unholy joy":

> All my loose soul unbounded springs to thee.
> O curst, dear horrors of all-conscious night!
> How glowing guilt exalts the keen delight!
> (lines 224, 228–30)

Pope's lines, though morally serious, are nevertheless witty and stylish as he ramifies Eloisa's pleasing guilt—Abelard's "fair frame" is "That cause of all my guilt, and all my joy" (lines 337–38)—and they can be used to make still another point: that though *conscious* often refers to deep guilt and its attendant sufferings, it can concurrently be used lightly and whimsically. The "conscious tail" of Gray's cat is sensitive and expresses joy, but there is also about this organ of pleasure more than a tinge of guilt in the adjective because it points to an imminent fall. Thus though guilt may lurk stealthily in Selima's undulating, serpentine tail, the imbuing of it with consciousness is primarily light and witty.[13] Cowper is often capable of using the term in contexts of guilt and suffering and also of large, optimistic religious meaning; but he too can use it whimsically, delicately, in a mood of playful self-censure. He sits before a domestic fire and reflects on minds that think and on those indisposed to any thought at all:

> Laugh ye, who boast your more mercurial powers,
> That never feel a stupor, know no pause,
> Nor need one; I am conscious, and confess,
> Fearless, a soul that does not always think.
> (*The Task,* 4:282–85)

One scholar has found Cowper's use of the term in this passage "epoch-al," a "pre-Romantic discovery of consciousness" that makes the decade of the 1780s notable.[14] Even though before Cowper wrote there had been a long philosophical debate about whether the soul thinks continuously—a tradition to which I shall return at the close—I am not sure that his *conscious* here means much more than the following when he says "I am conscious": I plead guilty now and then to having a vacant mind when I sit before my fire. The immediately subsequent passage, with its praise of the free play of fancy, may indeed be important in cultural history; but the use of *conscious* I have just quoted is not. At most a charming example of the "unballasting" of a word that had for many years carried a heavy freight of guilty moral meanings, it is neither unique or pioneering.

The *Conscious* of Innocence and Virtue

Only an exhaustive word-count, in the manner of Josephine Miles, with a careful assessment of meanings would show whether as the century progressed there was a bleaching out of the guilty stains in *conscious.* C. S. Lewis has suggested that when Hamlet says that "conscience does make cowards of us all," it is the fear of hell that should give us pause.[15] Whether between that day and Cowper's use of the word to mean guiltless guilt the word reflects an important change in religious *mentalité,* I am unable to say. But it is noteworthy that later dictionaries than the ones I referred to earlier—specifically Johnson's and Sheridan's—though they recognize both guilt and innocence in the noun *consciousness,* keep from their definitions of the adjective all overt or prominent traces of sin or evil.[16] If such lexical elimination of seriously guilty meanings from the word *conscious* reveals a wide consensus, this fact would represent, I believe, not the creation of new meanings for the term but a movement from one of the ancient polar meanings to the other. For we must recall that the heritage from Latin also includes the personification *conscia virtus,* which Virgil had used more than once and which appeared with noteworthy frequency in poetic translations and works influenced by the Latin classics. In Latin *virtus* could mean almost any kind of power, from force to moral goodness, though one supposes that the idea of power prevailed. It seems to have been different in Christian England where the term *conscious virtue* and its cognates seems mostly, though by no means always, to invoke goodness of character. As that moralization, if not Christianization, of the phrase took place, *conscious* came to be attached to so many ethical and psychological benefits that its guilt-associations seem to a somewhat less than systematic surveyor to have been, if not forgotten, at least strongly competed with. The personified virtues or values that wear the label *conscious* are impressive in number and dignity. The "conscious virtue" that the old Emperor in Dryden's *Aureng-Zebe* possesses even in his withered age (Act II, lines 395–97) may be the strength of a soldier rather than goodness—the aged hero may indeed be Virgil's good old wrestler Entellus *redivivus.* But when Dryden says in *The Hind and the Panther* that "conscious merit may be justly bold" (3:1381), when Pope finds that "conscious Honour is to feel no sin" (Bk. I, Ep. i, line 93 of Horace), when Johnson rejoices that the "conscious heart / With virtue's sacred ardour glows" (Horace, *Odes,* I, xxii; line 1), and perhaps even when Swift praises "conscious pride" ("Sir W—— T——'s late Illness," line 11), we encounter only a fraction of the many ethical valorizations of *conscious.* Admittedly my examples come from contexts of poetic exaltation—even at times from fairly direct translations—and are not entirely free of neoclassical artificiality. But consider a fine passage in Hume's prose: "Who is not struck with any signal instance of greatness of mind or dignity of character; with elevation of sentiment, disdain of slavery, and that noble pride and spirit, which arises from conscious virtue?"[17] This noble association of a grand civic spirit with the Virgilian term shows that the innocent *conscious* no less than the guilty *conscious* is vastly more important than a recurring flicker of poetic ornament.

What did *conscious* mean for Steele? It is Hume's meanings, though with somewhat less civic and more individual *éclat,* which I believe to be primarily present in his famous dramatic title, *The Conscious Lovers.* The term is capacious and sturdy and can easily bear the weight of honorific language from *Spectator* 75, par. 4: "Humanity and good Nature, fortified by the Sense of Virtue." In fact, the word *Sense* may be a close equivalent of *consciousness.* Fortunately Steele obliges us by using our term directly and in ways that show a self-aware word-definer laboriously at his task. Will Honeycomb describes a woman in a nearby box as follows:

> Behold, you who dare, that charming Virgin. Behold the Beauty of her Person chastised by the Innocence of her Thoughts. Chastity, Good-Nature, and Affability are the Graces that play in her Countenance; she knows she is handsome, but she knows she is good. Conscious Beauty adorn'd with conscious Virtue! (*Spectator* 4, par. 6)

The passage is highly revealing, to say the least. Steele lays heavy emphasis on the *science* (knowledge, of course, and a wide-eyed knowledge at that!) in consciousness. If Indiana and Bevil Junior in the play are conscious in this manner, they will inescapably know it. It is thus not sufficient to be honorable and chaste; you must be fully aware of your virtues and willing to discuss them at the proper time. Long before she can be sure of a happy resolution of her difficulties and while her maiden aunt continues to doubt Bevil Junior's sincerity, Indiana says of herself and her lover:

> . . . I'll wrap myself up in the integrity of my own heart,
> nor dare to doubt of his.
>> As conscious honor all his actions steers:
>> So conscious innocence dispels my fears.
>>> (last lines of II.ii)

The psychological effects of this inner assurance on the behavior of the hero and heroine are very salutary, however much we today may wish to turn away from such self-approving joy. Because guilt had so insistently lurked in the word *conscious,* Steele's banishment of it in his bold assertion of the value of what is elsewhere called the "pure Consciousness of worthy Actions"[18] had a wide resonance. It must also have been supported by an alliance with a powerful tradition, for Steele was far from being great enough to have been a solitary pioneer in effecting intellectual or emotional change. The tradition I shall discuss in a moment.

The resonance I detect as far away as Blake, who uses the word *conscious* four times, not once with any implication of guilt. On one occasion Blake uses the word indubitably of himself: a friend who had been kind to him he hopes to repay "with the courage of conscious industry," evidence that as late as 1804 a Virgilian personification with *conscious* could be used quite naturally in a quotidian context.[19] In another place Blake identified himself with the prophets who gave us "the Sublime of the Bible," and who were "consciously & professedly Inspired Men," a fact that nerved them and their followers to action.[20] A third instance is Blake's definition of the "strong Man," related to his concept of the prophet and also to his own concept of himself: he "acts from conscious superiority, and marches on in fearless dependance on the divine decrees, raging with the inspirations of a prophetic mind."[21] Fourth, Blake applies the term to one of his poetic characters, who is ultimately ground down by an envious community to despairing self-distrust—to what Blake sees as the real terror of dull, spiritless, and uncreative humility. But she had begun her career as an embodiment of beauty, freedom, charm, and love:

> Mary moves in soft beauty & conscious delight
> To augment with sweet smiles all the joys of the Night
> Nor once blushes to own to the rest of the Fair
> That sweet Love and Beauty are worthy our care[22]

Before she falls into lonely despair and outward conformity, Blake's conscious lover is much less concerned with honor, chastity, or even conventional modesty than Steele's. But they are alike in rejecting from their consciousness guilt, shame, depravity, each developing a version of Virgil's *conscia virtus*.

Such is the resonance of Steele's title. And now for a word about the tradition. Behind Blake's and Steele's consciousness there was of course the "conscious virtue" of many English writers who, in their attempts at one or another kind of poetic effect, at the very least kept the Virgilian phrase current. Behind Blake's "strong-Man"-Prophet there stood, at least for a while, Milton's Satan, who when he spoke to his followers on the burning marle of hell spoke as a dignified rebel "with Monarchal pride / Conscious of highest worth" (*Paradise Lost*, 2:428–29). Behind Blake's "conscious" Mary were the likes of Dryden's "conscious" Eleonora, who "Scarcely knew that she was great or fair" and yet paradoxically did:

> For to be conscious of what all admire,
> And not be vain, advances virtue high'r.
> (lines 100–101)

And behind Blake and perhaps also Steele was a version of Christian conscience powerful in Anglo-Saxon culture—not the inner judge and lawgiver I discussed earlier but "the blessed assurance," to use the dissenter's idiom, which was at once the consolation and inspiration of those believers who rested their spiritual awareness on Romans 8:16: "The Spirit itself beareth witness with our spirit, that we are the children of God." To be conscious of that witness—to "know with" that kind of inward energy—was considerably different from an awareness of an eternal judge or lawgiver. And it may be an irony of history that so strongly a Christian concept should have driven the *virtus* of *conscia virtus* back to the more primary pagan meaning of power and strength. For in order to restore power to consciousness Blake was purposely and often blazingly irreverent and even immoral in his rhetoric. Few others were so bold and individualistic as he, but no consideration of *conscious* in Protestant England could possibly ignore a tradition that was often charismatic and antinomian. God the Holy Spirit had breathed on the concept of consciousness.

The *Conscious* of Sensibility

Do you *know* or do you *feel* power within? Obviously no sharp separation can be made, though it strikes me as natural to say that we *know* an inner law and *feel* an inner energy. In other words, the content of consciousness affects its nature. The change that we have been noticing—from law to energy, from virtue as legal goodness to virtue as power—is a change in content. I believe there is a comparable shift in the suffix of the adjective itself—from science meaning knowledge to science conceived of as emotion. The dynamics of *conscious* shifts from "knowing with" to "feeling with," and the word takes its place in the complex history of sensibility.

It would, once more, be a mistake to set up a rigid contrast: Aristotle and Samuel Johnson were by no means the only thinkers in Western culture to emphasize that pleasure (and other emotions, too) accompanies knowledge and that in the end the two cannot be separated. Yet there is a scale of values running from reason to the heart, and human attention can register responses all along that range. Shared knowledge, one supposes, can theoretically be neutral enough; but the very fact that a secret is kept and shared tends to make the mutual knowledge tremble with fear or glow with emotion. The secret can eat like the canker worm, hell itself being an inexorable alliance with one's own preferences; but the secret within can also titillate—do I need to appeal to childhood experience? Such emotional associations perhaps explain why a word with *science* at its root should have entered poetry in the first place. And this much can certainly be said for even some of the most conventional personifications of poetic diction—that they often imply that the world is a great sensorium. The groves in Denham's *Cooper's Hill* (line 277) are "conscious" because they are associated with love and triumph; in Dryden's *Astraea Redux* (line 245) the winds that blow the royal vessel are "conscious of their charge"; Pope's "conscious morn" is painted with blushes (from Ovid: *Sappho to Phaon,* line 98); Gray's "conscious truth" possesses "struggling pangs" (*Elegy*, line 69); and Cowper's Deity, conceived of as a "conscious cause," exerts ceaseless pressure on matter (*Task*, 6:220). In these examples *conscious* is a means of uniting animated nature and human life in bonds of sympathy.

In the relations of man to man and of man to God the person we find a similar conflation of consciousness and sensibility. In one of his typically exciting sentences, the Restoration preacher, Robert South, says that "To be a friend, and to be conscious, are terms equivalent." The context of the remark is not, as one might think, that of the traditional classical essay on friendship, in which the friend is another self with whom we share knowledge. South's meaning is that a Christian man is a friend of God, from whom no secrets are hid, and that God is a friend of man, to whom divine secrets are totally revealed. For this sublime knowing-feeling together, even the noble word friendship is not strong enough, for South says, "Love is the greatest of human affections, and friendship is the noblest and most refined improvement of love."[23] An eighteenth-century writer might thus have quite naturally referred to the "conscious Enoch" or the "conscious Abraham," both of whom walked and talked with God.

Setting aside both religion and animated nature for the moment, we must consider how purely human intercourse provides an emotional consciousness that takes on a peculiarly eighteenth-century coloration, at least in the ensemble or pattern of association that formed around the *coeur sensible*. Thomson refers to "the conscious heart of Charity" (*Winter*, line 354); the author of *Spectator* 224 refers to the "pure Consciousness of worthy Actions" and assigns this heightened awareness to the "generous mind," for whom such consciousness is itself "an ample Reward" (par. 2). Let me show how, in translating a simple and moving scene in *The Odyssey*, the translator embroiders it with the language of sensibility. Nausicaa, led to believe that she is destined to remain a maid not much longer, asks her father to give her a wagon in which to carry her wedding garments. Modest about the coming event, she is of course vague about her true purpose, which she covers up by pretending to be concerned about washing her brother's clothes. But her father knows everything (*panta noei*) and provides the royal wagon at once. One may of course prefer Homer's simple directness—the girl addresses her father as παππα φίλ' (*pappa phil*) and Homer calls him πατρὶ φίλῳ (*patri philō*)—finding these brief simple words sufficient to convey all the necessary feeling. The eighteenth-century elaboration, however, is an interesting example of the sentimental associations of consciousness:

> . . . blushes ill-restrain'd betray
> her thoughts intentive on the bridal day:
> The conscious sire the dawning blush survey'd. . . .[24]

The sire would not have deserved the honorific *conscious* had he not immediately granted her request, for the adjective here means perceptive, loving, kindly, considerate of the girl's natural embarrassment.

The juxtaposition, in the translation, of Nausicaa's blush and the word *conscious* brings me to my own juxtaposition of sex and sensibility. In a revealing bit of Podsnappery, Mr. Podsnap regards his young daughter as "a certain institution" in his mind—by which phrase I take Dickens to mean the foolish father's tendency to abridge the girl's actuality so that he can respond, not to the real girl but to his own stereotype of her, which he keeps calling "the young person." It is that stereotype, not what Dickens intended Georgiana Podsnap really to be, that interests me now:

> The question about everything was, would it bring a blush into the cheek of the young person? And the inconvenience of the young person was that, according to Mr. Podsnap, she seemed always liable to burst into blushes when there was no need at all. There appeared to be no line of demarcation between the young person's excessive innocence, and another person's guiltiest knowledge.[25]

Christopher Ricks, who finds Podsnap "a very nineteenth-century figure," finds also that "the young person" embodies a paradoxical mixture of innocence and guilt which he finds romantic: "a disconcerting mixed feeling very different from the old clarity of demarcation."[26] But eighteenth-century explorations of the frontiers between innocence

and guilt reveal that the earlier period knew very well this disconcerting mix and had already challenged the "old clarity of demarcation."
The heroines of Otway, Richardson, and Austen, Sterne's portrayal of
My Uncle Toby and the Widow Wadman, several of the girls in Watteau,
Greuze, and Mozart's librettos, and Blake's virgin Thel often tremble
with mixed guilt and innocence on the edge of experience, a confusion
of which the blush was of course not always the overt sign.[27] Even the
seasoned goddess Juno, partly no doubt because of her desire to maintain matronly respectability, colors in the manner of Miss Podsnap when
in the *Iliad* she decides to distract Jove's attention from the battlefield
by using the aphrodisiac cestus she had borrowed from Venus. The
sexually aroused father of the gods suggests that he be allowed to
gratify his desires on Mount Ida in his golden cloud. As Pope translates
Homer,

> He spoke; the Goddess with the charming Eyes
> Glows with celestial Red and thus replies.
> Is this a Scene for Love?
>
> (14:373-75)

Maynard Mack says, rightly, that "Pope remembers [Milton's] Raphael
on angelic love";[28] to express her sense of delicate embarrassment, a
lesser though typical poet might have given to Juno "conscious" cheeks.
    On a much less exalted level but with the same psycho-sexual
dynamics, Richardson actually uses the word to describe the emotions
of the younger Sorlings girl, who permitted Lovelace to kiss her. She
immediately became *"sensible all over."* When her elder sister "popped
upon her," "the conscious girl blushed again."[29] Professor Sherbo would
have us read guilty for conscious,[30] but Lovelace is closer than the
scholar to the complex though humble and quotidian reality his creator
is developing: he believes the girl is truly innocent but only "confounded," embarrassed, and still hungry for his continuing attention.
I do not want us to forget what I said earlier, that *conscious* often
referred to overt and fixed feelings of sexual guilt. But I want us now
to confront a sensibility of the erotic, sometimes delicately colored
with guilt, sometimes not, which I find to be an important eighteenth-

century literary mode. Milton's "blushing" Eve is of course not guilty; she is clad in "Innocence and Virgin Modestie" (8:501, 511), and she also possesses "conscience of her worth" (502). Paradoxically, that "conscience" is not entirely unlike the consciousness of highest worth that gives force to Satan's confident rhetoric; to Eve it gives the dignified assurance, despite her modest fears, that she has a full right to require of Adam a formal suit for her hand. And yet Eve's skin, like that of Raphael's, is susceptible to the rosy red of angelic amorousness presaging the delights of the Edenic bower of bliss. Blake, who tried to create a more aggressive Daughter of Albion, free of guilty inhibitions, was an enemy of the blush. Milton and the eighteenth century were not. For the delicately complex mixture of guilt and innocence, of raptures at once desired and feared, conveyed by the blush, there could hardly have been a more appropriate word than *conscious.*

For the sake of completeness I must turn, however briefly, to the robust Dryden, who certainly respected female modesty and who could also use our term to denote real guilt. Neither applies to the love which Aureng-Zebe feels for his beloved's body: "my conscious Limbs presage / Torrents of joy, which all their banks o'rflow!" (Act IV, lines 540–41). Here the adjective refers to sexual arousal that appears not to be condemned, where human limbs stand as a not very subtle substitute for a more sensitive member.

In these ways, then—sexually and socially, delicately and robustly, institutionally and naturally—*conscious* was associated with feeling, and it may not be irrelevant to note that the Latin prefix *con* and the Greek *sun,* besides meaning *with,* were also intensifiers, adding the notion of *altogether* or *completely.* We should not therefore be surprised to find that influential and normative philosopher, John Locke, defining being, or self, in terms of sensibility. "*Self* is that conscious thinking thing, . . . which is sensible, or conscious [note the synonymy here] of Pleasure and Pain, capable of Happiness or Misery, and so is concern'd for it *self,* as far as that consciousness extends."[31] Similarly, though later, Abraham Rees, who duly discriminates the traditional ethical and theological meanings, nevertheless defines *conscience* in its self-reflective qualities, as "the source and cause of all that joy, or dejection of mind, of those internal sensations of pleasure or pain, which attend the practice of great virtues or great vices."[32] Clarissa may at times have wished that her heart did not so often misgive her; nevertheless, she felt that she had to trust it particularly when it gave powerful signals: "in so strong and involuntary a bias, the *heart* is, as I may say, *conscience*."[33] Thus once again conscience and conscious come into phase, and we see the profound moral seriousness of the conscious of sensibility that may underlie even its lighter manifestations.

The Philosophical *Conscious* and the *Unconscious*

If you conceive of conscience as based solely or primarily on the reason, you can perhaps regard daylight, waking introspection as sufficient for understanding the inner life. But the heart beats on in darkness and in sleep; and sensibility may, willy-nilly, bring us to the frontiers of the unconscious. At the very least we are led by our most recent definitions to ask: does the unconscious lurk in the eighteenth-century word *conscious*? I have already tried to show that in its range of greatly varied meanings, it is a complex word. Does it also possess the *structure* of a complex word? That is, do the surprising contrasts that William Empson found in words affect or reflect the very structure of *conscious*? We remember that he paused before the phenomenon of a word like *sensibility*, which was "rightly used to describe and praise discriminating reactions" but at the same time was "twisted round to describe and praise excessive reactions."[34] Well, *conscious* did, as we have seen, contain within it meanings as diverse as guilt and innocence. Centuries of religious introspection and evaluation had inevitably produced both acquitting and condemnatory responses in the consciousness. Our word is in itself neutral, even vacant, as we saw at the outset, and welcomes being filled up from the psyche or from whatever guides or forms the inner man. By its very nature, then—by its structure, if you will—the word is open to the conflicting meanings that have in fact been its referents. But I press on. Is the word also a primal word, with a sense inevitably antithetical to its basic meaning? Is it like Freud's *heimlich,* which refers to the home and the intimately familiar but which attracted to its orbit its very opposite, the *unheimlich,* the uncanny or the terrible?[35] If so, the *conscious,* already a complex word with greatly diverse and even contradictory meanings, would sooner or later become linked with the *unconscious.* Today we like to think in this way, and examples abound in contemporary criticism of our fascination with antithetical, even mutually annihilating words.[36] What is more natural than for us to think that conscious calls up the unconscious as host invokes the lurking enemy *hostis,* as host also calls up parasite, as constituting invites deconstituting, analysis paralysis, idealism skepticism; or, most commonly and basically, as rational logocentricity invokes linguistic nihilism.

The reality in eighteenth-century thought regarding the unconscious seems to be at once simpler and profounder, if the hypothesis I shall now propose has validity. But first we must note that the Restoration and eighteenth century certainly knew of the realm of the unconscious. Early in his career Dryden described the primal condition of one of his dramatic efforts "long before it was a Play; When it was only a confus'd Mass of Thoughts, tumbling over one another in the Dark: When the Fancy was yet in its first Work, moving the Sleeping Images of things towards the Light, . . ."[37] The realm of the unconscious was that of "the Chaos dark and deep, / Where nameless somethings in their causes sleep."[38] Both Dryden and Pope locate the sleeping prefigurations of art within the mind of man. Even Johnson, who was uncomfortable about fog and darkness in the psyche, certainly recognized the unconscious, at least in external nature. Imlac says that "all the notices of sense and investigations of science concur to prove the unconsciousness of matter," and *unconscious* means that matter is "inert, senseless and lifeless." But he does give to it "form, density, bulk, motion, and direction of motion"—the last two being noteworthy here. Johnson the amateur scientist and lover of experiments applied such active and dynamic "philosophic words" as the following from matter to the operations of the intellect: coalesce, dissolve, exhale, impregnate; elastick, volatile; attraction, oscillation, paroxysm, velocity.[39] Matter might indeed be unconscious, but it was far from being inactive or unproductive, as any chemist would know.

Let us return to human consciousness. In trying to show how the unconscious might conceivably operate there, I must recall a debate among the philosophers and psychologists of the eighteenth century regarding the existence of the self. Locke asserted flatly that we perceive our own existence plainly and infallibly: "In every Act of Sensation, Reasoning, or Thinking, we are conscious to our selves of our own Being; and, in this Matter, come not short of the highest degree of *Certainty*" (*Essay,* IV.ix.3). Hume's consciousness possessed no such certainty, though he used precisely the method of observation and reflection characteristic of his predecessor. Hume could never "catch" *himself,* as he put it; he caught only fleeting, particular glimpses of the self, and he therefore was forced to conclude that the self was only "a bundle or collection of different perceptions, which succeed each other with an inconceivable rapidity, and are in a perpetual flux and movement." The "I" is not an invariable identity, but only a succession of parts or a network of relations seemingly held together by some principle of union like soul or substance which we feign, by some cohering principle which we only imagine. When we sleep or after we die we surely lose identity. Hume means to say that by rooting our existence in perception and thought about perception, Locke had proceeded precariously. There are too many vacancies in our perception to permit the conviction of a continuous, identical existence.[40] The empirical tradition tended to lose permanent, unchanging, uninterrupted identity by anchoring it in consciousness, which experience can easily show has gaping vacancies within it.

Coleridge, on the other hand, though he found man to exist to himself only in moments, postulated a class of infinite beings, "who tho' not conscious of the whole of their continuousness, are yet both conscious of *a* continuousness, and make that the object of reflex consciousness."[41] Coleridge's subjectively derived "continuousness" of being (which man can shadow) had been prepared for by almost a century of philosophic and religious thought and polemics. Joseph Butler refused to believe that personal identity could be grounded in memory or consciousness: ". . . consciousness of personal identity presupposed, and therefore cannot constitute personal identity."[42] Later, Thomas Reid refused to identify consciousness with memory and preferred to separate the present conscious from all recollection of the past and even from simple present empirical perception.[43] Zachary Mayne, the putative author of an *Essay on Consciousness,* which proclaimed itself a pioneering work, separated consciousness from dreaming, from imagination, from all bodily perception and based it on "the Mind's Intellectual Nature and Essence."[44] And Berkeley, in a clearly pre-Kantian passage, shifted from "me" (the object of consciousness) to "I," its subject, which he distinguished sharply from color, sound, shape—indeed from all "sensible things and inert ideas": "... I know or am conscious of my own being; and that I myself am not my ideas, but somewhat else, a thinking active principle that perceives, knows, wills, and operates about ideas. I know that ... I am ... one individual principle ..."[45] We are not far away from Kant's "unity of consciousness which precedes all data of intuitions," not far from that "pure original unchangeable consciousness" which he named *"transcendental apperception."*[46]

What does all this have to do with the unconscious? Simply this: that the philosophy of idealism and transcendence implies it. By shifting from me to I, from object to subject, from the known to the knower, you must posit an entity that itself slumbers not nor sleeps, that structures reality, produces rational forms, and makes imaginative, intellectual, and linguistic linkages in sleep, trance, rapture, perhaps even in senility and states of forgetfulness. Ultimately it is God who will have to sanction what Coleridge was so passionately desirous of having—continuousness of being. But on the purely human level, if he wants continuous identity, man must place the soul outside memory, outside daylight perception, outside empirical consciousness. It is not an exaggeration to say that without this postulation of identity in the unconscious the whole fabric of religion and responsibility would collapse. It is thus that the conscious implies the unconscious. Indeed, the demand of idealistic philosophy for the assumption of continuous, coherent identity, of Being itself, calls into dialectical existence the realm of the unconscious. Such is the Great Implication of philosophy; it prepared the way for a remarkable extension of the idea of the unconscious in the Romantic period, an enrichment and sophistication we cannot discuss here.

Some post-Modernist theory seems to insist that language itself inevitably erects binary structures and that the unconscious would of course be implicated in the conscious by the very processes of thought and rhetoric. But such linguistic and epistemological fatalism is not, I believe, characteristic of the Great Implication of the unconscious that

I see in Berkeley and Kant and the lesser writers I have mentioned. As religious men who wanted to be free and responsible, all these were shocked by the gaps and vacancies in continuity left by the empiricists. Idealist-transcendental thought extended being into these interstices and so created a logical continuum. But it also vitalized and personalized that continuum, creating not so much a Great Chain of Being as what Pope called "the chain of Love" (*Essay on Man,* 3:7).

Samuel Johnson and Jane Austen

Does what I have called the Great Implication of the unconscious embrace Johnson and Jane Austen, neither one a professional philosopher but both authors who used the term *conscious* frequently, sensitively, and in ways highly relevant to their art and thought? Johnson's definition of *unconscious* is brief—almost dismissive, in a way that would be impossible in our own day or even in the Romantic period: the word for him means, *tout court,* "Having no mental perception." But the most recent student of the creative imagination has said that "Johnson probes the unconscious mind ... with a brilliant, stubborn persistence unrivalled before Freud. He is aware that the door is always open between imagination and every impulse, instinct, and emotion, at every level from the rudimentary to the sophisticated."[47] There is much to be said for this view, which had earlier been stated by Walter Jackson Bate. I should prefer, however, to put matters a bit differently. Johnson was of course aware that psychological links were automatically forged in the dark—that one vice, for example, could be magnetically attracted to another, sometimes a virtue to a vice, sometimes an excess to a defect—all that because of the very structure of the psyche, without volition, without choice. But such processes might easily darken reason or abridge freedom. In Dryden the fancy moves the "sleeping Images of things toward the Light [and now I finish the quotation given only in part earlier] there to be Distinguish'd, and then either chosen or rejected by the Judgment" (see n. 37). Whether the fancy in such an operation always works automatically, unconsciously, I do not know. But I do know that Johnson wanted all such activities brought into the light, by an act of rational volition. In noting that Swift believed men to be "grateful in the same degree as they are resentful," Johnson may in fact be confronting a link formed in the unconscious by the very nature and structure of desire. But he goes on: "This principle, with others of the same kind, supposes man to act from a brute impulse, and pursue a certain degree of inclination, without any choice of the object; for otherwise, though it should be allowed that gratitude and resentment arise from the same constitution of the passions, it follows not that they will be equally indulged when reason is consulted" (*Rambler* no. 4., par. 16). Thus there is an unconscious, but that unconscious is not fate. For Johnson, moreover, even the realm of the unconscious could be conceived of as partly self-created, a realm that is dark because the self-flattering eye chooses to make it so by willfully not observing it. "It seems generally believed, that, as the eye cannot see itself, the mind has no faculties by which it can contemplate its own state, . . ." That belief Johnson finds sophistical—and all too easy. It has "commodious consequences"—that is, it soothes the ego. "Self-love is often rather arrogant than blind; . . . We are secretly conscious of defects and vices which we hope to conceal from the public eye, . . ." (*Rambler* no. 155, pars. 2, 3). Note well that Johnson does indeed explore the unconscious, but with a searchlight that exposes it for what it really is—the "secretly conscious," a vastly different kind of realm, created by the self escaping itself, a realm, however, which can be reclaimed by the ethical reason.

> He therefore that would govern his actions by the laws of virtue, . . .
> must keep guilt from the recesses of his heart, and remember that
> the pleasures of fancy, and the emotions of desire are more dangerous
> as they are more hidden, since they escape the awe of observation, . . .
> (*Rambler* no. 8, last par.)

Johnson, as profoundly religious a thinker as the eighteenth century produced, surely realized, as Coleridge did later, that "the spiritual in man . . . lies on the other side of our natural consciousness," which is the realm of observed fact and of the combining, judging mind. This realm of "ulterior consciousness," truly "a land of darkness" to the average man, must be where the primary imagination does its eternal, ongoing work of translating the infinite into the finite—a realm very close to the unconscious I have postulated as necessarily present in all idealist philosophy. But both Coleridge and Johnson realized that human creation and action take place in a more illuminated place. For Coleridge artistic creation occurs in the secondary imagination, which is a power "co-existing with the conscious will."[48] And, as we have just seen, Johnson believes that the good life is created by the very same conscious will, which operates under what he calls, in the thrilling phrase I have quoted, "the awe of observation."

I do not know that such large philosophical considerations as these apply to Johnson's disciple, Jane Austen, or that she knew or cared much about the idealist-transcendental implication of unconsciousness or even of synapses made in the unreflecting psychic depths. I find possible Freudian double entendres in her work to be so infrequent as to be negligible,[49] though I do believe that her pages are often alive with amorous, even sexual excitement. One of the many instruments of rendering that excitement was Austen's use of the word *conscious,* which is varied enough to constitute a summary of the meanings we have explored and subtle enough to provide examples of the word's employment in high art.

The etymological meaning, involving both syllables of the word, is present. Near the end of *Mansfield Park* Fanny Price, her younger sister Susan, and Mr. Henry Crawford, now in pursuit of Fanny but of course inhibited here by the presence of the sister, go on a picnic in Portsmouth. In this situation he must content himself "with the indulgence, now and then, of a look or hint for the better informed and conscious Fanny" (III, x). Here the word means that Fanny knows more than Susan knows and that she knows it *with* Henry—knows, that is, everything that has gone before, including her coolness and his heat.

When at the beginning of *Emma,* the heroine experiences a "gentle sorrow," it comes "not at all in the shape of any disagreeable consciousness," where "guilt" can be substituted for "consciousness" without any violence whatever to the meaning (I, i). Exempted from that kind of consciousness at the beginning, Emma feels it in her relations with Harriet at the end, for the heroine's dangerous prevalence of imagination has led her to tamper with another's soul. Emma senses resentment in her protegé's letter now that Harriet has learned to whom Mr. Knightley's love is indeed directed: "It might be only her own [Emma's] consciousness [that is, a perception colored by a sense of guilt], but it seemed as if an angel only could have been quite without resentment under such a stroke" (III, xvi).

Variants of Virgil's *conscia virtus* appear everywhere in Austen; for example, the Fanny Price who has become beautiful might now be called the "conscious Fanny," as she is elsewhere, for, like Blake's Mary, the girl now "saw that she was approved; and the consciousness of looking well, made her look still better" (II, x).

Austen's considerable arsenal of effects includes as a favorite weapon *conscious* as sensibility, or heightened feeling, both with and without erotic coloration, but especially with. Toward the end of *Northanger Abbey* Catherine Morland introduces the man she loves and will marry to her mother: "With a look of much respect, he immediately rose, and being introduced to her by her conscious daughter as 'Mr. Henry Tilney,' with the embarrassment of real sensibility began to apologize for his appearance there" (see n. 2). Such sensitive consciousness can be very strong indeed, as Fanny Price learns when, after dismaying her uncle with her determined refusal of her suitor, she "walk[s] off in agitating consciousness" and finds "herself, as she anticipated, in another minute alone with Mr. Crawford"—a scene in which the "conscious" Fanny's emotions are complex indeed (III, i).

It goes without saying that the *conscious* in Jane Austen includes the social and ethical awareness that Johnson made fundamental in his teaching. Early in *Mansfield Park* Sir Thomas wants to "preserve in the minds of my *daughters* the consciousness of what they are, without making them think too lowly of their cousin" (I, i). At the end Sir Thomas has learned by hard experience that the cousin, Fanny Price, along with her brother and sister, possessed "the advantages of early hardship and discipline, and the consciousness of being born to struggle and endure" (III, xvii). What good consciousness included for Jane Austen appears in her judgment of Fanny's politely reared cousin Julia, who lacks "that higher species of self-command, that just consideration of others, that knowledge of her own heart [note this phrase well!], that principle of right which had not formed any essential part of her

Thus the critique of
Bevil is that where
he is not conscious
(of anything but his
virtue), he is pompous.

education" (I, ix). Austen had absorbed the Johnsonian lessons and seems also to have heeded Steele's implicit demand that the consciousness needs governance.[50]

But the term is artistically useful to Austen for other than ethical reasons. To "know with" oneself, to "know with" another, to be aware delicately, sensitively, erotically, even nervously and vividly if we remember that *con* is also an intensifier—these are the very traits that separate the artistically rounded character from the caricature. Great faults, even potentially self-destructive errors of perception, do not necessarily forfeit our sympathies if the character is "conscious"—witness the career of Marianne Dashwood in *Sense and Sensibility*. Opposed to such characters as these is that gallery of fools and knaves, of conventionally or pompously good characters, sometimes cruel, more often thoughtless. These are the unconscious ones. And the two hemispheres of conscious and unconscious are indispensable to one another, rounding out to an artistic globe.

I cannot say that these obverse realms in Jane Austen, though one requires the other, do indeed interpenetrate or "interinanimate" globally. But it is my claim that they do within the word itself—in Jane Austen and earlier—particularly when it embodies sensibility. Then the very word becomes a vital and organic world, where guilt and innocence meet and are sometimes revealed by the ambiguous blush, where shared secrets can have ambivalent relations, where sexual excitement joins charity and benevolence, where even awareness itself requires or impinges on the realm of dark, nameless somethings sleeping in a state of psychological preexistence, and even where gaps in the empirically guided consciousness imply the unconscious existence of continuous responsible being. *Conscious* then discloses the structures of human sensitivity; and to describe its complex interior dynamics, we may find the language of Wordsworth about "the best feelings of our nature" to be suggestive—

> feelings which, though they seem opposite to each other, have another and a finer connection than that of contrast. It is a connection formed through the subtle progress by which, both in the natural and the moral world, qualities pass insensibly into their contraries, and things revolve upon each other.[51]

2

Verbal and Visual Caricature in the Age of Dryden, Swift, and Pope

*A*mong *the greatest* achievements of English verse are the satirical lines devoted to Achitophel, Zimri, Baron Cutts the Salamander, Atticus, and Sporus. What shall we name these poetic paragraphs? Samuel Johnson called the Achitophel of *The Medall* a "picture" and referred to the "artful delineation" of character in *Absolom and Achitophel.* Of Pope's personal satires Johnson used the term employed by the author himself, by his contemporaries, and by Dryden; that term, *character,* has persisted to our own day.[1] Characters, however, are traditionally typical or categorical, not individual, and those of Pope, identified or not, are or seem to be personal. Then why not *portrait,* which Johnson in his dictionary defined as "a picture drawn from life"? Because, in spite of their many historical details and insights, the famous lines of Dryden and Pope can scarcely be regarded as realistic transcriptions, and we cannot ignore Johnson's important word *artful.* It is also a challenging word, although very few have risen to tell us wherein lies the art of a form that Dryden received as brick and that left his hands as marble, an art he regarded as difficult and "severe."[2]

Perhaps one should use the plural and ask what art forms satire assumed in neoclassical Europe. Some writers created situational satires, with great skill applying epic and heroic forms to contemporary situations or adapting the highly suggestive devices of Boccalini or Quevedo. *The Tatler* and *The Spectator* made short satiric narrative effective, and Pope suggested the progresses of Hogarth in his moral tale of Sir Balaam. Pope also created short conversational dramas along lines suggested by Persius and Horace. Dryden made "beautiful turns of words and thoughts" and "sounding" and "elegant" language his especial province.[3] And from rhetoric came the ideal of vivacious imagery, of *enargeia*, of visual palpability and lifelikeness.[4]

The art of satire also consisted in the making of pictures, formal pictures; and this aspect of satiric art, which is more and other than straightforward visual vivacity, has not been much discussed. Dryden said a "man may be capable, as Jack Ketch's wife said of his servant, of a plain piece of work, a bare hanging; but to make a malefactor die sweetly was only belonging to her husband."[5] The creation of pictures was one way to do better than a plain, bare hanging.

Analogy with the Visual Arts

It is widely acknowledged that the historical situation, which always provides the artist with his choices and opportunities, was in the Restoration peculiarly congenial to the collaboration of poetry and painting. The analogy of the visual and verbal arts is a hardy perennial that grew first in classical soil and flourished in Renaissance and baroque Europe. It lived to bloom in Restoration culture because it was nourished by the most exciting and ambitious intellectual enterprises of the period: British literary realism, philosophical empiricism, and natural science. In his ode "To the Royal Society," published in Sprat's history, Cowley refers to words as "Pictures of the Thought" and shows that he has a full-blown pictorial analogy in mind. He invokes the classical story of birds flying at painted grapes, recalls the examples of Rubens and Van Dyck, draws a precise comparison with portrait painting, and praises the painter for producing "The Natural and Living Face":

> The real object must command
> Each judgment of his Eye, and Motion of his Hand.[6]

Earl Miner has said that it was natural at the time of *Annus Mirabilis* to think of the "correspondences between art and action," so natural in fact that Dryden compared Anne Killigrew's turning to classical landscape with Louis XIV's depredations upon his neighbors.[7] Since satire was where the action was, it is not surprising that satire also strove to achieve the benefits thought to be conferred upon verbal art by attempting to imitate its visual sister. Marvell, writing as a political satirist, said:

> Painter, adieu! How well our arts agree,
> Poetic picture, painted poetry.

These lines come from Marvell's *Last Instructions to a Painter,*[8] a poem that excellently represents a genre in which the painter was summoned, advised, and instructed by the poet. This genre, used by Marvell himself, by Waller, and by a number of anonymous satirists, was one of the two or three most popular forms for political poetry in the Restoration. Juvenal came into post–Civil War culture in the very year of the Restoration with sumptuous illustrations by the prestigious engraver, Wenceslaus Hollar, whose engravings naively, suggestively, ambitiously, and vividly pictorialize the ancient satire.[9] Dryden called *Absalom and Achitophel* "a Picture to the Wast" and drew its motto (*Se Propiùs stes / Te Capiet Magis*) from the *Ars Poetica,* lines that, immediately following the famous tag *ut pictura poesis,* begin Horace's influential comparison of the two arts.[10] In a lighter vein Swift uses Horace's dictum when he writes an answer for the long-nosed Dan Jackson to a libel on his face:

> My Verse little better you'll find than my Face is,
> A Word to the Wise, *ut pictura poesis.*

Swift drives on with the pictorial language and even anticipates Hogarth's aesthetics:

> Let then such Criticks know, my Face
> Gives them their Comeliness and Grace:

> Whilst ev'ry Line of Face does bring,
> A Line of Grace to what they sing.[11]

Pope, in discussing LaBruyère's characters, says: "Tis certainly the proof of a Master-Hand, that can give such striking Likenesses in such slight Sketches, & in so few strokes on each subject."[12]

We have thus summoned the poets with whom we are concerned to witness to the close association in their critical consciousness of painting with satire. Their practice follows their profession, and their satirical verses recall motifs and genres of the visual arts. In a moving night scene by Marvell which begins, "Paint last the king, and a dead shade of Night," and has for its only light a weak taper, King Charles awakens in horror, muses on "th' uneasy throne," and sees an apparition, a nude whose arms behind her are interwoven with her tresses. The King is kind, but he soon shrinks back for her cold touch chills him. The airy picture vanishes, and "he divin'd 'twas England or the Peace."[13] The allegorical Virgin, so reminiscent of Botticelli's nudes, and the disturbed King meet in a tenebroso piece that also recalls Ribalta, Ribera, and the followers of Caravaggio. The poem "Advice to a Painter" (1673), perhaps by John Ayloffe, recalls the contemporary political caricature, for the Duke of York is verbally painted with the conversational balloon of the cartoon near his mouth:

> First draw him falling prostrate to the south
> Adoring Rome, this label in his mouth.[14]

Shimei appears in a formal portrait:

> His Hand a Vare* of Justice did uphold;
> His Neck was loaded with a Chain of Gold.[15]

The round and liquored Og, in a kind of seascape capriccio, rolls behind his linkboy, like a stout and tossing vessel coming into harbor behind

---

*A rod, staff, or wand symbolic of judicial authority. The Oxford English Dictionary quotes Dryden's line as its last example of this meaning.

its light.[16] Sporus at the ear of Eve is less biblical or Miltonic than graphic; he resembles countless engravings of the serpent in Eden with a human or an angelic face, his body wrapped around the tree as he offers the apple to Eve from his mouth: "A Cherub's face, a Reptile all the rest."[17] Pope's "frugal crone," who is dying and is attended by praying priests, appears in a mock *sacra conversazione* which illustrates the pictorialist critic's dictum that verbal art ought to catch the single and brief dramatic action on the canvas. Even at the moment of last unction, the stingy old lady still tries from her bed "to save the hallow'd taper's end":

> Collects her breath, as ebbing life retires,
> For one puff more, and in that puff expires.[18]

These circumstances—that the poet as critic associated satirical verse with visual art and that in his practice he embodied or recalled specifically pictorial forms—provide historical sanction for the nomenclature now proposed: that the satirical lines attacking individual persons be called by the visual term *caricature,* and that this art (which distorts but does not destroy resemblance)[19] be divided into two subspecies, *emblematic* caricature and *portrait* caricature. The adjective in each term is intended to invoke the most closely related visual art, the emblem for the first and the portrait for the second. (1) Emblematic caricature is not primarily concerned with resemblance, although it wishes unmistakably to strike an individual. It attempts to reduce the subject to ridicule and contempt by means of insulting comparisons. These comparisons are emblematic, or hieroglyphic (to use a term Swift liked), and tend, because of the mocking reduction involved, to become grotesque. (2) Portrait caricature strives not to be monstrous but to keep the representation credible and recognizable. It too seeks to render the original reprehensible or ridiculous by means of a distorting line, but it is concerned to maintain a realistic surface.

Emblematic Caricature

The emblem is shorthand allegory, and allegory is an extended emblem. Among the many literary and pictorial forms that satire mocked, reduced, parodied, adapted, or subverted are both the longer and shorter versions of visual allegory. The ceilings and walls of palaces and churches, the pictorialized pages of Ovid and Spenser, and the cruder or simpler icons of the emblem books provided opportunities that a pictorially oriented satirist did not neglect. Dryden's Flecknoe sits high on a throne, with all the accoutrements of dullness visually realized;[20] Pope's Dulness, though somewhat less pictorial in rendition, is surrounded by the "Four guardian Virtues" that support her throne, while Prudence bears her glass and Poetic Justice lifts her scale.[21] Pope's Obloquy dwells "Hard by a Sty, beneath a Roof of Thatch," attended by her train, her breasts marked by "ev'ry Collier's Hand."[22] Criticism in Swift's *Battle of the Books* takes her place in a pictorial stasis: "extended in her Den," she has eyes that turn inward, but her swollen spleen extends like a dug; and she is attended by blind Ignorance and Opinion, "perpetually turning."[23]

Swift, in a witty denigration of popular imagery, outlines the method of allegorical and emblematic caricature. He refers to "mystical" writing that "enigmatically" and "cunningly" shades meaning "under Allegory." He distinguishes between "Mythology" and "Hieroglyphick" and describes verbal forms that tell fables, draw comparisons, and make visual analogues for satirical purposes.[24] Swift may have rejected the mystical and emblematic seventeenth century, but he was steeped in its visual allegories and emblems. The artistic side of his satire may be viewed as the persistence of earlier emblematic forms, which he adapted to his purpose but from whose essentially hieroglyphic qualities he never departed. Sometimes he is overtly emblematic:

> Now hear an Allusion!—A Mitre, you know,
> Is divided above, but united below.
> If this you consider, our Emblem is right;
> The B——s *divide,* but the Clergy *unite.*[25]

When Swift, in an early Pindaric, called the French king a "Tennis-Ball of Fate,"[26] he was using a popular and conventional emblem. Saint Teresa saw the "devils playing tennis" with her soul, and one of Solórzano Pereira's *Emblemata* shows God dealing with kings as tennis balls.[27] Lady Acheson's thin body and face (she was Swift's friend, by the way) must have been more emblematic than realistic: chin and nose meet, the fingers are ten crooked sticks, the elbows are pointed rocks that gore a husband's side at night like the tusks of a boar.[28] The lady's portrait is drawn in an obviously exaggerating and wittily caricaturing line that will not disturb a friendship.

Swift's lines to Lady Acheson are a frank, spoofing, in-group, cease-and-desist kind of verse. He wants his friend to put on a few pounds and to stop staying up late and abusing her health. Even in friendship, as the *Journal to Stella* also shows, Swift finds emblematic caricature irresistible. If this kind of caricature be done in the green tree, what shall be done in the dry? What one would expect. When Swift, the incorrigible maker of emblems, fires his shots in anger, his ammunition is the inverted or perverted emblem, the grotesque. (All emblems that carry the weight of much meaning, even the serious ones, tend to run to the unnatural and the grotesque. Consider Dürer's rhinoceros or the outrageously constructed woman by Ripa who symbolizes Boethian intelligence.)

Artists had for centuries reduced men to grotesques. Leonardo created a terrible kind of visual comedy by greatly distorting his line but always remaining within nature and sometimes even within his own family.[29] Other caricaturists reduced men to vegetables, to objects or machines, and to animals; and they did so lightly or savagely. Arcimboldo created the head of a gardener out of leeks, onions, carrots, cherries, apples, and rutabagas and the head of a librarian out of books; the librarian's hair was an open book with leaves fluttering, his nose the spine, his ear the ribbons to tie the book.[30] Tobias Stimmer made a pontiff out of a clock, a candle, and a bell. Brucelli fashioned human figures out of kitchen utensils, as did English popular art, where maids were constituted of mops, pails, and brooms. Staffordshire potters made women into variously shaped bells. Hogarth saw men as periwigs, the head of a lawyer as a mallet, the head of a bishop as a Jew's harp, the head of a king as a guinea; he also constructed heads of weather vanes, hands of keys, and scarecrow faces of cloth and straw.[31] There is abundant visual precedent for the grotesques in Pope's Cave of Spleen:

> Here living *Teapots* stand, one Arm held out,
> One bent; the Handles this, and that the Spout:
> A Pipkin there like *Homer's Tripod* walks;
> Here sighs a Jar, and there a Goose-pye talks.[32]

This passage, incidentally, Fuseli had no difficulty in illustrating.

Men as animals had a long visual history—from Titian's substitution of monkeys for men in a travesty of the Laocoön to Hogarth's *singerie*—which stopped well within the period under consideration. Painters had, as Sir Thomas Browne said, "singularly hit the signatures of a Lion and a Fox in the face of Pope Leo the Tenth,"[33] and Richard Flecknoe saw these same animals (surely because they were emblematic) in the face of Cromwell, whose red nose also suggested "a bloody beak" and made his countenance that of a "bird of prey."[34] Alexander Pope's head appears on a rat's body in a famous caricature, and Dr. Johnson's on an owl's, "Old Wisdom Blinking at the Stars."[35] The Scriblerians compared William Broome, Laurence Eusden, and Ambrose Philips to tortoises, who are "*slow* and *chill,* and like *Pastoral Writers* delight much in *Gardens:* they have for the most part a *fine embroider'd* Shell, and underneath it, a *heavy Lump.*"[36] Count Heidegger's face was so ugly that without the ministrations of art it caricatured the human form divine, and so Pope used this "strange Bird from Switzerland," ironically the "surintendant des plaisirs d'Angleterre," the *Arbiter Deliciarum,* who rose from producing masquerades to being George II's master of revels, in a grotesque emblem: the sacred bird of the goddess Dulness is "a monster of a fowl, / Something betwixt a Heideggre and owl."[37]

Swift's animal grotesquerie—droll, savage, cruel, playful—is the most brilliant in literary history. His menagerie has weird, solemn, funny, nasty, or cute creatures, from elephants to those invisible vermin of the fable of the fleas which inhabit the trousers of Grub Street poets. All these creatures appear *sub specie civitatis,* caught in the regularity, purity, and urbanity of the language. And they sometimes appear as though in genre prints, the verse then becoming brilliantly phrased mottoes placed under the scenes. A beau, dressed for conquest, compares his figure in the glass with a print of a monkey open before him (a print, incidentally, which prefaces one of Gay's fables). The beau's eyes move from monkey to reflection, from the printed plate to the glass, with sublime unconsciousness distinguishing all the features in common:

> The Twist, the Squeeze, the Rump, the Fidge an' all,
> Just as they lookt in the Original.[38]

Swift's emblematic grotesques appear in Ovidian allegory, Aesopian fable, satirical genre picture, or brief caricature. In all these forms Swift is a typical maker of emblems, as was Dryden before him. Both used grotesques to establish meanings. Dryden's bestiary, as we now know, was not chosen whimsically or arbitrarily; it represents a skillful application to men and their institutions of traditional beast meanings from Aristotle and Pliny, from medieval allegory, and from emblems and proverbs of the Renaissance and the seventeenth century.[39] Swift's emblems also come from tradition, and his reductions bear moral and social meanings.

Once the essential or implied seriousness of Swift's reductions has been granted, however, we do them an injustice if we do not also see them as exuberant, playful, fanciful, and personal, written in fun and pique, in exasperation and hatred, in order to give their author pleasurable relief. The compulsive linking of man and animal, the artistically just, economical, and effectual yoking of opposites in grotesque reduction—this joining is the one copulation we can be sure Swift enjoyed.

Swift's "The Description of a Salamander" (1705) is a pure example of grotesque caricature.[40] Its reduction of man and men to a single animal is a personal vendetta broadened to include large social meaning. The force of Swift's poem is revealed if it is compared with Addison's later essay on the salamander, where the animal stands for a heroine of chastity, a woman, not unlike Pope's Cloe, of the minimal frigid decencies and no more.[41] Addison's lady, like the salamander, lives in fire without being hurt, "preserv'd in a kind of natural Frost." As he generalizes the already general type, Addison tends to forget the salamander and makes assertions that are relevant intellectually but not imagistically. The frosty lady makes no distinction of sex, admits males to her bedside, is scandalized by unreasonable husbands who make physical demands, declaims against jealousy, and does not understand temptation. The reductive comparison tends to disappear in abstraction and application. The caricaturing line is there but it is not tightly drawn.

Swift's concentration on the reductive image, once it has been introduced, is fierce and unrelenting. He begins by invoking the long tradition of confusing military men and animals: mastiffs are called "Pompey" and heroes are named after brutes. Modern heroes, since the invention of gunpowder, require a new image. Buckets and pumps being too low, what could better serve than that classical creature described by Pliny, the salamander? (John Lord Cutts, a Lord Justice of Ireland and a brave soldier whom Swift hated and made his butt, had, incidentally, been called a salamander for his intrepidity under withering fire.) This image now becomes the line of distortion, the caricaturing line that bounds the whole and links part to part in an imagistic reduction of taut and brittle brilliance. The creature, gaudy and loathsome, with a shining but spotted coat, comes out of its hole in a tempest and returns to it in fair weather. So Cutts; and so other generals, peers and beaux of the Establishment, who crawl out of their dunghills to shine in war but crawl back to mother filth in peace. The application is both individual and general: a fierce personal revenge joins a political attack on official militancy.

Salamanders not only live in flames; they also put flames out, for these creatures emit a purulent white matter that extinguishes fire. The discharge also corrupts, causing leprosy and baldness. If the sexual application that ensues is also intended for Cutts, the satire is of unprecedented and surely of unwarranted violence. When it is applied, however, to the irresponsible and predatory upper classes of Restoration and Augustan England who poisoned the flesh of English women, the emblem takes on the intensity and the cogency of Blake's attack on poisonous love in the Urizenic dispensation:

So have I seen a batter'd Beau
By Age and Claps grown cold as Snow.
Whose Breath or Touch. where e'er he came.
Blew out Love's Torch or chill'd the Flame;
And should some Nymph who ne'er was cruel.
Like *Carleton* cheap. or fam'd *Duruel,*
Receive the Filth which he ejects.
She soon would find. the same Effects.
Her tainted Carcase to pursue.
As from the *Salamander's* Spue;
And. if no Leprosy. a Pox.

Then I'll appeal to each By-Stander,
Whether this be'nt a Salamander.

In 1660 an engraving by Wenceslaus Hollar represented Juvenal's satires as cloven-footed satyrs, men with goaty legs and hams, in a stroke of wit more inevitable then than now when *satyr* and *satire* were often spelled alike.[42] Before 1683 Sir Thomas Browne called the drawing of men's faces with resemblance to animals "Caricatura."[43] Both Browne and Hollar, and their readers and viewers, would have understood precisely what Swift was doing and why I have called this kind of delineation "emblematic caricature." They would also have made the proper moral response to Swift's meaning, for Browne warned his reader: "Expose not thy four-footed manners unto draughts, and Caricatura representations."[44]

Portrait Caricature

At the opposite pole from the carefully selected, heavily distorted, a priori meanings and grotesque mischiefs of emblematic caricature stands portrait caricature, whose drive toward realism can perhaps best be introduced by considering the scene or landscape of satire. Isaac Barrow, in a sermon that enumerates the many forms of protean wit, referred to "a scenical Representation of Persons or Things."[45] The naturally descriptive in satire can be illustrated by Pope's brilliant portrayal of the place where George Villiers was thought, mistakenly, to have drawn his last breath, a scene described late enough to have been influenced by one of Hogarth's shabby interiors:

> In the worst inn's worst room, with mat half-hung,
> The floors of plaister, and the walls of dung,
> On once a flock-bed, but repair'd with straw,
> With tape-ty'd curtains, never meant to draw,
> The George and Garter dangling from that bed
> Where tawdry yellow strove with dirty red,
> Great Villiers lies—[46]

This kind of realism portrait caricature attempted to achieve, for it was partly the art of literal appearance.

Before considering the art of portrait caricature, we ought to consider the prestige, the pride of place, and the dignity of portrait painting, whose position was fully comparable to that which the emblem had enjoyed earlier. What Richard Flecknoe claimed for his verbal "Pourtracts"—that they give the "Bodies resemblance together with the disposition of the Minde"[47]—was also claimed for the original art, after the great revolution of seventeenth-century painting had transformed languid, generalized, or emblematical representation into the achievement on canvas of the unique and living face. The body was given breathtaking verisimilitude in oil and watercolors; it was said of portraits that "if we'll credit our own Eyes, they live."[48] But the countenance on canvas also expressed the mind—*index animi vultus;* and Johnson's "Epitaph on Hogarth" closed and summarized a century-long chorus of praise for expressive *visibilia* in portrait art:

> Here death has clos'd the curious eyes
> That saw the manners in the face.[49]

In Pope's earlier years portraiture was regarded as having reached its zenith. Nowhere else, said Steele in 1711, are portraits done so well as in England: if the Virgin Mary should want to be painted once more from life (she had earlier sat to Saint Luke), she would surely come to England for a sitting.[50]

At least from the time of Richard Flecknoe on, verbal descriptions of individuals, both panegyric and satirical, were regularly called portraits. The analogy with the art of painting, besides conferring prestige, had many implications for the verbal form, particularly in verse. It implied concentration on detail, physical and otherwise; the fact that Dryden's *Absalom and Achitophel* has portraits of only twenty-seven contemporaries in 1,030 lines, while Marvell's earlier *Last Instructions* strikes at eighty-four contemporaries in 990 lines, results from a determination to render concentrated and organized detail in rich abundance.[51] The analogy also has other implications closely related to concentration and organization: verbal portraits try to achieve a stasis, in which time does have a stop, or virtually so, without narrative drive or progressive logical development. They are bounded in space; one moves clearly from a single individual to another; and they resemble a framed, not a flowing, art. Verbal portraits also achieve the simplicity, the economy, the severity (to use Dryden's term once more), the linear sharpness, of visual art, and they possess these qualities—of being framed, individual, static, and graphic—even when purely moral and mental descriptions are being made.

If we read Hogarth, we view Dryden and Pope. Something is on display, usually an individual in a portrait, sometimes an individual in a *conversazione*. The portrait of Atticus, though clearly framed and presented with unrelenting concentration, begins and progresses nonvisually, in grammar; in a brilliant series of conditions contrary to fact, one protasis after another is followed by a climactic and resolving apodosis, which is, however, a sad question: "Who would not weep if Atticus were he?" Yet even from this sinewy syntax a graphic setting appears, subtly, gradually, unmistakably. Atticus rules alone, tolerating no brother near the throne. Where is it he rules? Not in Turkey, although there is allusion to Oriental tyranny and fratricide, but in a place of fools and flatterers, templars and wits. And where would that be? No place else but contemporary clubland, where the pontificating, expectant, and eager dictator sits at the head of the table,

> While Wits and Templars ev'ry sentence raise,
> And wonder with a foolish face of praise.[52]

The great Addison has been reduced to easy triumphs at Button's Coffee House.

The most important implication of portraits, as also of the less frequent *conversazioni,* must be more fully discussed. Whenever the art of portraiture was made exemplary by poet or critic, the claims of literal realism were being enforced. Pope, himself a painter, laughed at the dauber who, "not being able to draw Portraits after the Life, was used to paint Faces at Random" and then look around for someone on whom he could force the "likeness."[53] Pope's own satiric portraits drive relentlessly, as Professor Boyce has seen, to particularity and individuality, and his art tended to dissipate all principles of generality.[54]

From the Restoration on, the art of satire, as an accompaniment to philosophic and scientific realism, attempted to be historically credible. Locke recorded in detail the physical symptoms of the first Earl of Shaftesbury, permitting a modern diagnosis of the ailment as a suppurating hydatid cyst of the liver. A surgeon operated successfully and left the wound open, inserting first a silver and then a golden tube for drainage. That pipe, nicknamed "Tapski," entered the anti-Shaftesbury literature:

> The silver pipe is no sufficient drain
> For the corruption of this little man,
> Who, though he ulcers have in ev'ry part,
> Is nowhere so corrupt as in his heart.[55]

But realistic detail was not enough. The ambition was to achieve the whole man. According to Henry Gally, the great ambition of personal satire was to "draw a Character so to the Life, as that it shall hit one Person, and him only."[56] The great satirists were thought to have succeeded. Horace Walpole believed that Dryden "caught the living likeness" of Buckingham and that "Pope completed the historical resemblance."[57]

Was reality ever satisfactorily achieved? No portrait of Pope can be judged "absolutely faithful, unbiased, and complete."[58] We have doubts about most identifications, even those made in the eighteenth century. Even when we are absolutely sure of the historical original (Atticus is indubitably Addison, Zimri indubitably Buckingham), we cannot now be sure of the justness of the portrait, and, human complexity and partisanship always having been more or less what they are now, no one could ever have been sure. There are exceptions, of course: so penetrating was the realism of a Dryden that it can be counted on to guide historians into understanding contemporary characters. On the whole, however, we must conclude that the realism of the satirical portrait belongs more often to art than to history; specifically, it belongs to the art of appearance, to a desire, like that of Defoe and of Swift in *Gulliver's Travels,* to seem real and therefore to be rhetorically effective. Writers seemed impelled to act as though satire, like all the didactic art of the period, had to resemble a clear and undistorting glass before which one could adjust one's manners and morals. Yet distortion lurks in the very medium. A limited frame that sets off only a few short lines requires simplification and selection. Even Flemish portraits, for all their abundant detail, select and emphasize; and Boswell, who called his great *Life of Johnson* a Flemish picture, has cast over his subject a distorting ray. Trevelyan treated visual caricatures with rapture: "How wonderful a thing it is to look back into the past as it actually was"; but he lapsed into doubt a few months later and conceded that these drawings need not always be taken literally.[59]

Dryden and Pope give us not history but art, not literal truth but rhetoric, not transcriptions of reality but revealing distortions based on an appearance of reality, an appearance that is never destroyed. In other words, they have created caricatures, and we now move from the adjective, *portrait,* to the substantive, *caricature.* The term *caricature,* applied to the grotesque emblems of Swift, will arouse no objection, but if applied to the dignity of Dryden or to the subtlety of Pope, it may. Caricature is usually thought of as gross and greatly exaggerated. But need it be? Caricature, by historical definition, must not destroy resemblance, and the term itself should say nothing about the degree or kind of satirical distortion, whether light or heavy, comic or tragic.

Painted portraits can idealize or degrade, but in the classical age both the idealization and the degradation were lightly and delicately done. And under an austere ideal of realistic representation there is not much difference between departures up or down from the norm of nature. Hogarth's portraying pencil went in both directions. In his portrait of Simon Fraser, Lord Lovat, the leader of the Highland chiefs who wanted to restore the Stuarts, the pencil moves downward, that is, toward satire (see fig. 1.).[60] Hogarth, however, drew from life; he visited the chief after his capture and on his way to the trial that found him guilty and condemned him to death. In the etching Lovat's face is fat; his clothes bulge; he wears a wig; he gestures as though speaking and counting, the index finger touching the right thumb. Is any of this portrayal unnatural distortion? We cannot now tell, but we may venture to assert that the represented face has been touched by a sinister line. The eyes, matching the grossness of the countenance, look drunken. There is no humble fear of death, as the tongue wags and the fingers count. Surely this man is not one to be entrusted with the destinies of a nation. Not an emblem, but moving slightly in that direction, and not a grotesque either, but bearing the hint of a hostile and distorting line, Hogarth's *Lord Lovat* is insistently more than representation. What is it then? Even though the distortion is slight, it must be called caricature—portrait caricature—for its resemblance remains fully intact while the representation distorts to achieve satirical meaning.

So close to this technique are the great verbal portraits of Dryden and Pope that they too must be named portrait caricatures. No other term available from literary or art history will do as well. The portrait caricature in its apogee has transcended the sketch, that series of descriptive strokes with details from reality badly or miscellaneously organized. It is no longer the credo character, consisting of assertions about a person's beliefs and attitudes. It is not now an agglomeration of psychological details that merely add up to complexity. The remnants of these antecedent forms may still confer weight, veracity, credibility, conviction, but the lines to Zimri and Cloe are portrait caricatures of the same genre—though in a different medium—as Hogarth's *Lord Lovat.*

Sir Thomas Browne's definition of wit supports the application to Swift of the word *caricature.* Did Augustan England provide a foundation for Pope's art of combined representation and distortion which we have also called caricature? It did, very precisely. John Hughes in 1712 defined *caricaturas* as "preserving, amidst distorted Proportions

Fig. 1. William Hogarth after Hogarth, *Simon, Lord Lovat*. Etching. Yale Center for British Art, Paul Mellon Collection.

and aggravated Features, some distinguishing Likeness of the Person. . . ."[61]
Dryden, too, had a clear notion of caricature; in discussing the theory
of satire, he said: "To spare the grossness of the names [fool, blockhead,
knave, and the like], and to do the thing yet more severely, is to draw
a full face [the ideal of resemblance], and to make the nose and cheeks
stand out [the caricaturing line]."[62]

Hughes was able to define portrait caricature with precision and
Dryden was able to apply its elements to his art with easy knowledge
because it had been precisely defined and precisely practiced by its
Italian masters. Its inventor, Annibale Carracci, not only made caricature heads but analyzed and defended his practice. Bernini also practiced the art and brought to it at least a part of the genius that
transformed Counter-Reformation Rome.[63] The invention and practice
of mock portraiture was vastly more than a mere trick of line and
illusion. It was an attempt to grasp the truth beneath the surface through
superficial distortion, to enter more deeply into nature by deforming
it, to create a new kind of comic art by a new vision of deformity.

The Scriblerians asked, mockingly, "Is there not an Architecture of
Vaults and Cellars, as well as of lofty Domes and Pyramids?"[64] It may
be answered, seriously, that caricature, both in its Italian origins and in
its later English literary manifestations, was a countertendency to the
dominant idealism. High culture was capable of turning itself upside
down; *The Dunciad* is the other and sometimes concealed face of *The
Rape of the Lock*. The art of distortion is to the art of idealization what
bathos is to hypsos: an exact inversion, to which the same techniques
apply, though the direction is down and not up. The art of distorting
reality is the precise reversal of *la belle nature*. It is nature consum-
mately wrought down to a lower pitch.

Thus far I have attempted to define portrait caricature; to establish
its relations to the visual art it paralleled; to disclose its historical roots;
and to point out the verbal equivalents of frame, bounding line, concentration on a single individual, vivid *visibilia,* and pictorial or graphic
realism. No attempt has yet been made to define the verbal equivalent
of the caricaturing line, the distorting ray or linear movement which,
whether gross or delicate, is at the very center of caricature, the art of
distorted but not destroyed resemblance.

The equivalent in verbal portraits to the caricaturing line or ray of pictorial art is, I believe, usually intellectual or psychological or moral. Concentration on a single individual establishes a resemblance to portrait; emphasis upon a single mental trait or dominating intellectual feature within that person creates the caricature. Paradoxically, the distorting emphasis may not, to the author, have seemed to be caricature at all; in the conscious mind it may have been a serious effort to enter into both universal and particular human psychology, that is, an effort to disclose a human gestalt, to establish a doctrine about human nature, or to reflect a conviction that human evil is a central eccentricity, a departure from the divine or the human norm. The effect of caricature remains, however, whether the author strikes in daylight anger or mischief, creating a distortion with conscious malice aforethought; or whether he is expressing a seriously held doctrine of the ruling passion; or whether he is following the rhetorical practice of exaggeration for emphasis; or whether he is doing all these things under impulses of a nighttime demon in the unconscious. In the end the writer has produced not literal but caricatured resemblance, as the following examples are designed to show.

Pope's Wharton is consumed by a ruling passion, "the Lust of Praise," and on that mark alone the picture is focused, an example of distortion by excessive clarity:

> This clue once found, unravels all the rest,
> The prospect clears, and Wharton stands confest.[65]

Long before Pope made the ruling passion basic to some of his portrait caricatures, Evelyn associated that idea with the line or shape of graphic art: "And now we mention Picture, since the *Posture,* or *Stroak* of one single Line, does often discover the Regnant Passion."[66]

The caricaturing line in the initial portrait of Achitophel in *Absalom and Achitophel* reduces the complex historical Shaftesbury to an intellectual diagram. But what a diagram it is! A black-and-white, unshadowed, larger-than-life Satan, who threatens human stability because he is "Bold, and Turbulent of wit," "Restless," "fiery," "daring," "great," "Pleas'd with the Danger."[67] "Turbulent of wit": *wit* means *imagina-*

tion, and Johnson's great phrase illuminates the distortion within Achitophel: "Dangerous Prevalence of Imagination."

Zimri is also tortured out of shape by imagination. This "Blest Madman's" imagination, however, is a lightweight, dilettantish kind of thing better called *fancy,* a kind of parody of the fretting, restless imagination of Dryden's Shaftesbury. Buckingham is various, an epitome of levity, a spinning top that draws all unstable motion to itself, the whirligig of revolutionary energy. Nature's pencil had doubtless distorted the man into caricature before he ever sat to Dryden, but Dryden heightens the color and concentrates the line.[68]

Pope's caricature of Philomedé[69] begins, "See Sin in State," and ends by displaying State in Sin. Henrietta Churchill, the Duchess of Marlborough (if indeed she is the original), is an intelligent woman and a peeress who is drunken and promiscuous in public. The incongruity distorts in two directions: the noble position of wife is prostituted and a decently placed, privately confined, socially stable promiscuity is also prostituted, for the woman is

> Chaste to her Husband, frank to all beside,
> A teeming Mistress, but a barren Bride.

Such a lady cannot remain even a balanced incongruity, and the caricaturing line plunges her into action, into social and intellectual disgrace. Philomedé lectures mankind on refined taste and soft passion; but, like the dictator at a feast who analyzes the wine and meat but eats a plain pudding at home, this peeress, falling in an instantaneous plunge to Pope's underworld,

> —stoops at once
> And makes her hearty meal upon a Dunce.

Conclusion

Graphically vivid details had appeared in English character sketches almost from the beginning. In 1650 Sir Anthony Weldon, James I's onetime clerk of the kitchen, described his royal master:

His eyes large, ever rowling after any stranger came into his presence, in so much, as many for shame have left the roome, as being out of countenance; his Beard was very thin; his tongue too large for his mouth, which ever made him speak full in the mouth, and made him drink very uncomely, as if eating his drinks, which came out into the cup of each side of his mouth; his skin was as soft as Taffeta Sarsnet, which felt so, because he never washt his hands, only rub'd his finger ends sleightly with the wet end of a Naptkin, . . . his walke was ever circular, his fingers ever in that walke fidling about his codpiece.[70]

This portrait has breathtaking realism but, lacking pictorial analogues, it is perhaps not caricature.

Hudibras's beard is of the emblematic variety, like Swift's salamander. Butler elsewhere provides many visually vivacious details, often seeming to write clear libretti for his illustrator. His characters are paintable and "engravable," and we see his hero's face and features, his dress, paunch, sword, and horse. We also see his beard, with its tile and whey and orange-gray colors. That adornment, however, is more than a watercolor in subtle chromatic gradation. It is, to use Butler's—and Swift's—own term, "Hieroglyphic"; it is an emblem with many alternative meanings: a Samson head of hair, or a hairy meteor that presages the fall of scepter and crown, or a "Hieroglyphic Spade" that digs its own and the state's grave, or a martyrlike sufferer spat upon and tortured by red-hot curling irons.[71] Butler has given us an *emblematic caricature.*

Juvenal's sixth satire, the one devoted to women, is a characterization of women and their society; although mischievously unfair to the sex, as Dryden noted,[72] it is perhaps a just indictment of the society. As a social scene it has breadth, vividness, and much truth; and its tiny vignettes are as memorable as its occasional longer narratives. But this conversationally lively and flowing commentary on corrupt women in a corrupt city is not pictorial and not even very visual, for it lacks framework, living individuals,[73] and sustained pictorial concentration.

What Juvenal's satire lacks, Pope's *Of the Characters of Women* abundantly possesses.[74] The poem begins with a paragraph that recalls the motifs and poses of fashionable portraits and directly "quotes" paintings by Van der Vaart and Titian. Pope then presents himself as a painter, preparing his ground and colors. Through the rest of the poem he sustains the metaphor and gives us a gallery of twelve portraits, each bounded and framed, each portraying or seeming to portray a living person. For a caricaturing line Pope invokes the *donna é mobile* theme but sharpens that cliché into one of "Contrarieties" existing within one person. With consummate skill, varying this theme to make it adaptable to an individual and also keeping it uniform and clear to serve as a line of distortion running through the entire gallery, Pope paints a central incongruity into the vivid but bounded realism of each representation. He has thus achieved *portrait caricature.*

In England emblematic caricature virtually disappeared from poetry, and portrait caricature moved from couplets to the novels of Fielding, Smollett, and Dickens and also to the prints of Hogarth, Rowlandson, Gillray, and Cruikshank.[75] After Pope, caricature declined in poetry. Although Charles Churchill achieved some power through bold and direct assertion and through descriptive strokes that can draw blood, the art of organized distortion was gone. The taut visual line of Dryden, Pope, and Swift had slackened. The brilliant Byron admired Dryden and wondered that Wordsworth,

> The "little boatman" and his *Peter Bell*
> Can sneer at him who drew "Achitophel."[76]

And yet Byron, for all his admiration of the neoclassical masters, was not himself able to sustain a verbal caricature. He reduced Hogarth's complex portrait of Wilkes to a single line, calling him "A merry, cock-eyed, curious-looking Sprite."[77] Byron's situations are comic and, when cosmic, marvelously grotesque; his individual words ring, in and out of the teasing rhyme; his stanzas are flexible; his rhythms flow with colloquial ease. But where are the tightly drawn individual emblems of Swift? Where are the galleries of Dryden and Pope, with their framed pictures, their sharply etched and deeply bitten black-and-white engravings? They have all gone—at least out of poetry. With the disappearance of *ut pictura poesis* in satire and the languishing of the habit of looking to emblem and portrait for inspiration and example, the bounded but energetic line of caricature has also disappeared. Never, since Pope, has literary satire in verse been able to keep its eye on a single object with the same relentless pictorial concentration. Never again has a distorting poetic line been able to reduce a victim to visual incongruity. The verbal art of concurrent representation and distortion has had its day and has ceased to be.[78]

3

"Such, Such Were the Joys": The Boyhood of the Man of Feeling

We were all children once, having come into the world as tiny babes. This fact scarcely requires elaboration, and I leave it at once. But does it follow that our cultural life needed to create the bewildering and fascinating variety of children that appears in Western literature and art? Many of us grew up haunted by the sentimental waifs of Victorian painting and of the fictions of Dickens and Hugo—wide-eyed, suffering little creatures, the girls prematurely maternal. I have no doubt that the Victorians were repelled and touched by the children of another age—the children of Hogarth and the fleet-footed and nimble-fingered truants of Defoe's London streets. No modern American can completely escape the shame of the spoiled child in our midst; and who can forget that frightening example of disorder and early sorrow, the Hollywoodish boy in Nathanael West's *Day of the Locust?*

Other cultures too have produced what gives off the sickly-sweet odor of spoliation: there are those juvenile puff pastries filled with overripe fruit at whom Jane Austen winced and Smollett fulminated, the products of vainglorious fools and their extravagant wives. The infancy of Louis XIII—not the childhood, mind you, the *infancy*—reveals a sexual precocity that would have shocked a Victorian lady into insensibility but that titillated the ladies of the French court. The gross manners of the little Bourbon scarcely anticipate what the great French authority on childhood, Philippe Ariés, calls *mignotage* (the word could be translated "coddling")—the tendency to make of the baby a pink and fragile plaything that looks like china but tolerates handling like rubber.[1] Little Louis's aggressive self-displays and his offers of himself have a darker side that do anticipate the infantile sexuality and the childhood jealousy in Freud's analysis of that period of life once called the Age of Innocence.

The whole career of the child in art and thought moves, like so much else in our cultural history, between the poles of reality and stylization. In an example I owe to the late H. T. Swedenberg, we get a glimpse of a reality that can only be called raw, the plotmaker Titus Oates's boyhood:

> When he grew up, writes his mother, I thought he would have been a Natural; for his Nose always run, and he slabber'd at the mouth, and his Father could not endure him; and when he came home at night the Boy would use to be in the Chimney corner, and my Husband would cry to take away the snotty Fool. . . .[2]

To move from that grimy but very human threesome, unpromising in everything except future mischief, to the triangles of myth (Mars, Venus, and Cupid) and of sacred story (Mary, Joseph, and the Christ child) requires a great imaginative leap into symbol and emblem. But even exalted children like Jesus or Cupid have been subjected to the changing conventions of our history. Cupid, unknown in his more or less modern form until the late Middle Ages, appeared decisively at the end of the fourteenth century, but after that what an abundance of life and love he appears to have been present at, seeing and not seeing! And the Christ child himself swings between the extremes of human reality[3] and superhuman efficaciousness—now nude, masculine, hungry, loving; now the stiff emblematic child of hieratic art, his little hand raised in benediction. Alexander Pope's emblematic Messiah (in the

poem beginning "Ye Nymphs of Solyma") is both pagan and Christian—
the future Savior and also a little Hercules who takes in his hand the
"crested basilisk and speckled snake," surveying their "green and lus-
trous scales" and playing with "their forky tongue."

Pope's baby, innocent and powerful, is a long way from Wordsworth's vision of Hartley Coleridge, except that they are both symbols.
Wordsworth's boy is a mysteriously wild creature, whose nonsense
syllables express unutterable thought; a mystic voyager, whose boat is
suspended between water and air, a dewdrop, a gem, who at the touch
of wrong in the stained and staining world will slip out of life or reality
altogether.[4]

Wordsworth brings us a little beyond our subject in time, to the
Romantic child, whose influence is still strong in the land and whose
complexities are rich and resonant.

> Such, such were the joys,
> When we all girls & boys,
> In our youth time were seen,
> On the Ecchoing Green.

Those words are sung by the old folks who sit, in Blake's lovely design,
under a large oak, watching the children at play in the fading daylight
just before they are summoned home to supper and rest.[5] (The song
bears no hint of the irony that George Orwell gave it when, in his fine
essay "Such, Such Were the Joys," he exposes the parental and magis-
terial tyrannies that darkened his boyhood.[6])

The Romantic child is not only or always the transparently simple
and uncomplicated creature of Blake's Song of Innocence. He is also a
leader, the best philosopher, the father of the man, a prophet-poet, a
Christ-figure. In Wordsworth he is presented with considerable rhetorical inflation as a bearer of immortal intimations. But we must forgive
the pretentious language, for the poet is struggling to express our deepest and most elusive intuitions. Coleridge censured those who ignore
or scorn a preoccupation with childhood for not being "good and wise
enough to contemplate the Past in the Present," and he seemed to

desire "a virtuous and thoughtful sensibility" that is continuous in the self-consciousness and that reaches back to our earliest childhood. Failing to achieve this integrity with our former selves, we risk being "annihilated as to the Past," dead to the future, and fragmented into many warring parts.[7]

Coleridge fervently hoped that a continuity in consciousness with the past would bring joy and tenderness. But it did not. The Romantic child is compounded of tenderness and terror. A good emblem of that combination is Wordsworth's kitten, which is at once innocently sportive like an infant and predatory like a tiger.[8] The poets who call infancy tender, innocent, lovely, sportive, sinless, and who compare the child with a summer rose can also darken the scene with terror. Both these seemingly contradictory emotions of happiness and fear rest on something that is "elementary" and "primary," to use Wordsworth's large but just terms for our passions. And that something is the combined love and fear we associate with our mothers.

For Coleridge "Mother" was a word "clothed about with Death— Mother of Love, & Fear, and Holy Hope."[9] The fearsome aspect of that mother is what reappears in the lady Geraldine of *Christabel,* a witch-serpent-woman; in the cursing mother of the ballad *The Three Graves;* and in the "Nightmare Life-in-Death," the woman "who thicks man's blood with cold" in the *Ancient Mariner.*

Wordsworth, in contrast, called the mother the child's "one dear Presence," which "irradiates and exalts / Objects through widest intercourse of sense."[10] It is this presence which haunts the landscape of the poet, who calls nature the nurse, guide, and guardian of the heart. He gives new meaning to the ageless personification Mother Nature. The nature who speaks in the Lucy poems is maternally possessive, taking unto herself the dead child and raising her to maturity:

> This Child I to myself will take;
> She shall be mine, and I will make
> A Lady of my own.

The powerful—and almost grotesque—fancy continues as the dead child moves to puberty:

And vital feelings of delight
Shall rear her form to stately height.
Her virgin bosom swell.
   ("Three Years She Grew")

Wordsworth said that "remotest infancy" was "A visible scene, on which the sun is shining."[11] That sun was forever darkened in the poet's eighth year, when his mother died. And one way to appreciate the boy in nature is to understand that he is seeking his lost mother and now and then finding her. It has often been said that at the heart of Wordsworthian sensibility is nature. But in the heart of nature are enshrined a mother and child, the mother shadowy/clear, loving/admonishing, lost/regained, regained/lost, like Paradise itself, which, by her presence, is more often a nest than a garden.[12]

Does the pre-Romantic child of the eighteenth century appear to be the father of Wordsworth's and Coleridge's child? Does the maternal orientation of Romantic vision appear in the boyhood of the Man of Feeling? Do the alternations of joy and fear caused by the Romantic Mother darken and lighten the pre-Romantic landscape? Does the eighteenth century take literally the personification of Nature as Mother? The answer appears to be yes, if we can trust the witness of those writers we shall now summon in two minor works, by Henry Mackenzie and William Beckford, and two major works, by two creators of modern sensibility, Goethe and Rousseau.

Peter Coveney, an authority on images of childhood in literature, has said that "the creation of the romantic child came from deep within the whole genesis of our modern literary culture."[13] The emphasis should fall on the word *deep*. For it will not do to think that we can understand what took place by remaining on the surface—by considering only the overt representations of the child, sentimental concern with the child, tears over the neglected and suffering child, or direct love of the child. Our subject is more complex than overt expressions; it concerns a consuming nostalgia for the past, the persistence of boyhood into manhood, and the regression from adult responsibility and mature and personal social relations to a condition that sometimes looks like arrested development.

The surface values of that *locus* un*classicus* of pre-Romantic feeling, Henry Mackenzie's *The Man of Feeling* (1771), a work that became Robert Burns's bosom favorite and that ran through some forty-six editions, have long been considered: the advanced and humane view of the sufferings in Bedlam, the redeemed prostitute, the wronged father, the death of the dog, the worthy anticolonial sentiments.[14] It is more germane for us to inquire what kind of man this particular Man of Feeling is. Painfully shy but not an awkward booby, the hero with the delicate heart is especially bashful before his beloved, a Miss Walton, who is also sentimental, blushes easily, and throws Harley into a fit of weeping when she tells a moving tale or even makes an affable comment to an inferior. When Harley has tried the ways of men in the city and rejected them for a return to the country, the author forces him to confront Miss Walton. Before that, he writes a pastoral poem, in which, in the mood of Gray's *Elegy*, he longs for the quiet calm of death. The verses, though they are as pallid as the young man's complexion, must be quoted in part, for they set the stage for the climax. After a conventional, graveyard-school mood of longing for night, gloom, silence, and the moon, the languishing poet proceeds:

> Let me walk where the new cover'd grave
> Allows the pale lover to rest!

> When shall I in its peaceable womb,
> Be laid with my sorrows asleep!
> Should Lavinia chance on my tomb—
> I could die if I thought she would weep.[15]

The novelist grants the hero his death wish—in the following manner: Miss Walton, free of an old obligation and therefore fully available, is waited on by Harley, who is seized by his old shyness. In addition, he is deathly weak following recovery from a fever. The frail and trembling Man of Feeling has lost his taste for life, and he now longs for death and heaven even as he declares his love to Miss Walton. Her tears flow without restraint. He kisses her hand. His languid cheek reddens slightly.

She faints. He falls dead. Two pale and motionless bodies are discovered lying together. Such, such are the joys in love of the Man of Feeling!

The hero's divorce from life, his frightened rejection of London, his longing for death and a grave near his mother's, his tormented fear of the opposite sex, his conception of love as tears and tales of woe, with death and swooning at the slightest physical contact—surely all this suggests the prolongation of boyhood into manhood. No mother is present in the novel, since Harley is early an orphan; but the air is heavy with a maternal presence nonetheless, a presence that arrests development. And the melting feelings that drench the handkerchief of Harley remind one of what Freud called love with an inhibited aim—that is, normal, adult, physical love diverted to sentiment by an inability to cross what persisting childhood continues to regard as forbidden frontiers.

Burns loved *The Man of Feeling.* Byron adored virtually as a Bible the next work we shall consider, William Beckford's *Vathek* (written in 1782).[16] From Mackenzie to Beckford is a movement from tears to raging fears, to splendidly dark Gothic fancies. The obvious features of *Schauer-Romantik* in *Vathek* have been sufficiently described: the strange tower of fifteen hundred stairs (we remember that at Fonthill, in what Lord Kenneth Clark[17] calls a "sudden outburst of romantic rhetoric," Beckford later built a weird tower that fell to the ground), the pyramid of skulls, the flickering splendors of the Hall of the Eblis, where giant forms pace with hands on their burning hearts and female black slaves are mute and blinded in the right eye. The scenes recall Piranesi's *Carceri (Prisons)* and they anticipate the gigantic hellscapes of John Martin.

If in *The Man of Feeling* the mother is present only implicitly in the effects, here she dominates the scene, above and under ground. For *Vathek* is an overpowering sexual fantasy involving a diabolist mother, a wildly sensual son (the Caliph), and a young maiden who chooses doom with him rather than "innocent" love with another. The vampire-mother desecrates sacred objects, cherishes dead bodies, and has many strange curiosities to satisfy. But she is obsessed by two aims—dominating her son, who is all appetite and rage, and winning the favor of the powers of darkness in order to possess the wealth of the pre-Adamite kings. The Caliph himself does not succeed in offending his demon mother by his raging appetite for murder, by his aggressions toward young and pretty boys, or by any of his orgies of anger and hatred. But when he chooses to offer his passion to a beautiful girl, the mother pursues and overtakes her son, and the demonic woman is revealed as the law of avenging chastity. She brings the three of them—her son, the maiden, and herself—into an underworld of great men who have fallen through pride and knowledge, especially the forbidden knowledge of sexuality. One of the greatest of the fallen monarchs in the Hall of Eblis, Soliman, groans out his guilt: "I basely suffered myself to be seduced by the love of women, and a curiosity that could not be restrained by sublunary things."[18] This hell is one created by a chaste and diabolical mother for a son who disobeys her command to win Satanic wealth because he has been diverted by the love of a beautiful woman.

The canvas of *Vathek* is not entirely painted in lurid infernal red or in the ominous chiaroscuro of darkness visible. Between the perverted society of mother and son and final damnation in the Hall of the Eblis is a pastoral interlude, the love affair of Nouronihar (such is the impossible name of the girl whom Vathek later seduces to passion and damnation) and her effeminate cousin, Gulchenrouz. These lovers appear to be early adolescents or even preadolescents in the smooth, monosexual nature of their caressing:[19] theirs is the world of the scarcely differentiated Cupid and Psyche, a world of presexual play in a kind of Blakean Innocence. It is this world which the girl rejects for everlasting damnation. The only alternatives, then, that the probing, unstable, but unmistakably avant-garde imagination of Beckford presents us are these: (1) the Innocence of undisturbed tranquility and the pure happiness of childhood or (2) the horrible Experience of passionate love, which is tormented beyond all civilized tolerance. It is small wonder that the author of *Vathek* says in his preface that his novel is "a story so horrid that I tremble while relating it, and have not a nerve in my frame but trembles like an aspen."[20]

T. S. Eliot has said somewhere that "sensibility alters in us all from age to age whether we will or no, but expression is only altered by a man of genius." Mackenzie was able to reflect the newer sensibility, but his turgid, loose, jumbled style could not possibly have altered any-

body's expression in life or art. Beckford's tortured and haunted imagination could intermittently produce memorably rhythmic prose and
plastically conceived scenes that embody as well as illustrate sensibility.
But the men of genius we now turn to, Goethe and Rousseau, managed,
through language, to create the feelings and forms that affected the life-
and art-styles of subsequent ages, including our own. It may be of major
significance that the Oedipal triangle implicit in *The Man of Feeling*
and melodramatically present in *Vathek* is the very mold and frame
that shaped *The Sorrows of the Young Werther* and Part I of the
Confessions.

Sturm und Drang is the German version of sensibility.[21] Taking its
shape around 1770 and ending in 1778, its career was meteoric, and
its most famous result was Goethe's youthful novel, *The Sorrows*—or
more accurately *The Sufferings*—of *the Young Werther,* the first work
of modern German literature to gain world fame, a novel that affected
custom and habit as well as artistic taste. Young men dressed like
Werther, in blue coats and yellow waistcoats, and even suicide became
fashionable. The novel was imitated, discussed, and damned. In Leipzig
its sale was forbidden. The theological faculty in Denmark placed it on
the index. The resident bishop of Milan bought up the entire edition
and had it destroyed. But still its fame raged. In Vienna it was worked
into a tragic ballet, and the fireworks that accompanied the sad, this-
worldly events of the fiction invited the imagination also to contemplate a pious future and presented "Werthers Zusammenkunft mit Lotte
in Elysium," the redeemed but still loving pair sojourning in the Elysian
fields.[22]

Such fame surely means that Goethe had entered deeply into the
emotional revolution of this time, becoming a cause as well as an effect.
He was in fact the eye of the *Sturm,* the raw nerve of the *Drang.* No
one who wishes to take the psychological dimensions of *sensibilité* can
ignore *Werther.*

How is it to be understood? Read as a conventional love triangle—
Werther the lover, Lotte the beloved, Albert the betrothed and later
the husband—the book is intolerable. Engagements can, of course, be
sacred, marriages more so; and eighteenth-century Europe, least of all
provincial Germany, had not forgotten the solemnity of marital troth.

But it is likely that the courtly and intellectual societies of a Europe that was still pretty toughminded and skeptical would have laughed, as we tend to, at the drenched handkerchiefs and even at the suicide if they had really felt that the heroine was only a dutiful young Frau and the hero a mooning young painter who had come into the picture too late.

What then of the view of the socialist realist Georg Lukács that *Werther* was an earnest of the new bourgeois revolutionary inheritance, a kind of John the Baptist proclaiming a fuller development of personality than the *ancien régime* could tolerate?[23] That calm, orderly pharisee, the husband Albert, would then stand for the conventional society against which Werther's sensibilities clash. But can the frightened and fleeing Werther honestly be regarded as the harbinger of any kind of dawn—as a large and liberating force? As we shall see, the hero rides on no wave of the future but on a wash backward to his own past. Essentially and fatally nostalgic and regressive, Werther is scarcely the cutting edge of a transforming revolution. For Goethe himself the novel was not placed on the stage of a changing culture but within "the life-process of every individual" as a story of "ungratified desires" and "thwarted happiness."[24]

But what happiness and what desires remain ungratified? And how have they been thwarted? Goethe, of course, does not tell us in his criticism, but in his novel he does. Lotte, whose own mother has died, is presented from the very outset as a mother, even though she is yet unmarried. She is surrounded, like one of those Victorian child-mothers, with eight brothers and sisters. Kindly, intelligent (she reads Goldsmith), avant-garde in her taste (she sighs the name of Klopstock to Werther in the storm), mature and calm when other ladies whimper in fright, she is a leader even in the festivities, the establisher of order at the dance. Fresh, young, healthy though she is, she can scarcely be said to be what Shakespeare calls "a dish" or "a morsel" in any conventional love-sense. She likes older people and is liked by them. In her relations with Werther she is more often like a mother than a beloved, scolding him and even giving him sweets as though he were a little boy. Albert, the aggrieved lover and husband, is, as Lukács implies, a force for order, but it is a paternal order. Like the stereotypical father, he is undiscriminatingly on the side of established value and insensitive to the individual suffering that law and custom entail.

Invading a relation in which the young lady is perceived as a mother and the lover-husband as a father, Werther's role is not and cannot be that of a manly lover in any version we know from life or art: he is not a knight, a hero, a Marquis de Sade, a Casanova, a Don Giovanni, a Lovelace, a Tom Jones. No, entering the triangle that Goethe had prepared for him, he had to be a child. And so he is one of the most authentic and most illuminating, as he was one of the most influential, of the pre-Romantic children. Toward Albert he feels manly jealously only very seldom if ever (one or two twinges at most), but he does feel the jealousy of the child, mixed with admiring love. Werther looks to Albert as to the embodiment of stern duty from whom he half expects the ministrations of the rod. Before Lotte the child-man is most fully revealed. In her presence he kneels; toward her white form he stretches out his arms, like the Blakean child toward a swan or a lamb. She remains, until the climax, sacred, untouchable, an angelic apparition, and his response is childlike, his emotions diffused, as it were, through the whole body, as in preadolescence. To him Lotte had to be unobtainable, and of her—as did so many Romantics of their women—he obsessively uses the word *innocent.*

And so the one passionate embrace at the end, fully forgivable in another arrangement of persons, is here inevitably unforgivable. In these terms the situation is desperately hopeless and can only lead to suicide. Werther had in reality committed a dark sin, and any sensitive reader of the novel senses that a deeply felt taboo has been violated. He must reject himself with finality. And Lotte must also reject him—with almost as much finality. Without intending mischief, she gives the pistols to the boy, who gives them to Werther. With one of these, a "gift," as it were, from his forbidden beloved, he dispatches himself in an ugly scene. On the eve of his death Werther cries out, "Sin? . . . I am punishing myself for it. . . . I shall go before you! go to my Father, to your Father . . . [I shall] see your mother! I shall see her, shall find her, ah, and pour out my whole heart to her! Your mother, your image."[25] Against so powerful an Oedipal obsession the world outside has no chance. The violent severing of the ties of life is not melodramatic or gratuitous, but inevitable.

One of the richest revelations in all literature of the human psyche is Rousseau's *Confessions.* The first of its two parts (covering the period from his birth in 1712 to 1741) is perhaps the greatest of the late eighteenth-century novels of sensibility, a work less of history than of art. The first part of the *Confessions,* written at Wooton in Staffordshire many years after the events described, reveals the confessor in the grip of a powerful nostalgia that tends to dim the actual landscape of one of the finest of verbal scene painters while it provides a rich and varied landscape of the mind.

Like so many works of Western art, this one records a Fall from Paradise, and that unhappy event can be precisely located in the village of Bossey near Geneva, when young Jean-Jacques and his cousin are boarders at the home of a Protestant pastor and his sister. Here the boy first meets injustice, and even violence, when he is accused wrongly and punished insanely for what he had not done or even thought of doing, breaking a lady's comb. Before that event, all was trust, joy, innocence, his face and his words and his deeds mirroring exactly the honest desires of the heart. After the event, lies insinuate into truth, the ways of honest openness become devious, and the accusations and expectations of society virtually guarantee that forbidden fruit will be eaten. The sexual aspect of the Fall at Bossey is related not so much to the general human condition as to the particular character of Rousseau himself. In suffering the corporeal punishments administered by Mademoiselle Lambercier, her catechumen ate of the tree of the knowledge of good and evil. The lady was thirty, as Rousseau remembered her (actually closer to forty); the boy was eight. What the lady's feelings were we can only attempt to divine; the author leaves us in no doubt concerning the boy's: "the chastisement drew my affections still more towards her who gave it," and "there was [I quote here the translation of 1783], without doubt, a froward instinct of sex in it." The sensual floggings established a permanent association of punishment with love, and of a young man with an older woman. It also made supplication on the knees one of Rousseau's most typical love-postures, a physical and psychological position that tended to obviate normal fulfillment. So much for the Fall.

The character in Part I of the *Confessions* who is the radiant and magnetic cause and creator of sensibility in the confessor—the person toward whom his emotions flow and from whom stream the organizing impulses of his inner life—is Madame de Warens. She is twenty-eight when the sixteen-year-old Rousseau meets her in the lovely village of Annecy. This amazing young woman, herself a Catholic convert, soon makes one of the young Protestant vagabond she takes in, sending him to Turin for instruction and for his submission to the Church. She then undertakes to guide him, establish a home for him, love him physically and spiritually, and create for him a veritable Eden after the Fall. The first habitation is the house in Annecy, where nature is sweet and green, reminding Rousseau of the pastor's house at Bossey, the site of the Fall during the time of Protestant catechism. The house was neat, decent, patriarchal; the kitchen and cellar well stocked—it was all comfort, plenty without pomp. Here, as Jean-Jacques says, "I gave myself up to the sweet sense of the well being I felt in her company."

For that sweet sense Rousseau has some difficulty in finding language. He of course uses the terms of his age—*sensibilité,* emotional sensibility, acute sensibility, feeling, affection. But preciser definition is necessary. He finds his new feelings more voluptuous than friendship but less impetuous than love. He decides that they must necessarily arise from a heterosexual relation, to which he applies such terms as *sentimens affectueux, tendres, doux, exquis.*[26] We are at the very center of Rousseau's sensibilities, and, remembering that he helped create the age that followed and has powerfully influenced our own, we must look more closely.

We do not have to look far before we see that in the heart of his heart this boy, who had lost his mother in childbirth, has recovered one in Mme. de Warens.

> From the first day the sweetest intimacy was established between us, and it continued to prevail during the rest of her life. "Little one" was my name, hers was "Mamma," and we always remained "Little one" and "Mamma," even when the passage of the

years had almost effaced the difference between our ages. The two names, I find, admirably express the tone of our behavior, the simplicity of our habits, and, what is more, the relation between our hearts. To me she was the most tender of mothers.... And if there was a sensual side of my attachment to her, that did not alter its character, but only made it more enchanting. I was intoxicated with delight at having a young and pretty mamma whom I loved to caress.[27]

Such was the nature of the idyll at Annecy. It continued essentially the same at Les Charmettes, when Rousseau was in his twenties. Since Les Charmettes can be said to be a prototypical Romantic garden and retreat, we should examine its features. It is there that "Maman" brings her "Petit" a ravishing calm, which consists neither of transport nor desire, though it is called an inexpressible delight. The place is modest, the house comfortable, the surroundings rural, the garden terraced, a chestnut plantation nearby, a vineyard and an orchard not far away. The whole place was a sanctuary, somewhat "wild and aloof." It was a place, Rousseau says compulsively, where "true happiness and innocence dwell," where life is "innocent and peaceful, free from all wickedness, grief, and distressing want."

A more precise description reveals that Maman remains an instructing elder, intimately caressed but not always moved; that a stable "father" is present; and that a usurping "brother," manlier than Jean-Jacques, introduces the serpent of jealousy into the Garden and finally causes departure to the world outside. An Oedipal nest, this Paradise had to be lost—not by a retributive death and suicide, as in *Werther,* but by expulsion for sin. Even before its end, the idyll had been streaked with menace. Vapors and hypochondria darkened the bright Geneva air, and the fears of a Calvinistic hell threatened, for dangerous frontiers had been crossed. Les Charmettes was Paradise (temporarily) Regained. It could not last, since it was created by regressing affection and life-denying isolation.

We get a perspective on it if we go outside the boundaries of Part I to the end of Part II of the *Confessions,* when Rousseau takes up the last retreat described in his autobiography, the island of Saint-Pierre, about a mile and a half in circumference, which belonged to Berne and lay in the very middle of the lake of Bienne—a place conducive by its very geography to separation from the world and to natural retreat. It provided all the necessities of life, a pleasing variety of landscape, and only one house, large, comfortable, and nestled in a hollow which protected it from the wind. It had all the features of what we now know to be the features of a Rousseauist nest, its chief quality being the emotional response it evoked: nostalgic, regressive, and isolationist. Here, as Rousseau says, "I was . . . taking leave of my age and my contemporaries, . . . bidding the world farewell." This was to be a "happy land of sleep," where the idleness is that of "a child who is incessantly on the move without ever doing anything, and at the same time it is the idleness of a rambling old man whose mind wanders while his arms are still."[28]

It may be objected that by focusing on a late—and actually unrealized—idyll dreamed by a man of about fifty-three, bitter now at the adversities created by hostile and persecuting contemporaries and perhaps justifiably paranoiac, we are projecting a false view on the idylls of the greatest of the eighteenth-century men of feeling. But is it really so? If the argument of this chapter is sound, we have moved almost inevitably to the isolation of St. Pierre in Berne by a clear path that leads to it from Bossey and the Protestant pastor's home through those most important enclosed gardens created by Maman at Annecy and Les Charmettes.

Blake seems to have perceived the permanent threat to human nature and society created by situations that prolong the boyhood of the Man of Feeling. In that grim and early masterpiece, *Tiriel,* a story of parental and societal tyranny, Blake has created a pseudo-Eden. In it live Har and his sister Heva. The two bathe together, guarded by a mother Mnetha; they sleep together, like children, and are watched by their mother. They talk like children, are frightened easily into breathless terror, and sit like children beneath an oak tree waited on by their mother. They play with flowers, and run after birds. Then, tired, they go to bed, "and in the night like infants sleep delighted with infant dreams." It is a real shock, then, to consult the illustrations and find that Heva is a largish woman of uncertain age and that Har has a long white beard. Blake's aged children grow out of Rousseau's last vision in the *Confessions,* where he dreamed of an idleness capable of beguiling both a child and an old man. "Such, such were the joys" that prolonged the boyhood of the Man of Feeling.

Lukács has said that "every great socio-historical revolution brings forth a new man."[29] In the eighteenth century that new man was the Man of Feeling. He did not win the day everywhere or easily. Against his challenges Smollett erected the Tory ideal of industry in the country, the healthy and modest ambition to make two blades of grass grow where one grew before, where diligence is rewarded, and where luxurious, extravagant wives die off conveniently. Samuel Johnson resisted, as both a public and private man, "the dangerous prevalence of imagination" (*Rasselas,* chap. 44), showing the hideousness of monomaniacal subjectivism and the disorders that attend that creeping sensibility which invades the recesses of the heart. And Jane Austen, who was painfully aware that a dark and powerful sensibility could destroy the integrity of life, erected traditional country order and sturdy country good sense against its ravages. But it is a tribute to the power of the movement that Johnson was not unaffected by it (he was "Johnson Agonistes," to use Bertrand H. Bronson's memorable phrase);[30] that Jane Austen's girl of sense, Elinor Dashwood, even after the spectacle of Marianne's destructive sensibility, does move in its direction; and that Smollett's self-portrait, Matt Bramble, mellows into a version of the Man of Feeling, engagingly, eccentrically picturesque and full of love for his natal place.

The examples I have given of paralyzing or life-denying isolation in the elysiums of the Age of Sensibility do not permit us to regard it simply as a period when what Jane Austen somewhere called "fettered inclinations" became unfettered. Such release might have been healthier, for then—to adapt Samuel Johnson—guilt might have been kept from the recesses of the heart and "the pleasures of fancy, the emotions of desire" might have been less dangerous, since they would neither have been hidden nor have escaped "the awe of observation."[31] Diderot, in a stunning defense of following natural inclination, confines those released pleasures to the vacation: "Put on the costume of the country you visit, but keep the suit of clothes you will need to go home in"; "be monks in France and savages in Tahiti."[32] Escapes into nature often led to delusion, since the rural haunt could not permanently allay or evade the pervasive and insufferable nostalgia:

> Hence, viper thoughts, that coil around my mind,
>   Reality's dark dream!
> I turn from you, and listen to the wind . . .

Since nature was required to absorb the shocks and convulsions of the denied and starved heart, it is not surprising that the windy lute might emit screams "of agony by torture lengthened out."[33] Coleridge's dejection was of course not that of Wordsworth, who did not always love or worship nature either; in fact, he sometimes attacked her violently, as though to ravish her. His transactions with the natural world began manic and ended depressive:

> We Poets in our youth begin in gladness;
> But thereof come in the end despondency and madness.[34]

Mario Praz believed the *roman noir,* the Gothic novel, and the taste for horror in dark forests, gloomy caverns, cemeteries, and storms developed directly out of the *fêtes galantes* of the age of Watteau, Boucher, and Zoffany—that terror arose from the feminine rococo and was caused by an age of delicacy in which women dominated.[35] There is truth in his observation. We have seen again and again that a powerful mother seems to pull the Man of Feeling back to permanent boyhood and make heaven and home kindred points. Men seem not to progress but to return. The leaders of sensibility do not advance to a brighter dawn, they all seem to wish to go home again.

German-Swiss longing for home (thought to be an absolutely ineffaceable *Heimweh*) became, as we learn from Alan D. McKillop, a ruling passion in our period.[36] Its music was that bagpipe tune called the *Ranz des Vaches* or the *Kuhreihen* (the cry of the cowherd), wild, irregular, and beautiful. Such, such were its joys that it brought back the scenes of home, hearth, and childhood; and these joys could be so intense and intoxicating "that if at any time [the Swiss] hear [the melody] even when abroad in foreign service, they burst into tears; and often fall sick, and even die, of a passionate desire to revisit their native land." We have given reasons why this bit of dubious folklore should have captured the imagination of Akenside, Rousseau, Byron, Scott, Goldsmith, William Wordsworth, and James Beattie, whom we have just quoted. No Swiss peasant may ever have sickened or died on hearing the *Kuhreihen*. But Werther and Mackenzie's Harley sickened and died of their sophisticated version of *Heimweh*, while Vathek and Coleridge were damned by theirs. The Jean-Jacques of the *Confessions* and the Wordsworth of the Lucy poems and of some episodes in the *Prelude* were artistically beautiful but socially ineffectual angels looking homeward. This investigation suggests irresistibly that the influential and much-praised pre-Romantic and Romantic sensibility, which I admire as powerful, was partly and insistently compounded of a gripping nostalgia for the nest.[37]

4

Eros and Psyche: Some Versions of Romantic Love and Delicacy

*I*n *1819 Keats* wrote his "Ode to Psyche" and hailed the immortalized maiden as the "brightest" and the "loveliest vision far / Of all Olympus' faded hierarchy"—superlatives fully appropriate to his own conceptions and to one interpretive tradition (the erotic) which he and his age inherited. But when the poet also saluted her as the "latest born," we must, for the sake of proper perspective, qualify his utterance. Psyche may indeed have come too late for the most ancient of vows and "too, too late" for the most naive and simple of "fond believing" lyres; but her story has in fact been in Western consciousness from at least the fourth century B.C. right up to the present time, when C. S. Lewis adapted the legend in his parable, *Till We have Faces,* and when Joyce Carol Oates gave the title of "Cupid and Psyche" to a story about a love and passion that moves from a vague longing and dread through fulfillment and almost simultaneous disgust to the warmth and safety of a marriage that is loveless but yet impregnable.

The millennial interest in the fable told by Apuleius in *The Golden Ass* has produced periods of intense preoccupation. Of these uses of the legend none is more interesting, varied, and profound—none pos-

71

sesses greater implications for contemporary life and manners—than the obsessive concern of pre-Romantic and Romantic writers and artists. Hellenistic, Roman, and early Christian culture had produced at least twenty surviving statues of Psyche alone, some seven Christian sarcophagi that used the legend, and a set of mosaics on a Christian ceiling in Rome from the early fourth century;[1] and of course to late antiquity belongs the distinction of having produced the seminal telling of the tale by Apuleius in about A.D. 125. But what we possess from that remote time is thin and lacks the power to engage the modern spirit. The allegorizing and erotic responses made in Renaissance, Mannerist, and Baroque culture produced monuments of painting that the later period cannot rival; but the impregnation of literature by the legend was slight, and the intellectual or moral content was often only a perfunctory and dutiful addendum. The revival of the story in the aesthetic movement of the late Victorians and early moderns has its examples of beauty, particularly in Rodin and in the lush harmonies and occasionally piercing melodies of César Franck's *Psyché,* a tone poem for chorus and orchestra; but the long retellings by Morris, Bridges, and John Jay Chapman oppress with luxuriant sweetness and remain of interest only as period pieces.

These latest literary renditions of Apuleius's story bear out Douglas Bush's contention that "no myth has been retold in English more elaborately than that of Cupid and Psyche."[2] But the late eighteenth and early nineteenth centuries provide us with more than elaborateness: for then there existed an imaginative affinity for the story that actively sought relation to its best manifestations in the past, that was widely diffused among all sorts and conditions of men, that penetrated deep into the spirit of geniuses like Canova, Keats, Blake, and that must have satisfied profound psychic and social needs.

Nothing shows cultural penetration and diffusion more clearly than popular caricature and humor. Rowlandson laughs at a "Life-Class" and shows on a shelf several classical busts: along with such "chestnuts" as the Farnese Hercules and the Venus Pudica stand Cupid and Psyche embracing. Gavin Hamilton puts Lord Gawdor in the studio of Canova, coolly contemplating the famous rescue of Psyche by Cupid. One of the remains of antiquity most admired in this period of fervid Hellenism was the Duke of Marlborough's gem, a cameo portraying the marriage of Cupid and Psyche, by all standards the best known ancient representation of the climax of Apuleius's story—a gem that Cipriani painted, Flaxman copied, and Bartolozzi engraved (fig. 2). It was so famous that when in 1797 Gillray wished to caricature the long-delayed nuptials of Miss Eliza Farren, actress, to Lord Derby, who had been paying her court for some sixteen years, he created a delicious travesty of the Marlborough onyx, in which the groom Cupid is not merely pudgy but paunchy, the Psyche is not only a shade taller than her godly lover (as on the gem) but towers up to twice his height though she is only half his girth, her face insistently virginal with a pointed chin and nose, her chest very flat, her veil heavy and impenetrable, and her Psyche wings folded as she is being led by Hymen to the nuptial bed (fig. 3).

Gillray's parody would have been less devastating in his own day and less delectable in ours had it merely been the merry reduction of a solemn and ancient marriage mystery. But it was also a spoof of overly refined allegorizing. Gillray has made a heavy and ordinary wedding band of the gold that had all too often been beaten to airy thinness by the neo-Platonists. For it was being said that the marriage represented on the ancient cameo symbolized the restoration of nature, when man's life will be renewed and when divine love and the soul will be reunited. Flaxman, a better artist than thinker, accepted the Pythagorean interpretation (Psyche, the earthly soul, unites with Cupid, supernal desire), which consorts well with his insubstantial linear forms. Thomas Taylor, the Platonic thinker of the Romantic period, who always did his best to dissolve corporeal grossness, makes the fable reek with ethereal ambrosia: Psyche is beautiful as every human *soul* is before it is "defiled by matter"; but she does tend to "reel" for a while in bodily desire, from which she needs to be rescued by an unearthly love that is pure and lofty. Back of Taylor lay centuries of allegorizing and spiritualizing. Gloster Ridley in 1747 made a Christian sermon of the story. The influential antiquarian Montfaucon in the early eighteenth century eliminated all sexuality from the examples he selected from antiquity— Psyche is a human moth who becomes an immortal butterfly. The religious seventeenth century allegorized the tale in expected ways, the English tending to make it a kind of allegorical *Paradise Lost* and *Re-*

Fig. 2. Sherwin after G. B. Cipriani, *The Marlborough Gem*. Ancient onyx. From Jacob Bryant, *A New System, or An Analysis of Ancient Mythology,* 3 vols. (London, 1775), 2:392, plate 11.

Fig. 3. James Gillray, *The Marriage of Cupid and Psyche*, published 3 May 1797. From George Paston, *Social Caricature in the Eighteenth Century* (London, 1904), fig. 78.

gained, but without Milton's Christian emphasis on the body. For Cal-
derón, Psyche's union represented the marriage of the Church to Christ—
another example of the kind of insistent spiritualization that transformed the Hebrew eroticism of the Song of Songs into Christian allegory. It would be of little value to follow this interpretive trail past
Boccaccio, Beroaldus, and Fulgentius, who interpret the tale directly,
all the way back to Plotinus and Plato, who do not, but who define love
in such a way as to reduce or limit the physical, elevating it to the
realm of immutable, eternal, and insubstantial ideas. As Erwin Panofsky
has pointed out, a powerful allegorizing strain *can* drain a conception
of all visual and palpable reality, as it did in the *dolce stil nuovo,* where
Cupid is made so spiritual that he cannot be described visually.[3]

One learns to suspect such fanatical unworldliness, even when it
comes under the aegis of a Plato or a Plotinus. Too often it looks like
headlong escape from a reality that frightens or disgusts. To penetrate,
for example, the full reasons why Coleridge denied the existence of
Cupid as a separate being would take more space than we have, but it
might help us understand the shuddering withdrawals that everywhere
characterize his private utterances about love: "I like not your Cupids—
Love exists wherever there is Goodness but it has no other Shape quite
and exclusively its own."[4] The child of Eros and Psyche, Pleasure, has
also been spiritualized beyond all carnal recognition, even though
Apuleius baptized her with the rather fleshy name, *Voluptas.* One turns
with relief to Samuel Johnson, who said, "When we talk of pleasure we
mean sensual pleasure. When a man says, he had pleasure with a woman,
he does not mean conversation."[5]

What Apuleius inserts into his novel strikes one as a fairy tale with
earthly and human meanings, a story of universal wish fulfillment, with
possibilities here and there of appropriate allegorization but with few
invitations to total etherealization. It is narrated by a crone to console
and divert a grieving and frightened girl who had been seized by bandits
just as her mother was putting her wedding dress on her. I *re*-narrate
it here with inserted references to relevant visual illustrations, since
one purpose of this essay is to derive from painting and sculpture a
perspective on the poetry discussed. Psyche, the heroine and protag-
onist—for this is a female-oriented story—is introduced at once, a

beautiful virgin, so ravishing that, even though a mere mortal, she sup-
plants Venus in receiving the homage of the adoring multitudes. (The
adoration of the virgin Psyche has not been much painted, but when
the seventeenth-century Neapolitan Luca Giordano portrayed the worship of Psyche in a picture now owned by the Queen, he created a
Virgin Mary and disposed the worshippers in a religious scene of adoration, making of the Cupid who appears in the sky a Christian angel.)
The jealous Venus now decrees that Psyche is to fall in love with some
outcast of a man, not realizing that her rival does not at all like her
lonely condition however revered she is and that she has come to hate
her own beauty. When Apollo orders her in a riddling erotic command
to marry a "viperous and fierce thing" whom even Jupiter fears, the
girl is quite prepared to leave her family, and, nothing daunted, she
does in fact go to the appointed place, an action which is treated rather
like entering a tomb than approaching a wedding altar. She is suddenly
transported to a goodly palace, where invisible servants prepare rich
banquets and where nightly she receives the visits of an invisible lover
who consummates their marriage. Knowing her husband only by touch
and smell, she is aware that his hair is curly and fragrant, his skin sweet,
smooth, and tender; but she is not satisfied without full sight. Urged
on by her jealous and unhappily married sisters, Psyche arms herself
with a dagger to be prepared to behead a serpent if in fact Apollo's
prophecy proves true and with a lamp to behold the husband, whoever
or whatever he is. The light reveals to the disobedient and excessively
curious girl Eros himself, a bright and delicate being with pure white
wings. (This scene, perhaps the most frequently and variously illustrated of all, led Fuseli to realize its female-erotic implications in a
drawing that presents the god as a man fully grown but passive and
Psyche as the aggressor in violence and curiosity leaning with sinister
force over the sleeping form.) Dropping hot oil on his wings, Psyche
awakens the god of love, who flies away, leaving her now to be the
victim of her divine mother-in-law's envy. A neglected and jealous Venus, a frustrated and impotent Cupid—such disorders make "Pleasure,
Grace, and Wit" disappear from human society, where now even a modest display of natural affection is considered disgusting—a situation
not unlike that of Blake's day, when the Eternals laugh at marital chastity

in England and say: "Have you known the Judgment that is arisen among the Zoa's of Albion? where a Man dare hardly to embrace his own Wife for the terrors of Chastity that they call By the name of Morality."[6] Psyche is now given a set of tasks that are literally impossible to perform. But helped by nature and divinity, by small beings like ants and great beings like Jove's eagle, she accomplishes them all. Not without grave risks, however: for example, after the nearly successful survival of her last trial the curiosity that had earlier impelled the girl to look upon her divine lover now impels her to open the box that contains the beauty of Proserpine, the female ruler of Hades. She falls instantaneously into a deathlike swoon, from which she recovers only when Cupid comes to her rescue. (That scene, another favorite of the illustrators, was made the subject of a splendid picture by Van Dyck, now at Hampton Court Palace, in which a Venus-like Psyche, richly and fully feminine, nevertheless recalls the dead Christ of a Lamentation, while a lively eager young Cupid descends like an Annunciation angel to awaken his bride.) The rest of the story moves quickly to triumph and apotheosis. Cupid arouses Psyche with a prick of his arrow, pleads his and her cause with Jupiter, who bestows on him the kiss of favor, decreeing that Eros must be forever wedded to the girl he has seduced. The gods receive them in rites celebrated in high Olympian fashion as Cupid and Psyche recline in the place of honor and Venus, now fully reconciled, dances while Apollo plays. Cupid and Psyche produce a child called Voluptas, or Pleasure, and the tale ends on a note of triumph, joy, and stability.

So the story, though plainly and pleasantly told, is rich and complex enough—as all fairy tales are—to justify the many varied interpretations which succeeding centuries have accorded it.

It is worth noting that at least three interpretations of the legend were prominent in the age of sensibility and Romanticism. One, the erotic or sometimes the erotic-uxorial, extends from the full-bodied, highly differentiated figures of antiquity (fig. 4) through famous frescoes by Raphael and Giulio Romano to Keats's pagan and voluptuous pair sleeping in the deep grass. The second introduces us to one kind of delicacy, that of gentle and unsullied innocence tremulously approaching experience and longing for it, the kind that appears in the

Psyches of the amazingly abundant and virtually unknown private art of Romney and in some of Blake's masterpieces, notably the *Book of Thel*. It may also be seen as present in Gérard's *Psyche* (fig. 5), whose soft and smooth body recalls the *biscuit* beloved in salon statuettes and in faïence, but whose developed breasts, plaintive eyes, and general attitude reveal an adolescent girl awaiting with quivering anticipation the mysterious coming of sexuality. The third interpretation embraces another kind of delicacy, one involving both lovers, the delicacy of narcissistic similitude and involution that reaches its climax in the love poetry of Shelley's maturity. It is this last response to the tale, difficult to define but insistently present in the late eighteenth and early nineteenth centuries, that will command the rest of our attention.

Plato, who recommended the transcendence of earthly love, would not prove helpful in explaining the obvious relish of a Keats contemplating Cupid and Psyche in amorous embrace, nor would the philosopher's view of intellectual love illumine that which is universally human in the tremulous and virginal desires of the modest, delicate, and threatened Psyche. But his postulation of a third sex, the androgynous—a unified condition to which we all supposedly long to return—may give us a perspective on the kind of Psyche-love in the period of sensibility and Romanticism that we now confront. But even here the embodied concept as it appears in the complex art of a Blake, Shelley, or Keats is vastly richer than the philosophic source or sanction. Thomas Love Peacock's Rhododaphne, who as earthly love is tempted away from hearth and home only to be felled at the end by a shaft from the quiver of heavenly love, may indeed come directly out of the *Symposium* and the *Phaedrus*. But androgyny in Shelley is much more complex in its constituents and in its origins, and bears only a superficial resemblance to Plato and the contemporary Platonists, who admittedly provided the envelope for much of Shelley's thought. Shelley's drive toward unisexuality is a basic force in his personality and art—one that is to be identified or associated with his interest in the hermaphrodite, in incest, and in homoeroticism, all these in turn related to his invincible self-scanning and perhaps partly unconscious self-projection.

Narcissistic delicacy is also of complex origin and long growth. Once more, it is the visual arts that provide the long and proper per-

Fig. 4. *Amor and Psyche*. Ancient Statue.
Museo Nazionale delle Terme, Rome. Alinari/
Art Resource, N.Y.

Fig. 5. François Gérard, *Psyche Receives the First
Kiss of Love*. Painting. Louvre, Paris. Alinari/Art
Resource, N.Y.

spective and also the concrete manifestations that capture our attention and engrave essential meanings in our consciousness. Correggio, that enormously popular painter, whose full influence on the eighteenth century and the Romantic period has never been fully assessed, created in one of his most beautiful paintings, *The School of Love*, in the National Gallery, London, a gorgeously fresh and delicate Venus, endowed with wings like her son Cupid, whom she instructs in erotic lore. The feature of the picture that strikes deepest is not the similarity of mother and child but the similarity of Venus and Mercury, who, but for the lack of breasts, almost reduplicates in his delicacy and effeminacy the Venus who accompanies him. Flesh of my flesh, as Adam said; soul of my soul, as Shelley would say. Correggio is not here portraying the Cupid and Psyche legend, but his presentation of a male and female both so alike in delicacy and beauty that they become almost indistinguishable is characteristic of later artistic versions of the legend. Even when he is a man and not a mere boy, Cupid's delicacy is not lost, as Pierino del Vaga shows by portraying an Eros with a visible *membrum virile* who is as feminine in face and musculature as the Psyche who examines his body. Spence in his *Polymetis* prints a plate in which Cupid and Psyche are virtually homosexual beings; and Romney presents a pair who are about to kiss, a painting not of passion but of the most delicate sensibility and tenderness, in which Cupid and Psyche are very much alike indeed, he, if anything, slenderer than she, his body more graciously and lightly modeled. And so it goes all through and even after our period—in Bartolozzi, Cumberland, Blake, and Gibson in England; Kratzenstein and Abilgaard in Denmark; Gérard in France (fig. 5)—and above all in Canova in Italy.

It is Canova who represents the climax of homogeneous delicacy in portraying Cupid and Psyche. His statue of Psyche alone presents a modest, downward-looking girl, her hair bound by a fillet, nude only to the waist, with extremely delicate hands and a look of bemused wonder, longing, and tenderness on her face as she contemplates a butterfly held between her fingers—a contemplation of herself, as it were, or of her own sexuality, or certainly of her own iconic sign, for she was supposed, as an emblem of the soul, to wear those wings (cf. fig. 7). Later, when Canova portrayed in marble the rescue by Cupid of

Fig. 6. Antonio Canova, *Amor and Psyche*. Statue. Louvre, Paris. Alinari/
Art Resource, N.Y.

Fig. 7. Canova, *Amor and Psyche*. Statue. Louvre, Paris.
Alinari/Art Resource, N.Y.

the unconscious Psyche after her trip to the underworld, he has the pair embrace and unite for a kiss, portraying that moment at which Psyche has barely returned to consciousness (fig. 6). Both bodies are equally delicate, both equally eager for union, the two together making one new androgynous whole—a fitting emblem of the Platonic *ur*-sex, if there ever was one. Even when, as he does in a still later sculpture (fig. 7), Canova has Cupid and Psyche stand with bodies apart, he scarcely differentiates them. Although Cupid's smooth, almost preadolescent pudenda are visible, he is highly effeminate and boyish; and Psyche, though equally delicate, may if anything be even slightly maturer as both gaze at the butterfly Cupid holds in his free hand. Such delicacy and similitude, similitude to the point of consanguinity, has of course been interpreted as "spiritual," "mystical," "immaterial," "Platonic," "exalted," and "ennobling," and Psyche has been called "creatura gentil—vaga angioletta"—that word *angel* again, which was used obsessively for over a century to describe a woman too rarefied for sexual desires.[7] But for Canova's true effect Flaubert's response is closer than that of the allegorizers just quoted—Flaubert who, when he saw Cupid and Psyche kissing, himself kissed the unconscious Psyche—"my first sensual kiss in a long time."[8] But a special kind of sensuality it is. Canova turns us in the right direction when he says that the kind of beauty he creates transports us back in time to "blessed innocence." (Actually, it seems closer to the sensuality of Freudian childhood.) Praz may be wrong in attributing Canova's effect to what he calls the artist's "idiosyncracy," a term he also used for the homoerotic tastes of Winckelmann; but the critic is surely right in seeing that the love portrayed in Canova is "preliminary," "contemplative," a kind of "adolescent eroticism," refined and passionless when compared with that of Raphael or Romano but with its own kind of sexual intensity, even though it can never be described as normal, adult, erotic.[9]

It is in fact compounded of the incestuous, the homoerotic, and the narcissistic—all of which, together and separately, became very prominent in that breakup of institutions and that soaring, or roaming, of the spirit that we witness in the coming of Romanticism. For over a century—from Dryden and Otway to Byron and Shelley—English poets were under the spell of the Song of Songs and its lyric apostrophes to voluptuous consanguinity: "Thou hast ravished my heart, my sister, my spouse;" "a garden inclosed is my sister, my spouse;" "Open to me, my sister, my love, my dove, my undefiled" (4:9, 12; 5:2). Coleridge, who philosophized about almost everything, philosophizes also about this. Longing for a heterosexual love that is "perfectly pure" and also "tender, graceful, soothing, consolatory"—all adjectives that could be applied to the Cupids and Psyches of this our last category— he takes heart from the fact that sisterly affection precedes the conjugal and makes the latter more "pure" and constant. Thus he finds, not a separation of family love from marital love, but a "beautiful gradation of attachment" that links child, cousin, sister, wife.[10] The smooth reduction of men and women to unisexuality and the love of sibling similitude are both close to the many portraits of effeminate men and to homoeroticism. Fuseli, who was very, very far from sharing the emotion we are now describing, was nonetheless capable of expressing it, so close was he to the tendencies of his times. As though consciously aware of the sexual synonymity of the innumerable Cupids and Psyches of his day, he himself transformed the Eros and Psyche of the Capitoline Museum in Rome (fig. 4)—two erotic adults, as we have seen—into a drawing entitled *Zwei einander küssende Frauen,* a sepia drawing close not only to his ancient model but also to his own highly sexual *Eros and Dione.*

It should not surprise us that the hermaphrodite seems to have become an obsessive symbol to the age of sensibility and Romanticism. Not, however, the Renaissance emblem of a Hermaphrodite who meets death—destruction by Juno's sword, Phoebus's water, and Mars's version of crucifixion—and is portrayed hanging by one leg from a tree, his head plunged in water, and a long spear through his body. Nor is Erasmus Darwin's pseudoscientific analysis typical nor Fuseli's combination of Michelangelesque hero and whorish temptress in one body. More typical is the sentiment that as the bodies join, the souls mingle, and that that love is the most beautiful which attaches itself to similars and ultimately attains the One. The view took tight hold, one that has not relaxed in our own day when Jung attempts to link incest to an androgynous archetype in a primordial unity, or when G. Wilson Knight asserts, somewhat too ecstatically, that in *Epipsychidion* Shelley stood "on the brink of a new state of being," moving mankind to "full sexual and bisexual integration," or when powerful currents driving toward the liberation of both the sexes from repressing conventions sweep us toward an undifferentiated commonality of men and women.[11]

The phenomenon we have noted—the physical assimilation in art of the bodies of Cupid and Psyche, which for centuries had been kept clearly and separately masculine and feminine—was of course allegorized in our period, as were the associated phenomena of the sister-spouse, homoerotic attachment, and the hermaphrodite. Later Walter Pater retold in crystalline prose the story of Cupid and Psyche, and the translator admits to having cooled the passion of Apuleius to what he calls *gravity.* Pater's Marius resists the temptation to see Cupid—and here he is being anachronistic—as Dante's "Lord of terrible aspect" or even as Praxiteles' earnestly erotic Love. Instead, the hero longs for "the ideal of a perfect imaginative love, centered upon a type of beauty entirely flawless and clean."[12] And "fleshless" and "sexless," we may wish to add, for there is evidence from Gray to Pater that Platonic thought has provided escape from unwanted or feared sexuality.

Even when there is no desire either to escape or mortify the flesh, there is a persistent tendency to reduce sexual differences and to spread, through all the relations of life, female gentleness. In Coleridge's Golden Age, what he called "the blest age of dignified Innocence," the sexes did exist, but with "just variety enough to . . . call forth the gentle restlessness and final union of chaste love, . . . by the natural affinity of their Beings."[13] Thomas Love Peacock is generally more robust than that, but in that pretty pagan poem of his to which reference has been made he praises the love of one soul in two bodies, the attraction of the similar and the neighborly that he makes prevail over the dangerous, tempting love of the earth and the demonic—his delicate, homogenous love being the source of

> All feelings that refine and bless,
> All kindness, sweetness, gentleness.[14]

Peacock, who wrote *Rhododaphne* right in the midst of the high Romantic achievement of the late teens of the nineteenth century, brings us to his friend, Shelley, who embodies, in one way or another, all the closely related trends we have been noticing—interest in incest, love of the hermaphrodite, and the creation of men and women in mirror images of one another. In fact, Shelley is the climax of such fusions as these. Never before or since has union been so intimately united or similars so passionately assimilated. From Shelley's pen we have no translation of Cupid and Psyche, no poem that is directly built on its foundation, and, if the concordance can be trusted, no direct references at all in the poetry to Cupid or Eros or Amor and no mention of Psyche by name. But Shelley knew the story and was enormously impressed by it—of that there can be no doubt—and Mary, at his instigation, had undertaken a translation.[15]

If the body and the mind are as closely related as they seem to be—ruffle the one and you ruffle the other, said Sterne—Shelley's spirit must have been effeminate, for his appearance, voice, and manner were those of the delicate hermaphrodite of art, and it was even said of him that he belonged to a kind of intermediate sex. It would be easily possible to exaggerate the ambivalence of so persistent a lover and so fertile a sire as Shelley actually was. But certainly the portrait by Severn shows the poet smooth-faced as a girl, sad in expression, with large limpid eyes—not unlike many of the Psyches that were painted in his own generation and the preceding one. Of Shelley's use of the hermaphrodite, we shall say something when we consider the poetry. Of his personal impulse toward the homoerotic and the incestuous, much has been said by biographers and biographically oriented critics. Shelley was literally haunted by the idea of incest, and several have found in him unmistakably bisexual tendencies.[16] But his first love affair, with Harriet Grove; his more than normal dependence on his sisters, made more acute by love disappointment; the friendship with Hogg—so intense and its temporary breakup so shattering; his tendency toward passivity; and his lifelong search for the woman who would bring him passionate warmth—all these which seem to unite in the nympholepsia of his brief years, we leave for those who can bring professional psychological insights. But there can be no doubt that Shelley's work and thought illustrate the Cupid-Psyche assimilation we have been considering. "Sister" remained one of Shelley's dearest literary words, the word for his heart's deepest desire; and his obvious echoing of the sister-spouse phraseology of the Song of Songs has erotic overtones of the deepest significance. In fact, his ideal in love was like that of Chateaubriand both in life and in the novelette, *René*—"mi-sorarale, mi-amoureuse, donc doublement proche."[17]

Conceptually, Shelley was capable of stating the ideal of amorous consanguinity, which in its largest context he related to love for community. Beginning at the mother's breast and growing with our growth, a desire for similarity distinguishes the human condition—"something within us which more and more thirsts after its likeness." That thirst Shelley elsewhere calls a "miniature" or "a mirror" of the "intellectual self," of "our entire self," an "antitype," "a soul within our soul that describes a circle around its proper paradise."[18] In *Alastor,* the vision the poet has in the vale of Cashmire brings before him a "veiled maid," "talking in low solemn tones."

> Her voice was like the voice of his own soul
> Heard in the calm of thought; . . .
>
> (lines 153–54)

And in *Laon and Cythna* the loving hero and heroine are brother and sister—a relationship that was changed to lover and friend when at the publisher's request the poem was revised into *The Revolt of Islam.* Shelley's defense, in the preface, of the original incest is conventional Enlightenment libertinism—like that of Diderot: the poet wanted to shake people out of their complacency, out of the trance of the ordinary, to break down outmoded opinion, and so weaken moribund institutions, transferring disgust and hatred from what is only a "crime of convention" to the deeper malevolence that underlies oppression and intolerance. But more important than such philosophizing is the artistic glow and texture of Shelley's verse on the love of Laon and Cythna— like the white and roseate intensity of Canova's smooth marble. In fact, Canova's *Amor and Psyche Kissing* (fig. 6) is an artistically close analogue to the love of the heroine and the hero as it is first presented— sisterly, adolescent, marmoreal, with an unmistakable eroticism that binds the similars together. For we remember that the adventure of

Laon and Cythna begins as a boy and a girl unite with a divine serpent in a rare and beautiful boat whose prow is made of moonstone. The ensuing adventures are exciting and sometimes heroic and even bloody; the ideals fought for by the protagonists are always humanitarian; the woman is often the leader and the saint. But through the ebb and flow of victory and defeat, of trial and danger, the delicacy of the sister-spouse love persists, love that had developed from childhood and that develops in a series of pictures that remind us of our Psyche in danger, of our Psyche's bridal night, and of our Psyche apotheosized as a heroine who struggles through fire and flood to martyrdom and victory. And like the Cupid and Psyche of legend, Shelley's pair rear a child, and are ultimately united in a vague Shelleyan paradise, the "Temple of the Spirit," where we may be sure that the love that should govern the world will forever burn and where the loving similitude of erotic sympathy will continue to feed on itself as like begets like. For just as Laon and Cythna resemble eath other, so the daughter resembles the mother, and "a light of liquid tenderness, like love" flows through the pearly convolutions of one, self-enclosed, delicate, pink, and intricate shell (if we may be pardoned a pseudo-Shelleyan image in response to the authentic poet). And from that central shell—or, if one wishes something more organic, from that self-contained network of vein, artery, tube, and canal—comes the energy that sends the Shelleyan mind spinning through space and time in its search for ultimate meaning.

Rosalind and Helen, a poem that is autobiographical in ways we cannot now discuss, contains two stories, each one devoted to a title character. Rosalind's story is that of deep love for a brother, which was frustrated by a father who knew the truth of the relationship; and of a subsequent marriage to a marital tyrant—an old, selfish, hard, guileful man who provides a contrast to the beloved brother (a situation not unlike that of Sieglinde, Siegmund, and Hunding in Wagner's *Die Walküre*). That brother remains the soul of Rosalind's soul even though she is condemned to exile and accused by her husband in his will even after that tyrant's death. Helen's story is that of a marriage to a poet who suffers torture and finally dies—an idealist, an attacker of institutions, a dreamer who made twins of love and life, though illness and death denied him the consummations of either. If Rosalind's half of the poem is incestuous, Helen's is narcissistic, for surely in Lionel, Shelley contemplates, loves, and sympathizes with himself—an introspection, really, that is symbolized by physical and spiritual union with Helen, in which mind fuses with mind ("like springs [that] ... mingle in one flood") as the blood of shared emotion flows "thro' the veins of each united frame."

Epipsychidion is one of the intensest love poems in the language, a climax of Romantic love sensibility, and it is useful to inquire where that intensity lies. It must be rescued first from attempts to Platonize all physical meaning out of it. Shelley, it is true, often expresses the desire for the supernal and the immortal—but this desire is not to escape physical passion but to prolong and embody it in forms that will keep its tremulous energy alive. The poem must also be rescued from attempts to make it a gauzily veiled seduction of Emilia Viviani or an expression of imagined rapture with a newly discovered virgin. No, the poem is that special kind of Shelleyan eroticism that unites similars. The object of this new affection repeats the images of the poet's oldest affections, going back to the earliest adolescence: Emilia is a "sweet sister," a "Spouse! Sister! Angel!" Shelley the lover springs up like "one sandalled with plumes of fire." Whence does he spring? From "the caverns of my dreamy youth." And that dreamy youth, we know, was always seeking a "soul out of my soul," "my heart's sister," who in this tremblingly ecstatic idealization of the physical that is generalized all through the body as in adolescence, that burns and is "yet ever inconsumable" because it does not attain normal climaxes, and that loses a sense of separate identity because "I am not thine; I am a part of *thee.*" The poem is gorgeous in color and piercing in tone, and its climax in the isle of bliss is expressed in some of the loveliest verse ever created. If we are to describe this ecstasy exactly or understand what it means we must relate it to the narcissistic delicacy of the Cupids and Psyches that look alike and not to Shelley's own view that he was dealing with ideas rather than with articles of real flesh and blood: "you might as well go to a gin-shop for a leg of mutton as expect anything human or earthly from me."

It was precisely because he did not deal with what looked like real flesh and blood, with human beings in recognizable human situations, that Mary Shelley was unhappy about *The Witch of Atlas,* our final example of Shelleyan involution in his love imaginings. The poem is an airy-fairy excursion beyond space and time into the realms of pure fancy, sometimes serious and sometimes playful, an Ariel-like and Puck-like excursion to the farthest reaches of the mental universe—a tissue of filmy dew and feathery softness that does, however, dart and flicker like mischievous flames. The Witch herself impresses one as a primal force in Shelley's own view of imaginative life; she is also primal in our view of Shelley and his age. She lives alone on Atlas's mountain when we first encounter her, the daughter of a mother who is one of the Atlantides and who lies "enfolden / In the warm shadow of her love- liness." She is not, however, self-generated, for she had been impreg- nated with the sun. The Witch, like her mother, is a self-enclosed form,

> A lovely lady garmented in light
> From her own beauty.

Like so many eighteenth-century and Romantic conceptions of love and poetry, the Witch is a civilizer of savage natures; and Silenus, Pan, Pria- pus, pygmies, polyphemuses, centaurs, satyrs all come to be tamed and subdued by her wonder and her mirth, their grotesque incongruities and dangers evaporating under her spell. Like Guido Reni whom the period—and Shelley himself—so much admired, like the beloved Bo- lognese eclectics, and above all like Canova, she smooths out the un- couth and distorted. Climactic in another quintessentially Shelleyan sense, the Witch preserves the lost sounds of earliest childhood, and no vision—least of all that of love—is lost in this lovely lady's cave. Once her love-scooped boat is in motion—what would Shelley do with- out a bark or pinnace?—the Witch can outstrip the wind and embarks on adventures that are too complex and numerous to follow, though they are all delightful. We pause to notice the love-implications—that she follows the lightning which is compared to a serpent, that she loves to observe "naked boys bridling tame water snakes," that she endows the beautiful with control, that she brings fulfillment to coy lovers, allowing them to find happiness in marriage that is "warm and kind." Acknowledging that she herself may find love later on, Shelley now presents her as chaster than Diana, "like a sexless bee," tasting all blossoms but confined to none. In other words, she is poised delicately, like a Canova Psyche, between childhood and womanly fullness. Among the sweet visions she scatters is one that is quintessentially Shelleyan in its suggestions of similitude:

> A pleasure sweet doubtless it was to see
> > Mortals subdued in all the shapes of sleep.
> Here lay two sister twins in infancy;
> > There, a lone youth who in his dreams did weep;
> Within, two lovers linked innocently
> > In their loose locks which over both did creep
> Like ivy from one stem.

And when the Witch creates a companion for herself, she kneads together fire and snow—a "repugnant mass" which she then tempers with "liquid love" and so creates "a fair Shape," gentle and strong, its bosom gently swelling, its wings "dyed in the ardours of the atmosphere," a being of sentiment and beauty and delicacy, who can, however, propel the pinnace with his wings and drive it toward the sun or moon. This being is a kind of Cupid—not of course the sensual Cupid we have discussed earlier but the smooth Cupid of indeterminate sexuality, whom the Witch names Hermaphroditus:

> A sexless thing it was, and in its growth
> > It seemed to have developed no defect
> Of either sex, yet all the grace of both.

In basic ways—both are now sexless—Hermaphroditus is the mirror image of its creator.

If images of love like those of Shelley's Witch and Hermaphroditus or of Canova's Cupids and Psyches represent as profound an expression of human desire as I think they do, one would be surprised if they died with Shelley or his age. And of course they did not. In art Thorvaldsen embodied the slender, delicate, and almost unisexual forms of tender youth in his Cupids and Psyches, as did Burne-Jones in his. Beyond direct renditions of the legend like Bridges's, Morris's, or Chapman's, already alluded to, the ideal remained deep in nineteenth-century consciousness. The image of the single sex continued to be compelling. To Comte, for example, the ideal human being was the hermaphrodite, and to Jung the androgyne was the archetype of the collective unconscious.[19]

Delicacy in Shelley may have bordered on the perverse, and a life devoted to a nympholeptical search for a Psyche who was sister and spouse ended in the bitterness of *The Triumph of Life*. But Romantic love had many-hued wings, and delicacy often resulted in other than tragic issues. To take but one example: Blake's lovely watercolor illustrations of Milton, which soften the asperities of the great Puritan poet into visions of gentle beauty and love, constitute an achievement impossible without the eighteenth-century transformation of the fierce Eros or the naughty Cupid into a more stable and delicate form, an achievement of grace in an age when sexual coarseness, grossness, or levity invaded even the highest circles and the brightest minds. To the shift from raw or robust eroticism to tender and sentimental love, the Cupid and Psyche legend made its contribution—a legend that itself records a triumph of femininity that a modern psychoanalytical interpreter calls a revolution similar to that signaled by the cry, "Great Pan is dead!" at the close of pagan antiquity.[20]

In this chapter we have confronted three kinds of response to Apuleius' fable: the erotic and two versions of the delicate—innocence seeking and undergoing experience and self-contained or homogeneous love in its subtle and perverse and beautiful manifestations. Perhaps those should be seen as a continuum, and we should regard the delicate in its finest manifestation as the flowering of a plant whose root is deep in erotic earth. Milton knew our legend, and he hailed the triumphant Cupid as "celestial" and his "dear Psyche" as an "eternal bride," the mother of youth and joy. This Miltonic summit is perhaps less a neo-Platonic division of the physical from the spiritual, less an abstraction of earthly meanings into bodiless ideas than it is the crown of organic Christian growth. The process of refinement in the eighteenth century, although it is not Christian, is also gentle and continuous; and Milton, rather than Plato, may provide the proper image. The exaltation of being from "first matter" to that which is "more refin'd, more spiritous, and pure," the poet enforces with the following metaphor:

> So from the root
> Springs lighter the green stalk, from thence the leaves
> More aerie, last the bright consummate floure.[21]

All the portrayers of delicate love, from Otway and Richardson to Rousseau and Shelley, have skirted the edge of abnormality and perversion. But at its best delicacy in love is a "bright consummate floure," whose roots lie deep in human physical desire but whose blossoming is one of the finer growths of sensibility and of the Romantic imagination. And the achievement of delicacy we have discussed anticipates an influential modern idea, that to feminize life may in fact be to civilize it.[22]

PART

II

Fig. 8. Guido Reni, *Michael the Archangel*. Painting. Church of Santa Maria della
Concezione. Alinari/Art Resource, N.Y.

5

Dryden's Grotesque: An Aspect of the Baroque in his Art and Criticism

The Baroque and Grotesque in Dryden's Theory and Practice

In the Church of the Capuchins in Rome, Guido Reni's *St. Michael* portrays the archangel about to plunge his sword with a powerful thrust into the body of Satan. The face of St. Michael wears an expression of smooth, graceful, detached, and somewhat effeminate calm that we today may find superficial but that the late seventeenth and the eighteenth centuries admired as ideal beauty.[1] In contrast to the victorious angel is the fallen devil, his face bearing suggestions of hair, his forehead wrinkled, his eyes dark and somewhat slanting, his nose pointed, his body muscular and powerful. Although threatening and ominous even in defeat, Satan is far from being the stock devil of folk legend. He is in fact fully human and looks a little like a middle-aged Italian (fig. 8).

Dryden knew of this painting. In "A Parallel of Poetry and Painting," written in 1695, he translated a long passage from Bellori, which included a letter by Guido about his *Saint Michael*. In the letter the painter discusses both his archangel and his devil. The angel he describes in terms that Dryden regularly used to express ideal beauty—

an idea of perfection formed in the imagination. The devil—an embodiment of the "contrary idea of deformity and ugliness"—Guido says he tried to blot from his remembrance.[2]

The painting embodies several baroque features: a conflict between good and evil in which good triumphs, a strong accent on the ideal humanity of the good figure, a subordination of landscape and background, the omission of the monstrous, and the achievement of success in an atmosphere of threatening turbulence. These and other features of the baroque appear almost everywhere in Dryden—in historical poem, heroic drama, satire, opera, and great ode.[3] But the painting—with Guido's letter about it—provides emblem and motto for this essay, not for general stylistic reasons but because the Satan portrayed—human and plausible and threatening—is precisely the kind of grotesque that Dryden was to develop in the decade of the sixties. Besides, Dryden, like Guido, tended to develop his grotesque as part of an antithesis. Both the grotesque and the contrast that contains it will be the focus of our attention in examining the main literary works of the poet's striking, formative,[4] difficult, and relatively unstudied early years.

Maximillian E. Novak has already called attention to the matter we are studying—"the baroque concept of playing the grotesque against the beautiful."[5] And Dryden himself stated the same principle, applying it to the theater: "Thus in a play, some characters must be raised, to oppose others; and to set them off the better ... thus, in my *Tyrannic Love,* the atheist Maximin is opposed to the character of St. Catherine."[6] One of Dryden's mentors, Ovid, himself a master of the grotesque, led the English poet's awakening "Invention and Fancy" into an attractive psychological locus for a modern concept of the grotesque: "*Ovid* images ... the movements and affections of the mind, either combating between two contrary passions, or extremely discompos'd by one."[7]

If the intellectual and stylistic habit of powerful contrast is eminently baroque, then so is the dark and distorted evil which that contrast brings into view. In the 1660s a poet whose eye and imagination were trained to absorb visual effects had the following vivid grotesques available to him from the baroque theater: fauns, satyrs, serpents, dragons, wild men of the forest, Medusas, mermaids, animals with human heads, Silenus, peasants at their feasts, comic masks.[8] Baroque and Mannerist painting contributed the signs of the Zodiac, weird metamorphoses based on Ovid, dreams, caprices, *bizzarrie*, Bacchic scenes, cockfights, Pan, Polyphemus, emaciated saints, severed heads, and horrendous details of plague, pestilence, illness, and damnation.[9] The walls of a cultivated man's *musée imaginaire* in the late seventeenth century were likely to be hung with all manner of memorable grotesquerie.

In his own infrequent uses and definitions of *grotesque* Dryden appears to be fully conventional. He associates it with the visual:[10] with clowns, the "Dutch kermis, the brutal sport of snick-or-snee," "the fine woman [who] ends in a fish's tail."[11] The term is used to refer to forms, details, and combinations that are heterogeneous, unnatural, false, deformed, hideous, deviant, fantastic, bizarre, extravagant, and laughable. Following Montaigne, Dryden applied the term to literature and found its equivalent in that lowest form of comedy, the farce.[12] The grotesque could provide pleasures, but these tended to be "accidental," not essential, unless the imitation was skillful.[13] So great was the prestige of natural and idealized representation in Dryden's scale of literary values that *grotesque* as a term of criticism was pejorative and not very important.

It was far different in his art and that of his contemporaries, where the presence of energetic and unforgettable representations of distorted reality and unnatural nature forced Dryden the critic to come to terms with the grotesque. In returning to a contrast that looks obsessive, between Venus and the lazar, Dryden kept asserting the right of the artist to represent leprous, beggarly, repulsive reality.[14] In 1668 he called *Bartholomew Fair* the "lowest kind of comedy" but conceded it was art because the low was "heightened" and intensified: though the "original be vile," Jonson "hath made an excellent lazar of it."[15] And in 1670 he defended his own portrayal of moral monstrosity in *Tyrannick Love:* "there is as much of Art, and as near an imitation of nature, in a *Lazare,* as in a *Venus.*"[16] In coming to accept critically as subjects of art the beggar as well as the monarch, the tyrant as well as the good king, the monster as well as Venus, Dryden's best teacher must have been himself. For there was a strain of the realistically grotesque in his poetry from the very beginning. The famous smallpox sores on the fair skin of Lord Hastings need not detain us. But the Swiftian portrayal in Dryden's first published poem of the aged as "Times Offal," with "Catarrhs, Rheums, Aches,"[17] presages a preoccupation with the grotesque and ugly during and beyond his apprentice years.

The grotesque in Dryden breaks out of the lexical confinements of criticism. It exists in life as well as in art. When men "fall into" it, they become fools or knaves on and off the stage. The grotesque can be a psychological and social condition. Dreamers, fanatics, lunatics, lovers who "rage" like Dido, the rabble who are as "blind" and "wild" as the Cyclops, the "Ghosts of Traitors" who join "Fanatick Spectres" on London bridge for a witches' Sabbath, the much-flattered heroes of Homer—a race of "ungodly man-killers" who murder, destroy God's images, and "never enjoy quiet in themselves, till they have taken it from all the world"—and those "good salvage Gentlemen" the critics and even Dryden himself who resembles them ("He is like you, a very Wolf, a Bear")—all these are versions of the grotesque who inhabit that literary-courtly-social-political-religious-learned milieu that Dryden made so peculiarly the subject of his art.[18] *Impossibile est* the grotesque *non describere*—because men living together were so adept at producing monstrosities. Dryden may have rhetorically heightened but he did not create "the lurid Anglican depiction of Catholics"[19] that appears in his verse:

> An hideous Figure of their Foes they drew,
> Nor lines, nor Looks, nor Shades, nor Colours true;
> And this Grotesque design, expos'd to Publick view.

This grotesque Dryden goes on to call an "Aegyptian Piece" with "barking Deities," "perverse," "unlike," a "daubing," a "Monster Mishapen," "ugly," like a "*Holland* emblem," full of "malice" and fit for "a Fiend."[20] Dryden's grotesque, broadly considered, is the result of an imperfect society pressing in on the mind of a sensitive and articulate observer.

The grotesques Dryden created during the 1660s differ from the grotesques of his mature polemical writings in poetry and prose in being less obviously, less consistently the objects of laughter and hatred. That is, Dryden seems to have had feelings about the earlier distortions

rather more mixed than he reveals later when his rhetorical and satirical techniques are more refined and his own commitments more single
and clear. The probing, inquiring young mind open to all the contemporary currents—naturalistic, skeptical, irreverent, even cynical—is
more ambiguously poised, and the grotesque formulation can contain
alloys of reason and sense, of attractive power and energy. It happens
that the wickedness and folly portrayed in the sixties had a sublime
side to it: Dryden's rhetoric in giving the devil his due is often brilliant
and blinding.

The grotesques of the sixties fall into three chief categories: the
social grotesque, the grotesque of superstition, and the grotesque of
power. Each example of these is presented in a contrast that has a
positive side. Sometimes these contrasts appear as in the massed opposites of baroque art, sometimes as argument.[21] The word-combats
range from "the amatory battledore and shuttlecock" that Saintsbury
deplored[22] to the rhymed theology of *Tyrannick Love*. The contrasts
are serious or comic, heroic or tragic. The arguments and the discussions, so often dismissed as frigid and unnatural in drama, could often
have fatal consequences in the action: Dryden said, "on the result [of
argumentation and discourse] the doing or not doing of some considerable action should depend."[23] It will be my aim to describe both
the grotesque and the positive value against which it is developed.

The Social Grotesque

Dryden was invincibly a public poet, his chief themes concerned with
men and their institutions. It is not surprising, then, that he should
early have thought of the grotesque in social terms. This category may
be regarded in three subdivisions: (1) the grotesque of passionate individualism that attacks the order of a good society that must be bound
by principles of honor and loyalty; (2) the grotesque of ridiculous folly,
which is exposed by a fashionable society in which a sublimely bungling
fool cannot operate; and (3) the grotesque of hypocrisy produced by
a nominally Christian society that in actuality is fiercely commercial
and aggressively imperialistic.

In *The Rival Ladies* and *Secret Love*[24] the grotesque is, typically,
developed in an antithesis, but that antithesis lies within the good peo-

ple. The evil is frustrated by a rigorous individual application of the ethical and social will. The danger represented by the grotesque of lawless passion and individualism remains, as it should in tragicomedies of the "platonic" variety, a threat only, a threat obviated in the happy denouement.

The response Dryden intended to elicit in *The Rival Ladies* (published in 1664), the second of his plays to be written and the third to be acted, was admiration for the ideal of honor and loyalty. Dryden seems to develop, in a formulation that today would be regarded as sexist, separate ideals for the man and the woman. For the man, the ideal against which the threatening grotesque is developed is loyalty to his word and to the social institution of betrothal. For the woman, it is loyalty to the first passion, the strong implication being that unattached, promiscuous passions forever changing their object constitute peculiarly dangerous and grotesque behavior in a woman.

It is clear that the ideals of male chivalry and of female loyalty and faithfulness are threatened by passions that Dryden twists into the grotesque. Gonsalvo's love of Julia arises like a fire of straw and is bluntly characterized as fury and madness. The fire does not burn itself out but grows as the play proceeds. In the end it is honorably put out by the good, knightly hero, himself a courteous man who respects social law and who quenches his passion out of respect for betrothal and for a rival's prior claims.

Julia's love is more complex in its nature and in its potential dangers. At the beginning she seeks a convent as a temporary asylum because her love is all desire ("Inclination") and offends virtue in its lack of judgment. Her love is like "the Day-dreams of melancholy Men":

> I think and think on things impossible,
> Yet love to wander in that Golden maze.
> (3.1.56–58)

Toward Gonsalvo her emotions range from grateful friendship and potential love to loathing, at least professed loathing. She is willing to make this concession at the end to Gonsalvo: "Were I not Rod'rick's first, I should be Yours." But in the end Julia must remain true to her first passion, which is admittedly "faulty" but so violent that its object could be changed only with grave danger:

> My violent Love for him, I know is faulty,
> Yet Passion never can be plac'd so ill,
> But that to change it is the greater Crime.
>
> (5.3.69–72)

An austere and perhaps even cruel idea! But the fickle Restoration seems to have known from experience the mad folly of allowing *la donna* to be *mobile*. Ferdinand in *The Tempest* laments the female propensity toward variety:

> Nature has done her part, she loves variety. . . .
> . . . No, no their Nurses teach them
> Change, when with two Nipples they divide their
> Liking.
>
> (4.1.106, 109–10)

Variety in love, so often wittily sung to light and delicate airs in Caroline gallantry, was apparently safest as a male privilege; from it woman must be guarded at all costs. But in this play male loyalty is a virtue too; as Gonsalvo says, in concluding the play,

> Beauty but gains, Obligement keeps our Love.
>
> (5.3.280)

In *Secret-Love, or the Maiden-Queen* (performed in 1667, published in 1668) we are concerned with the serious plot in verse, not with the pert and high-spirited prose of the comic subplot. The grotesque is here, as in the earlier "platonic" play, developed within the character of the heroine, the queen who has fallen in love beneath her and is the victim of passion, jealousy, and desires that alternate between love and violence. By her own confession, the Queen goes mad with love and shame: "O whither am I fallen?" (5.1.281) But in the end the distraught monarch renounces her love, approves the marriage of her beloved Philocles to her rival Candiope, dedicates her nobler love to her people, and even attains a rich, sable beauty as duty prevails over disruptive passion:

> Behold how night sits lovely on her eye-brows,
> While day breaks from her eyes!
>
> (5.1.430–31)

Philocles, ignorant at first of the Queen's passion for him, must struggle with ambition and desire when he learns of it:

> Sure I had one of the fallen Angels Dreams;
> All heav'n within this hour was mine!
>
> (5.1.434–35)

In both his "platonic" tragicomedies of love and loyalty Dryden uses an enlarging biblical, astronomical, and planetary imagery, showing that the stakes are high and that the social grotesque of lawless passion possesses its own kind of menacing dignity.

In *Sir Martin Mar-all* (performed in 1667, published in 1668) Warner, the servant, provides the ideal, and a most unusual one it is, seeming to anticipate the democratic aspirations expressed by the clever servants of Beaumarchais and Mozart. Warner is a Truewit, clever, sexually adequate, articulate, and an aggressive and imaginative master of the social mores of his society. He wins the lady, the high-spirited Millisent, because, in addition to his demonstrated mental and his promised physical potency, he is revealed at the end as a kinsman of a nobleman. He is, for all that, a Neander, a new man, and one may think that Dryden, consciously or not, must have put a good bit of himself into the servant-hero who rises in the world through mother wit, invention in plots, and skill in music and verse.

Against that social ideal of witty and successful energy, the grotesque of comic folly is developed in the invincible fool, Sir Martin, who does indeed "mar all" attempts by cleverer people to make him win his goal in love. Like Pope's personified Dulness, Sir Martin's bumbling folly grows and grows, finally able almost to propel itself. The fool, who rises like a balloon from abject repentance at the moment of failure to a sublime and impenetrable ambition as he undertakes each new plot, is not God's fool embodying the wisdom of simplicity and goodness. He is Nature's fool placed in Restoration society—as Rose says, he "has a rare way of acting a Fool, and does it ... naturally" (2.2.30–31). Totally incapable of mastering the Way of the World, he cries out, "I think there is a Fate upon me" (5.1.223). And so in fact there is, for the man is a wrench in the social machinery of his day, a grotesque created by the world where cleverness, a good memory, the ability to act, and skill in the arts open the doors to progress.

Sir Martin is a comic grotesque of the purest variety. Mentally and socially malformed, a distorted Gothic country figure, he is a throwback to another time and another place, set in a new and glittering milieu. When acted by Nokes, he must have been almost unbearably amusing to Dryden's contemporaries, as a total antithesis to the witty, successful, well-oiled machines of the Restoration beau monde. Pepys saw the play perhaps as many as ten times and judged it to be "undoubtedly the best comedy [that] ever was wrote."[25]

In placing "Christian" conquerors on the soil of the New World, Dryden seized an opportunity to develop a stunning variation of the social grotesque. Men professing the faith of Western Europe in a loving, forgiving, self-sacrificing God, confront the sun of natural religion and, bathed in its light, are exposed as avaricious, sadistically cruel, and intellectually tyrannical. The Spanish conquerors represent what Blake called the Abomination of Desolation, religion wrapped in war, and it is a measure of the intellectual boldness of the young Dryden that he was able to draw so unvarnished a grotesque of elements present in his own "Christian," commercial, and imperialistic culture.

The grotesque is developed against the dreams of the Golden Age revived by the sight and news of primitive men in the age of American exploration. In 1662 Dryden described the Indians Columbus had found as

> ... guiltless *Men,* who danc'd away their time,
> *Fresh* as their *Groves,* and *Happy* as their *Clime.*[26]

In *The Indian Emperor,* first performed in 1665, Dryden's hero, Cortez, replies to Vasquez's view that all is wild and savage in the New World:

> Wild and untaught are Terms which we alone
> Invent for fashions differing from our own:
> For all their Customs are by Nature wrought,
> But we, by Art, unteach what Nature taught.[27]
>   (1.1.11–14)

By the character of Montezuma, a noble savage adhering to the natural lights of his natural faith, those grotesques, the evil Christians, are most harshly judged as perverted, unnatural creatures.

In *The Indian Queen,* performed in 1663 ("the first fully formed heroic play to be acted in London,"[28] a collaboration of Howard and Dryden), Montezuma, always larger than life, reveals at the outset both passion in his love and also fury in his wars; yet he rises by the end of the play to keen and accurate perception, tolerance of the opinions of others, generosity to his foes—qualities becoming a well-tempered, magnanimous hero. In Dryden's own play on the American theme, *The Indian Emperour,* Montezuma once again begins faultily: his lionheart caught in the toils of love, he cuts a somewhat pathetic figure, weary of flesh and passion and racked with psychological "agues and Feavers" (2.1.109). But as before he ends as a noble natural hero, superior in character to all save Cortez, and at the close even dramatically superior to him.[29] Montezuma's moral stature shrivels almost all around him— the wild Indian rebels, his own timid and flattering priest, and above all the conquering Christians. Courteous, proud, tolerant (with a rela- tivistic view of religion), and loyal to his natural lights, he is the un- spoiled, natural ideal against which the Christians, lay and clerical, are revealed as grotesques. The light that exposes them is the light of his own natural father, the sun. What a stunning and noble contrast it is to the hellfire with which the priest threatens the noble savage! Monte- zuma says to the orthodox priest who tortures him:

> Thou art deceive'd: for whensoe're I Dye,
> The Sun my Father bears my Soul on high:

He lets down a Beam, and mounted there,
He draws it back, and pulls me through the Air:
I in the Eastern parts and rising Sky,
You in Heaven's downfal, and the West must lye.[30]

How the Christians shrivel in that natural light—they who preach orthodox doctrine while applying the whip and turning the wheel, who lust for women and for gold, and who profess a frowning Religion and are impelled by "holy avarice."[31]

Dryden's social grotesque is a complex and growing concept. In the two "platonic" plays it takes the form of an interior threat within the character of the good persons, the threat to human order of indulging disruptive sexual fantasies and desires. In the comedy the grotesque is an unconquerable folly that has to be displaced by the new man who rises from a hitherto unrecognized status. And in the Indian plays the grotesque grows within a Christian society that yields to the temptations of gain and the intellectual tyranny that beset it recurringly.

The Grotesque of Superstition

It is typical of the probing, tentative, and skeptical mind of the Dryden of the sixties that he should invert his antitheses. We have just beheld a good primitive setting off, in high relief, the social grotesque of Christian villainy. We now consider several socially tempered and benevolent men and women, both pagan and Christian, whose goodness sets off the fierce destructiveness and death-dealing energies of primitive men and women.

On the positive side of this contrast stand three characters from the plays of the decade, the first being Acacis in *The Indian Queen,* a Mexican prince, the son of the usurping Zempoalla—whose violent blood he has not inherited, although his brothers and sisters have—and of a dead father, a mild and gracious ruler from whom he has inherited gentle virtue, noble mildness, and civility. These virtues appear as he releases prisoners, nobly loves the good Orazia, shows chivalry to his rival Montezuma, remains loyal to his friend and his beloved even unto death. His own hand administers that death, and the entire, somewhat ambiguous world of *The Indian Queen* acknowledges the loss of a good and gentle man, charitable and noble, although an Indian pagan.

If Acacis is *homo naturaliter Christianus,* Cortez is the converse, *homo Christiane naturalis.* He possesses the natural virtues of the pagan just as the pagan possesses the Christian virtues of humility and charity. Dryden in this period reveals his scorn of confining religious creeds by producing benevolent heroes, baptized and unbaptized. Cortez is, as we have found, hardly a towering hero, and Montezuma upstages him in the final torture scenes of *The Indian Emperour.* But a hero he surely is, courteous as a lover, tolerant as a thinker, faithful to his promises. In the end he regrets deeply the bloody night perpetrated by Christian grotesques and pagan fanatics alike, and he puts an end to the flame, the sword, and the rack.

Berenice, the pagan Roman turned Christian in *Tyrannick Love* (performed in 1669), is the third example of the civilized norm, so complexly constituted already of the gentle natural man and the gentle Christian man. Berenice's civility is of sterner stuff than that of the males in the other plays, and her honoring of convention strikes a modern as chilling and perhaps even cruel. She prefers death to the breaking of the marriage vows that tie her to a criminal whom she hates. She frustrates a plot by her lover, whose love she chastely reciprocates, against the tyrant-husband, whom she loathes—a woman whom her lover describes as "Too ill a Mistress, and too good a Wife" (5.1.448). Nevertheless, Dryden gives her a Christian death of beauty and dignity, in full hope of an unsullied union with her lover in the other world. And one would have to say that his heroic woman, this staunch upholder of the virtues of order public and private, this somewhat aggressive instrument of necessary social law, joins Acacis and Cortez as an exemplar of love and loyalty, of the tempered personality whose fires are controlled by the pledged word and responsibility to society.

Against such an ideal Dryden presents the grotesque of wild, savage men and women, of vengeful passions, lawless beliefs, arrogant cosmologies—the grotesque of the elemental superstitions of primitive personality. This grotesque is, like its ideal counterpart, complexly constituted, appearing to be of two kinds: the grandly impressive, the protoheroic—the stuff of which true heroes could be made if the direction were different and the controls stronger; and the contemptible and loathsome, the ridiculously and dangerously subhuman or monstrous. Zempoalla is of the first variety and the monsters and sailors in *The Tempest* are of the second.

Zempoalla, the Indian Queen, with a few changes in the chemistry of her nature, could have emerged as finely tempered steel. But as Dryden and Howard present her, she is a cauldron of seething, primitive passions that boil in her blood and the blood of her children in the sequel play, *The Indian Emperour.* Zempoalla is a usurper, itself a dreaded role in Dryden's category of crimes. She desires the blood of the great, good man whom her gentle son Acacis wishes to spare. She is as passionate in love as she is violent in bloodlust, wishing to possess and command the person of Montezuma. A woman of dreams as well as rages, she seeks out the darker gods of night and the deep places of the earth and the mind; and she courts the elements, wild animals, and serpents, always associated in Dryden's mind with the older grotesques of superstition and supernatural evil. When these prove ineffectual, Zempoalla turns skeptic, rejecting them and their priests, shrieking out her impieties, threatening to burn the temples of the tyrants of the sky and earth who insist on leaving the soul in perplexity. Coming to believe that the gods are ruled by fate, whose harsh decrees determine the world's course, Zempoalla now and then reminds one of the Restoration naturalist and unbeliever, to whose arguments Dryden was of course fully exposed. Still, Zempoalla is not a metaphysical unbeliever; she is rather a frustrated believer, whose unbelief is the result of rage rather than ratiocination. The pagan queen hates virtue—and this is perhaps the most serious charge the play levels against her—considering it

> ... only heat
> That reigns in Youth, till age findes out the cheat.
> (3.1.98–99)

In this grotesque of wild blood and hot brains, Dryden anticipates his Maximin and pushes the grotesque of superstition to the frontiers of the grotesque of power.

Such majesty of evil the grotesques of the Davenant-Dryden *Tempest* do not possess, and we confront now the other type of superstitious grotesque, the bestial, ridiculous, but potentially dangerous low characters, Caliban, Sycorax, and the rabble. The monsters of this Restoration adaptation of Shakespeare do share with Zempoalla primitive passions and superstitions, but they are at the other end of the same category of grotesque.

Caliban is of course pure grotesque, closer than any other creation of this period to the abstract definition from the visual arts discussed earlier. He is a modification of Shakespeare's Caliban, whom Dryden admired as a dramatic creation and whom he characterized as possessing "all the discontents and malice of a witch, and of a devil, besides a convenient proportion of the deadly sins; gluttony, sloth, and lust are manifest; the dejectedness of a slave is likewise given him, and the ignorance of one bred up in a desert island."[32] Somewhat demythified, as are almost all of Shakespeare's unnatural or supernatural beings, Caliban remains grotesque, an uneducable human-animal—"What have we here, a man, or a fish?"[33]—lecherous, drunken, abject, doomed to a subhuman existence.

His sister Sycorax possesses approximately the same "virtues" as her brother, and the two together add to the monstrousness of the antihumanity they present by committing incest. Trincalo, who has learned that this lady had a "Witch to her Mother" and the Devil "for Father," comes upon the two in *delicto* that is uncommonly *flagrante:*

> ... I found her under an Elder-tree,
> upon a sweet Bed of Nettles, singing Tory, Rory, and
> Ranthum, Scantum, with her own natural brother.
> (4.2.107–109)

This unlovely, loving pair mingle with the sailors; and of the commerce of the islanders with the Italians Dryden makes lively and interesting drama. The sailors become rabble—grotesques of a subhuman variety, true brothers of the island naturals. The satire does not attack the lower classes per se: as humble sailors on their stout ship, fighting the storm at the beginning or going home at the end, they are admirable enough. But drunken, bawdy, lusting for power, trying to create a state and falling apart in the process, choosing a king, and playing at being dukes and viceroys—they then sink to the dregs of democracy and would pull down, if they could, all nobility, rank, station, decency, and order. So the sailors, separated from their rightful leaders and joining the monsters, become like them—only worse; and the island-creatures also sink lower for their commerce with the rabble:

> . . . The Monsters Sycorax and Caliban
> More monstrous grow by passions learn'd from man.
> (4.3.270–71)

With this kind of grotesque, essentially serious, Dryden permits himself to be playful, as in farce. And there is hoyden comedy as Trincalo courts Sycorax, whose "dear Blobber-lips" long for the boatswain's whistle and thirst for his wine (3.3.12).

When taken as a whole, Dryden's grotesque of superstition may be viewed as a modified Horatian monster with a head of some magnificence (Zempoalla's, say, the head of an angry and damned rebel). But the creature ends in a fish's tail—the "human" beasts of the Enchanted Island.[34]

The Grotesque of Power

The climax of the grotesque Dryden created in the sixties comes at the end of the decade in the character of Maximin, the villain of *Tyrannick Love*. As we have already said, that tyrant is anticipated in Zempoalla, lawless, passionate, and impious. It may be asked why I do not place the Indian Queen and the Roman Emperor in the same category of grotesque. To do so would obscure the essential differences between the characters and their respective cultures. The American Indies being conquered by Christians stand at a great imaginative and moral distance from imperial Rome being converted to Christianity. The first is a place of nature, the other of overripe institutions. Though Zempoalla is not a monster like Sycorax, she is closer to the island of natural superstitions than is Maximin. The queen lusts for power and tries to use it, but Maximin's power is wielded within institutions the Restoration would recognize as like its own—a powerful ruler abusing his prerogative, a hater of those familiar Anglo-Saxon institutions, the Senate and mixed government. Zempoalla is an exotic pagan confronting good natural men in her own culture. Maximin is also a pagan who nevertheless resembles Cromwell or a French or Spanish Bourbon and who faces pure and primitive Christian thought and character within his own state. Zempoalla faces a natural order than can be insulted with more or less impunity. Maximin faces a supernatural order against which his impieties are blasphemous.

The positive values against which Maximin's impious love and dangerous exercise of power should be seen come from both within and outside the play. The Prospero of *The Tempest,* a play written only two years or so before *Tyrannick Love,* provides one antithesis. Dryden and his collaborator waver somewhat in the presentation of his character, but the intention is clear: Prospero is supposed to be a good man of essentially benign power, trying first to train and then, failing that, to restrain the wild, natural man in his charge. Somewhat stiff and calculating in his dedication to safe social conventions for his children and excessively aware of the danger to them that love can create, he is nevertheless flexible. Each daughter is treated differently, and his plans are accommodated to rapidly changing conditions and accidents. All in all, Prospero is realistic ("How much in vain it is to bridle Nature"), generous (he will give Ariel his freedom), modest and even skeptical about his art ("perhaps my Art it self is false"), humble before mystery ("man's life is all a mist"), and pragmatic about the supernatural (if a fatal event is good, it is from heaven; if evil, from ourselves).[35] He anticipates the humanistic, ethical, disciplined, and dignified eighteenth-century man. Although indubitably wise, he is occasionally a bit stuffy and often cliché-ridden—an Imlac of the Restoration. And perhaps even a Voltaire or a Goethe! For this benevolent, demythologized ruler wants the magical island to become "a place of Refuge to the afflicted" (5.2.261–62).

It is of course not against Prospero in another play but against Saint Catherine in *Tyrannick Love* that Maximin, the grotesque of power, is developed. As one would expect from the lover of verse arguments, Dryden makes his Christian heroine a formidable dialectician, so successful in debate that her opponent, the pagan philosopher Apollonius, is converted and therewith carried off to his death. Her religion is in its essence the purest gospel—severely inward, austere, noble, exalted. The prohibitions against sin are, as in the Sermon on the Mount (Matthew 5:27–28), extended deep within to the very innermost psyche where desires are born. According to the heroine-saint, the Christian cannot even desire another's goods, and "we proscribe the least immodest thought" (2.1.218). Saint Catherine's own modesty is awesome and superhuman, if not inhuman. When the lusting but frustrated emperor has decreed a bloody end for the saint and her mother Felicia— the flesh will be torn away in "gory Gobbet[s]" until the beating heart is exposed—Catherine worries more about an immodest exposure of her body than about her and her mother's joint torture on the wheel and the spike: "Let not my body be the Tyrant's spoil" (5.1.251–307). And yet the queen is a woman of human feelings, as the great temptation provided by her mother's weakness and desire to be spared suffering reveals. Rejecting Maximin's foul lust, his gods, his empire, and his bed, Catherine goes to her death a fully responsible creature, willing her own demise and accepting the immediate consequences of her action (5.1.281–89). We are fortunately spared, by a Christian *deus ex machina,* from the sight of blood and rent flesh; and Catherine goes to a baroque death, one that could be represented by a great seventeenth-century Italian master in a house of prayer. But not by Bernini perhaps—for in Catherine of Alexandria there is no hint of the sensual, no recollection of that other Egyptian queen Dryden was later to represent on the stage, no combination of Ovidian voluptuousness and Christian sweetness.[36] The baroque of Catherine's climactic death is, rather, that of the purer, milder, blander Bolognese eclectics, the Carracci. It is a pure "spousal" scene, with the heavens radiant and the air filled with music and light and love.

Against so lofty an example of Christian thought and Christian style in life and art, the answering grotesque must, in its own way, be equally "pure." No outrageous, outlandish monster will do; only the highest, most dangerous evil, the evil of power. Since Christianity was embedded deep in culture, its solutions being theoretically within the power of every citizen and every leader, the threat to it must be plausibly immediate and real. And so Dryden has made it. If Catherine versifies Tillotson, Maximin recalls Hobbes.[37] Guido's Satan was said to resemble Pope Innocent X; Dryden's Maximin is a Western, even an English, Satan, now and then so close to Dryden himself that the following lines of Maximin might have been spoken by a member of the King's party in *Absalom and Achitophel:*

> The silly crowd, by Factious Teachers brought
> To think that Faith untrue their youth was taught,
> Run on in new Opinions blindly bold;
> Neglect, contemn, and then assault the old.
> Th' infectious madness seizes every part,
> And from the head distils upon the heart.
> And first they think their Princes faith not true,
> And then proceed to offer him a new;
> Which if refus'd, all duty from 'em cast,
> To their new Faith they make new Kings at last.
> (2.1.143–52)

Yet, however plausible his ideas, Maximin develops into a bitter, relentless tyrant who accepts no free will but his own, who regards the unfettered conscience as his greatest rival, and who would bind free reason with the hideous chains of intellectual and moral bondage. By the end the tyrant has become a full grotesque, decreeing and describing torture and then calling for "the sport" to begin. And in his death Maximin, raging at his own gods, roars out what we today would call black humor. The dying villain shakes his fist at his gods, declaring his everlasting enmity:

> ... Henceforth I and my World
> Hostility with you and yours declare:
> Look to it, Gods; for you th' Aggressors are ...
> Your trade of Heav'n shall soon be at a stand,
> And all your goods lie dead upon your hand.
> (5.1.593–99)

He and Placidius, next to the Emperor the most wicked of the characters, stab one another. Maximin sits dying upon the body of his *quon-*

dam officer, whom he gratuitously stabs again and again. As the tyrant dies, he imagines his own flight heavenward, a grotesque parody of Saint Catherine's martyr journey to bliss:

> And shoving back this Earth on which I sit
> I'le mount—and scatter all the Gods I hit.
>
> (5.1.633–34)

In dispatching Hobbes-Maximin, Dryden has created a scene of great grotesque energy, and the Emperor—hideous, bold, leering, and fiercely attractive—brings his half of a powerful baroque contrast to a fitting climax.

Maximin also brings the decade we have been studying to a fitting and summary climax. A grotesque of power, he recalls the grotesque of superstition. Grimly serious, he nonetheless has a touch of comic verve, and this *"Son* of a Thracian *Herds-man, and an* Alane *Woman"* is in his last hours not entirely unrelated to the rabble of *The Tempest* who play at being king and viceroy.[38]

Dryden and the Supernatural

Maximin is, as we have seen, a Satan who is fully human. He approaches the magnificent lineaments of Milton's mighty figure in *Paradise Lost*, which had appeared only three years before the publication of *Tyrannick Love*. To achieve the human grotesque of such plausibility and power must have cost Dryden a good deal of energy and even anguish, an anguish born out of his having to face the very disturbing matter of supernatural and metaphysical evil. No study of Dryden's grotesque in the sixties would be complex enough or complete if it ignored the marks of struggle one sees upon the poet in this, the period of his great apprenticeship. These signs appear in many strange and baffling ways: awkwardness and embarrassment in dealing with the supernatural, an excessive and inappropriate merriment in dealing with the diabolical, some infirmity of purpose and unsteadiness of aim in portraying his heroes, the dazzling virtuoso alternations in vigorous argument between equally plausible alternatives, and above all the heightening and lowering of the tone with confusing swiftness. The subject is extremely elusive and will have to be dealt with cautiously.

Dryden's treatment of the supernatural in general throws light on his handling of the diabolical grotesque in particular. In the preface to *Tyrannick Love,* in which he defends his right to portray the grotesque of evil that Maximin represents, he affirms, somewhat defensively one feels, his own faith in Christianity. He also declares that the drama ought to "second the Precepts of our Religion" in decently representing "patterns of piety ... equally removed from the extremes of Superstition and Prophaneness."[39] One must of course take Dryden at his word and respect his sincerity. At the same time one cannot ignore the many ironies and incongruities that surround this austerely Christian play, with its superhuman ideals of inward purity, played before an audience in part devout, and in part bawdy and loud, an audience that included scoffers, libertines, and the Merry Monarch himself. It was said that Nell Gwynn, who played the part of the love-martyr Valeria, became the King's mistress during the play's run—a fact which, if true, compounds the ironies, for the play was written to honor Charles's queen, Catherine of Braganza. That Nell as Valeria caught the roving royal eye may be no more than rumor, but it is fact that at the end of this most Christian play Nell spoke a naughty and merry epilogue as she was being carried off by the bearers just after she had stabbed herself for her lost love. Calling the bearer a "confounded Dog" for taking her away, she rose to speak the lilting lines that begin: "I am the ghost of poor departed *Nelly.*" Scoffing at her posthumous condition as a love martyr in a religious play, she said:

> I'm what I was, a little harmless Devil
> For after death, we Sprights have just such Natures
> We had, for all the World, when humane Creatures.
> (Epilogue, lines 4–6)

We are suddenly, after the baroque world of Catherine's death, in the land of Restoration gaiety that looks ahead to Pope's Ariel in *The Rape of the Lock.*

Such sudden change in tone from the sublimely serious to the wittily ridiculous was perhaps one of the young Dryden's concessions to his merry and irreverent age. If so, he made it often enough for one to feel that there was something far from uncongenial in the skeptical mockery that is now and then allowed to dissipate the solemnity. We have noticed how Zempoalla and Maximin can suddenly turn and rage against the gods and their priests. Although the Christian Dryden shared their dislike of priestcraft, he never treated the Christian Trinity with similar irreverence. And yet the examples that follow scarcely reveal humble piety before supernatural mystery. In *Annus Mirabilis* God himself extinguishes the flames that are devouring London:

> An hollow chrystal Pyramid he takes,
> In firmamental waters dipt above;
> Of it a brode Extinguisher he makes
> And hoods the flames that to their quarry strove.
>
> (stanza 281)

Samuel Johnson, who disliked religion in verse and who wanted grandeur to be kept general, found the image "unexpectedly mean," and Sir Walter Scott deplored the wild mixture of metaphors from candle-snuffing to falconry.[40] Prospero's supernatural ministrations never put him in the role of a celestial firechief, but he is sufficiently embarrassed to wonder if "perhaps my Art it self is False" (*Tempest* 3.5.154). In *The Indian Emperour* Dryden comes close to parodying *On the Morning of Christ's Nativity* (lines 173–220): just as the coming of the Christ child sent the pagan deities whirring through the air, so in Mexico the new Christian God will drive away the native deities from their beloved earth, a God who, in a bitter final irony, turns out to be Gold:

> A God more strong, who all the gods commands,
> Drives us to exile from our Native Lands;
> The Air swarms thick with wandring Deities,
> Which drowsily like humming Beetles rise
> From their lov'd Earth, where peacefully they slept,
> And far from Heaven a long possession kept.
> The frightened *Satyrs* that in Woods delight,
> Now into Plains with prick'd up Ears take flight;
> And scudding thence, while they their horn-feet ply
> About their Syres the little *Silvans* cry.

> A Nation loving Gold must rule this place,
> Our Temples Ruine, and our Rites Deface.
> (2.1.25–36)

The contemporary of Hobbes, the member and apostrophizer of the Royal Society, is not at ease in Zion! Dryden's vision of the supernatural reveals, in his earlier years, a curious mixture of embarrassment, distance, and a humor which is wry if not black.

If the portrayals of supernatural good boldly approach the irreverent, the portrayals of cosmological evil go over the border. Dryden of course had inevitably to be concerned with the devil: anyone setting his hand to the creation of grotesques would sooner or later encounter the father of all grotesquerie. The young Dryden was absolutely relentless in reducing the "black Gentleman" (*Tempest* 3.2.46) to a comic grotesque. In his "first attempt ... in *Dramatique Poetry*," *The Wild Gallant*, performed first in 1662, the hero Loveby has much to do with Satan (who is only one of the *dramatis personae* in disguise). He meets the devil outrageously tricked out "à l'antique," jokes with him, treats him as an old friend, uses him to flick at churchmen and fanatics, praises him as a "very honest and well-natur'd fellow," chides him when he does not reveal the source of the unexpected gifts of money. Loveby gets cozy enough to allow the devil to call himself Loveby's "Genius," and he addresses Loveby as "my Son," leading him in the end to his beloved Constance and the person who marries them. Evil spirits appear in the play and are mercilessly laughed at, as are those who believe in them. One old fool believes that the females of his household and also he himself are pregnant by the agency of the devil. Surely Dryden is joining the younger wits of the Restoration in laughing at the devil-superstitions of their elders.[41]

Horseplay with the devil and his minions was not new to the drama. But even in devil farces Satan was taken seriously, sometimes carried off by a Vice to the place of torment. Ben Jonson's devil is an ass, not because he is laughable or because he is only someone else in disguise but because he is outwitted in evil by men who are worse than he.[42] Dryden's purpose, however, is not to satirize evil as stupid but to laugh at the devil himself, his very existence. He dethrones Satan from a place of fear in men's minds to an object of their comfortable laughter. In *The Tempest* he and his collaborator continue the gay demystification of the supernatural evil being. The Italian nobility on the enchanted island are hungry and thirsty and have a vision of what Gonzalo especially longs for—"Boyl'd/Bak'd, and Roasted" meat. Eight fat, well-fed spirits enter with a cornucopia. Gonzalo, thinking they are devils, cries out, "O for a Collop of that large-haunch'd Devil." For a feast at that moment the Christian will risk even damnation: "if the black Gentleman be so ill-natur'd, he may do his pleasure" (3.2.34–35, 39, 46–47).

Dryden's merry way with Satan and devils make it difficult to believe we are in the age of Baxter and Bunyan, an age when Satan was very real and very much feared and when orthodox opinion urged that disbelief in supernatural evil was a first and inevitable step to atheism. And of course Dryden's age and the immediately subsequent one reacted strongly. Writing in 1673 Richard Leigh attacked the supernatural in heroic plays, not only "Heroes, more lawless than their *Savages*" but also "notional *creatures, Astrall* Spirits, *Ghosts, & Idols.*"[43] Two years before Dryden's death, Jeremy Collier censured Dryden's *An Evening's Love, or the Mock Astrologer* (performed in 1668). Its first act includes a scene set in a chapel, a "sacred place" to the Christian polemicist but one Dryden desecrated with ridicule of devotion along with the other world, Scripture, and the sanctions of the pulpit. Collier was especially offended at the ridicule of supernatural evil, the making sport, at the close of the play, with "Apparitions and Fiends": "One of the Devils sneezes, upon this they give him the blessing of the Occasion, and conclude *he has got cold by being too long out of the Fire.*" Granted that Collier's conscience was excessively tender—he was capable of being outraged at the charming opening lines of *Absalom and Achitophel*—and granted too that he came late in the day and may have taken much too seriously the Restoration joke. But is it hard to see why the faithful would wince, since they believed with Collier that the Scriptures provided "a frightful Idea ... of hell," described in "all the Circumstance of Terror," as a "solemn warning"? Dryden had in their eyes "diverted himself with the *Terrors of Christianity.*"[44]

Dryden's ambiguous way with the supernatural has complicated our analysis of his early grotesque. It should not obscure his twofold achievement in the sixties: the casting out of the demonic, allaying the power of the superstitious grotesque by laughing at it and burying it; and transferring evil to the mind of responsible men and to society. He shifted the focus of evil from super-nature to nature, from a postmortem hell to present reality. Satan does not cease to exist, only the excessively grotesque and farcically inhuman devil does. Satan is reborn as a human figure, vastly more menacing than the cloven-footed and horned monster of superstitious legend and primitive belief. He becomes the superstitious tyrant, Zempoalla, and that antiman, the towering grotesque of power, the Emperor Maximin. These grotesques make war, as Satan always has, on humanity itself and the structures it has erected for stability and self-realization. And these grotesques, along with others we have studied, reappear in Dryden's greatest work. The grotesque social fool is born again in Buckingham, Achitophel revives the grotesque of lawless and destructive power, and the grotesque of untamable passion, primitive and unstable, reappears in Antony.

To prepare for that great human achievement—the creation of grotesques that threaten psychological peace and corporate safety— Dryden had to exorcize unnatural silliness, to cleanse the mind of supernatural fears and to allow it to concentrate on real and present dangers. He abandoned or modified the older and cruder grotesques of emblem art, or mannerist and baroque hells, of the distorted fancies of *capricci* and *bizzarrie,* and even of Shakespearean magic.[45] The last scene (5.2) of the Dryden-Davenant *Tempest* is eloquent. It is the fate of those "mishapen creatures" (1.223), as Gonzalo calls them, the children of a powerful witch, simply to be left behind. Caliban, who is now over his illusion that the drunken sailors were gods and who now, with his sister, admires those "brave Sprights" (1.228), the Italian gentlemen, has to submit to rejection, as though there were no room for him and his kind in the new dispensation. And when Sycorax offers to come with her sometime husband and keep him warm in his cabin, Trincalo replies: "No my dainty Dy-dapper, you have a tender constitution, and will be sick a Ship-board. You are partly Fish and may swim after me. I wish you a good Voyage" (2.251–53). And so the grotesques are remanded to the sea, out of sight, out of mind—to that oblivion, in fact, where Guido had wanted to consign the Satan that appeared at the bottom of his painting.

Little in human culture appears to be permanent. And Dryden's attempts to exorcize metaphysical and cosmological evil, transferring the grotesque to the human plane where human reason and will could subdue it, opened up enormous possibilities for realistic, social, psychological, and moral art. But in the Romantic age and in post-Romantic cultures the grotesque of deep, permanent, and universal evil—fatal, deterministic, unassailable—revived and was remythologized. To return to the painting (fig. 8) which I made the emblem of this chapter, we find that Hawthorne's Miriam in *The Marble Faun* rejects Hilda's love of the dainty and beautiful Saint Michael and calls for a "smoke-blackened fiery-eyed demon, bestriding that nice young angel, clutching his white throat with one of his hinder claws" (chap. 20). Dryden might have said of Hawthorne and his century, or of Joyce and our century, what he could not have said of the eighteenth century, but what he did say of the seventeenth century as it and his own life came to a close: "Thy Chase had a Beast in View."[46]

Dryden's grotesque belongs, as we saw at the outset, in the framework of the baroque. Just as Dryden throughout his life continued to produce versions of the grotesque, so the larger ambience of the baroque continued to nourish his spirit. In what he termed "the descriptions or images" of that early "Historical Poem," *Annus Mirabilis,* the pompous decorations of baroque allegory constantly appear. The heroic plays continue to develop those massive baroque contrasts of light and dark, good and evil, that we have considered to be the essence of the antithesis that contains the grotesque. One great historical satire at least, *Absalom and Achitophel,* unfolds a grand baroque display, massing its opposed legions as though on the canvas of a Last Judgment. *All for Love* may recall one of the central themes—and even visual arrangements—of seventeenth-century art, Hercules at the Crossroads, and the great odes embody such obsessive baroque subjects as Saint Cecilia and such insistently baroque habits of thought as the virtual deification of authority. Dryden's imagination submits easily to upward-sweeping and curving forms of the plastic baroque, filling his sky with angels who descend and ascend. And the commerce of earth and sky is accompanied by grandiose celebrations of music, poetry and painting, secular and religious, not unlike the exaltation of the icon in the propaganda art of Counter-Reformation culture.

The grotesque, however, although it is developed primarily in connection with—or more precisely *against*—baroque idealization, is also related to that side of Dryden's spirit that has been called neoclassical. At the outset I described Guido's painting as baroque. It is more accurate to call it baroque and neoclassical. Guido imitated Raphael, who in turn had imitated ancient marbles in creating the delicate, lovely, decorous humanity that endeared him to the subsequent centuries. For Dryden's age and the eighteenth century, Guido's and Raphael's much-loved "air" became a paradigm for graceful, urbane, and fully human reality. Dryden has often been regarded as the founder of English neoclassicism, but he is more properly thought the inheritor, refiner, and propagator of a native strain emanating from Jonson and earlier writers. Of that strain he makes a spiritual countermovement to the exalted, religious, authoritarian, and highly decorated baroque. It cannot be ignored that the baroque of Dryden takes on a special quality by coexisting with a powerful desire to imitate the decorum of the classics, to refine the language, to discipline the imagination, and to transform the brick of crude satire to the marble of Horace. And this society-oriented virtuoso, who worked to develop sweet and sounding numbers and condensed, precise, and worldly speech, was also not unaffected by the neoclassical ambition in his creation of the grotesque. For it was, as we have seen, his accomplishment to transfer the grotesque from the supernatural to the natural sphere—to demythologize it and make it a more human and socially effective literary form.

Viewed broadly, the grotesque has its proper context not in the baroque alone but also in what may be called—if we are permitted to use the term loosely and suggestively—neoclassical empiricism.[47] The grotesque may in fact be the fruit of a union that brought together an imaginative energy that pushed upward toward the sublime, boldly risking the abyss of the bathetic, with an intellectually sharp, civilized, and this-worldly rationality that tried to apply the *frein vital*[48] to all human concerns.

6

Samuel Johnson and the Concordia Discors *of Human Relationships*

S*amuel Johnson* has become legendary as an opponent of cosmological, metaphysical, social, and moral systems. Although he was preoccupied with topics that then and now concern the community of scholars, he refused with greater verbal vigor than anyone else in our tradition to "commit the social science," a phrase given us by W. H. Auden which ought to please all who are disturbed by the submission of complex human behavior to paradigms, parameters, interfaces, and laws of mathematical probability. But however much opposed to intellectual formulae, Johnson was committed to antithesis as an organizing principle of perception and expression, and we might pause to ask why he so frequently thought in terms of contrast, the polarities of which he frequently applied to human life. Since he more than once quoted the ancient dictum that mediocrity is best, he must sometimes have erected verbal extremes in order to locate the golden mean between them.

More often Christian than classical, the Johnsonian contrast also served the serious purpose of opposing good to evil and the rational to the foolish, with a purpose of getting man to make a clear-cut ethical choice. Occasionally Johnson creates Christian paradoxes that seem to respect the pervasiveness of Incarnation, and the reader is asked to accept both the transcendental and the immanent, both the general and the particular, both the universal and the concrete. Most frequently and most essentially, the binary structures of Johnson were intended to display the human condition—to exhibit "the real state of sublunary nature, which partakes of good and evil, joy and sorrow, mingled with endless variety of proportion and innumerable modes of combination."[1] A Johnsonian antithesis can serve the cause of pleasure, showing the boundaries of possibility open to man, a kind of Dan-to-Beersheba range in which the imagination can sport and frisk at will. The "course of the world, in which . . . at the same time, the reveller is hasting to his wine, and the mourner burying his friend,"[2] can even heal the mind by its very contrasts. The "vicissitudes of the world, . . . day and night, labour and rest, hurry and retirement, endear each other" and so "keep the mind in action."[3] When a man has sunk into himself and suffers from the "frigid and narcotick infection" that arises from being alone, there is only one remedy: to make "an immediate transition . . . to diversion and gaiety." But such a recourse in which "levity and chearfulness" disencumber the mind from "awe and solicitude" exists only because of society and its endearments (*Rambler* no. 89; 4:107–9). And that brings us to our chief concern—to love, friendship, and marriage and also to the antithetical structures that Johnson applies to these human relationships.

On the subject of love, the young Sam Johnson is chillingly conventional. His poetry presents girls as "beauteous virgins," whose breasts are "snowy" and whose kisses are "balmy." If they are cruel, they are pursued by snaky furies; and since love is "wily" and desire "vain," the fiery destructive affection that inflames all sentient nature ought to be resisted as the mind turns to the "lambent glories" of friendship that never descend to fools and villains.[4] And yet by 1746, when Johnson addresses competent though certainly unexciting octosyllabic lines "To Miss ⸺ on Her Playing upon the Harpsichord, . . ." he becomes more interesting than usual, clearly adumbrating the important antithesis that is our subject. The lady addressed in this poem, Alicia Maria Carpenter, is a musician, a fact that leads Johnson to write:

> Mark, when the diff'rent notes agree
> In friendly contrariety,
> How passion's well-accorded strife
> Gives all the harmony of life.[5]

Johnson here recalls Manilius's famous phrase *discordia concors,* which he was to use or adapt later at crucial moments in his criticism of both art and life.[6] Thus the poem of 1746 contains the seeds of one of his most illuminating antitheses. The ancients seemed to derive the idea of discordant harmony (or harmonious discord) from nature—from its clashing elements and its drive toward unity. Johnson is of course not averse to learning from nature: "there is an instinctive natural affection in parents towards their children." But he is surer of the values of ethics and religion developed in civilized social contexts: "Sir, natural affection is nothing: but affection from principle and established duty is sometimes wonderfully strong."[7]

That kind of wise and disciplined affection arises between the bachelor Hymenaeus and the spinster Tranquilla (*Rambler* nos. 113, 115, 119, 126, 167). Both these witty, experienced, and thoughtful people respect the good estate of marriage even though neither was able to find a suitable partner despite an extensive survey of mankind and womankind. Finally, Johnson brings the two together in a pleasing union to which he is able to apply the great phrase, *concordia discors.* Two dynamically contrasting qualities constitute the full truth about this union, "in which caprice and selfishness had so little part." The first is similitude, the second difference. The similarities consist of a rational realism that protects the pair from "visions of felicity which human power cannot bestow." There is little disparity in either birth or fortune. The minds of both are, like the mind of a good poet—even like the mind of Imlac himself—well stocked with "stores of novelty" on which the couple can draw for a long time. Thus these seasoned lovers are "eminently qualified to give mutual pleasure," possessing as they do similitude of faith, manners, and virtue and so sharing good prospects for both time and eternity. Johnson glows with approval over such fruitful harmony, and in his epigraph he applies to them lines from

Martial in which "smiling concord" will dress their nuptial bed and Venus herself bless the happy union (*Rambler* no. 167; 5:120–21, 123).

But deep conformity of character, experience, interests, and abilities constitutes only one half of the truth about this ideal relationship:

> Tho' our characters beheld at a distance, exhibit this general resemblance, yet a nearer inspection discovers such a dissimilitude of our habitudes and sentiments, as leaves each some peculiar advantages, and afford that *concordia discors,* that suitable disagreement which is always necessary to intellectual harmony. There may be a total diversity of ideas which admits no participation of the same delight, and there may likewise be such conformity of notions, as leaves neither any thing to add to the decisions of the other. With such contrariety there can be no peace, with such similarity there can be no pleasure. Our reasons, though often formed upon different views, terminate generally in the same conclusion. Our thoughts like rivulets issuing from distant springs, are each impregnated in its course with various mixtures, and tinged by infusions unknown to the other, yet at last easily unite into one stream, and purify themselves by the gentle effervescence of contrary qualitites. (*Rambler* no. 167; 5: 123–24)

The intellectual structure here displayed is rich and complex. Johnson not only brings similitude and difference together in effervescent union; he carefully defines the kind of similarity that lays a good foundation and the kind of diversity that ferments into delight. Between this union of opposites in friendships and marriage and the union of opposites in metaphor and wit there is a striking similarity, to which I shall return in conclusion.

Now it is necessary to draw a distinction between a subtle and nuanced idea like *concordia discors,* which can be flexibly and creatively applied to the phantasmagoria of human life, and a worthy yet somewhat rigid and limited idea like that of the golden mean, which can all too easily become formulaic. In *Idler* no. 100, Tim Warner seeks a wife. What guides him is an aridly classical, stoical, and methodical desire to achieve the *aurea mediocritas.*

My resolution was to keep my passions neutral, and to marry only in compliance with my reason. I drew upon a page of my pocket book a scheme of all female virtues and vices, with the vices which border upon every virtue, and the virtues which are allied to every vice. I considered that wit was sarcastick, and magnanimity imperious; that avarice was economical, and ignorance obsequious; and having estimated the good and evil of every quality, employed my own diligence and that of my friends to find the lady in whom nature and reason had reached that happy mediocrity which is equally remote from exuberance and deficience.[8]

Tim Warner, following "happy mediocrity," is not unlike Pope's Cloe,[9] who is content to dwell in frigid "decencies" forever, and he gets in Miss Gentle exactly what he deserves—a female Prufrock, who measures out her life in coffee spoons: "she allows herself to sit half an hour after breakfast, and an hour after dinner; while I am talking or reading to her, she keeps her eye upon her watch, and when the minute of departure comes, will leave an argument unfinished, or the intrigue of a play unravelled" (p. 307). An amusing lesson, this, about the grotesque mistakes that beset those who airily or mechanically apply ideas to reality.

The idea of the golden mean is not always or completely out of favor with Johnson,[10] but in his long view it cannot surely have seemed so feasible or pregnant an ideal as *concordia discors*. Tim and his Miss Gentle (a precisianist, "a good sort of woman" but by no means "a good woman") are vastly different from the wise and witty Hymenaeus and Tranquilla, characters who truly breathe and exude the Johnsonian aether. Perhaps the superiority of *concordia discors* to the golden mean will appear if we examine more carefully each of its elements, first similitude and then difference.

In applying the ancient idea of elemental strife-harmony to marriage, Johnson uses not Manilius' *discordia concors* but Horace's *concordia discors* (see n. 6). Why did he prefer *concord* as the substantive? The answer appears if we consider the absolutely basic importance which Johnson attaches to similitude in lasting human relationships. But first we must notice that, though he was capable of distinguishing between love, friendship, and marriage, Johnson saw far more and far deeper similarities between them than most pre-eighteenth-century cultures ever had. Of his five *Dictionary* definitions of *friendship,* the first two are obviously the most important, and they reveal that Johnson found this condition to border upon love: "1. The state of minds united by mutual benevolence ... 2. Highest degree of intimacy."

In *Rambler* no. 18 Johnson finds marriage to be "the strictest type of perpetual friendship" and says that it must be based on "confidence, integrity," "virtue," and "piety" (3:103). And in his sermon on marriage, he finds an "exact conformity" between it and friendship, even though the two states must of course be distinguished. The chief distinction, however, is one of degree: marriage is friendship "exalted to higher perfection. Love must be more ardent, and confidence without limits."[11] Johnson's notion of marriage is as exalted as that of Clarissa, who calls it "the highest state of friendship."[12] Johnson the satirist sometimes approaches Swift in unrelenting exposures of romantic folly and of the self-destroying illusions with which the thought of marriage often seduced human beings from rational vigilance. But his wholehearted commitment to the beauty and value of both marriage and friendship is so profound that it must be regarded not only as a dutiful commitment to a Christian ideal but also as a response to the deepest necessity of his being. Of friendship he wrote, "Life has no pleasure higher or nobler than that of Friendship" (*Idler* no. 23; 2:72). And of marriage he said in a letter to his friend Joseph Baretti, "I do not ... pretend to have discovered that life has any thing more to be desired than a prudent and virtuous marriage" (*Life,* 1:382).

Viewing love, marriage, and friendship from these ideal heights, Johnson was in a position to see what was salient in them, and for him that was a profound and impregnable similitude of manners and sentiments. Johnson is absolutely unrelenting in enforcing this requirement—and with good reason. With stubborn realism he disbars differences in religion, disagreements about politics, and temperamental incongruities from true friendship in or out of marriage. Even virtue itself is not enough: "That friendship may be at once fond and lasting, there must not only be equal virtue on each part, but virtue of the same kind" (*Rambler* no. 64; 3:341). Whatever I shall say later on about the importance of zestful contrast and opposition, let it always be remembered that for Johnson similarity is the bedrock. Without it, "exchange of endearments and intercourse of civility may continue, indeed, as boughs may for a while be verdant, when the root is wounded; but the poison of discord is infused, and though the countenance may preserve its smile, the heart is hardening and contracting" (ibid. p. 343).

There is abundant precedent in the Western tradition for the ideas I have been explicating, though I find more eloquence and greater profundity in Johnson than in any of his ancient predecessors. His application of the exalted classical definitions of friendship to marriage, where he makes friendship the defining and absolutely requisite quality, has more recent antecedents and relates Johnson to the great fusion of sex and sensibility that reached a fuller and more impressive expression in the eighteenth century than in any century before his. Like the sentimental writers, with whom he has not often enough been compared, Johnson regards as a "crime" parental control over the youthful choice of a partner. Although he believes in the indissolubility of marriage, he does not wish it to be encumbered with unnecessary vows—vows to obey parents, vows to fulfill externally and internally imposed conditions, vows that arise from additional, unwanted, and unnecessary demands.[13] He also calls for the better education of women, to permit them to assume that position of equality which friendship inevitably demands. "Depend upon it, no woman is the worse for sense and knowledge" (*Life,* 5:226). The critic who believed that love was too frequently the subject of the drama also believed that the "violence and ill effect [of love] were much exaggerated; for who knows any real suffering on that head, more than from the exorbitancy of any other passion?" (*Life,* 2:122). And though it is his moral duty to point to the unhappiness of many marriages and give his own deeply considered reasons for such unhappiness, Johnson is forceful in asserting that "an accurate view of the world will confirm, that marriage is not commonly unhappy, otherwise than as life is unhappy" (*Rambler* no. 45; 3:243). Even in his view of the personal letter he has a profound sense that it can and indeed must minister to the fostering of love in friendship and marriage. He disputes with those who believe that ease and lightness are the only standards of the familiar letter; instead, we must "try every inlet at which love or pity enters the heart," one purpose being "to preserve in the minds of the absent either love or esteem; to excite love we must impart pleasure" (*Rambler* no. 152; 5:47). I have earlier tried to show that in some Romantic and pre-Romantic art similitude can be perverse and narcissistic.[14] From that taint Johnson's views are completely free. They are in fact healthy and simple: marriage and friendship depend upon love, love depends upon pleasure, and pleasure arises from similitude. Without basic concord the whole fabric of social intimacy would dissolve, leaving not a rack behind.

An endearing scene in Boswell records a disagreement between Goldsmith and Johnson on the question of whether people who disagree on capital points can continue to live in friendship together. Goldsmith declares for the negative, and he adduces arguments from the classical tradition intended to show that friendship requires the same preferences and the same aversions. Johnson surprisingly declares for the possibility of friendship between those who disagree on basic issues. As the argument proceeds, Johnson becomes heated: "Sir, I am not saying that *you* could live in friendship with a man from whom you differ as to some point: I am only saying *I* could do it" (*Life,* 2:181). Is this only another example of Johnson's contrary disposition in argument? Or does it, as I believe, point to his other requisite for friendship, the need for difference—the kind of yeasty difference he made prominent in the good marriage of Hymenaeus and Tranquilla? Even when he is praising the totally admirable, unclouded love that exists in the Burney family, one senses that he is calling for more than similitude:

> I am willing... to hear that there is happiness in the world, and delight to think on pleasure diffused among the Burneys. I question if any ship upon the ocean goes out attended with more good wishes than that which carries the fate of Burney. I love all that breed whom I can be said to know, and one or two whom I hardly know I love upon credit, and love them because they love each other. Of this consanguineous unanimity I have had never much experience; but it appears to me one of the great lenitives of life; but it has this deficience, that it is never found when distress is mutual—[15]

Johnson admires the "consanguineous unanimity" of this attractive family, no doubt of that. But he confesses to having had no experience of it himself and to wondering whether it can survive mutual misery. Johnson is obviously addicted to the chemistry of contrast in human relations, even in intellectual matters: "genius, whatever it be, is like fire in the flint, only to be produced by collision with a proper subject" (*Rambler* no. 25; 3:139). His temperamental inclination toward the adventuresome, the bold, the fullhearted, and the mental stimulation of conflict supports his theory of *concordia discors,* where of course the discordant is a requisite element.

Both Johnsonian theory and temperament loom up strikingly against the language and thought that the Western tradition had commonly devoted to the praise of concord and the censure of discord. In such writers as Spenser, Shakespeare, Donne, and Milton, concord is sweet, heavenly, angelic, divine, and sometimes virtually identified with God himself, who is the "author of peace and lover of concord." Correspondingly, discord is foul, evil, hellish, divisive—and usually in complete separation from the good. Johnson's *Dictionary,* which of course reflects the central usages of the English tradition, records this eloquent and moral kind of praise and censure, with respect to the words we are examining. But amidst the epideictic rhetoric of many of the quotations, the *Dictionary* here and there shows that there had been in antecedent culture some anticipation—though without Johnson's boldness—of his praise of the discordant and his belief in good contrariety.[16]

When we come to inquire more precisely of what the salutary oppositions in human relationships actually consist, we encounter some difficulties and must immediately make some exclusions. One is willing to believe that in his own marriage, which Johnson remembered for so many years with fervent love and devotion, "the little disagreements which sometimes troubled his married state" were not always repented of and may indeed have been cherished as a contribution to a wholesome *concordia discors.* When Mrs. Piozzi asked him "if he ever disputed with his wife," he replied, "Perpetually" and gave some examples that he seemed to recall with tender amusement. When the same lady asked if he "ever huffed his wife about his dinner," Johnson replied, "So often . . . that at last she called to me, and said, Nay, hold Mr. Johnson, and do not make a farce of thanking God for a dinner which in a few minutes you will protest not eatable" (*Life,* 1:239 and n. 2). At least some of the differences between Tetty and Sam were recollected in a tranquility that made them seem spicy rather than nasty or mean. But surely the same can scarcely be said of the tensions in Johnson's own private ménage, where there was "much malignity":

> At home we do not much quarrel, but perhaps the less we quarrel, the more we hate. There is as much malignity amongst us as can well subsist, without any thought of daggers or poisons.[17]

Johnson surely rules out of fruitful human intercourse nagging, frustrating, joyless contrarieties. The differences that enliven a successful *concordia discors* must be suitable, manageable, and far from divisive. They must exist in a context of deep-lying and cheerful similitude.

Johnson once wrote, "Happiness is enjoyed only in proportion as it is known; and such is the state or folly of man, that it is known only by experience of its contrary" (*Adventurer* no. 67; 2:387). And we remember that Johnson found that the contrasts in nature and life of day and night, labor and rest, endear each other and activate the mind. But here again one must be careful to avoid forcing Johnson into a position which he would have found repugnant, the position adopted by many Deists and other optimistic creators of theodicies in his day—that such contraries to the good as ill health or poverty or deprivation are necessary to the universal scheme of happiness. And Johnson was far from believing that we should "continue in sin, that grace may abound" (Romans 6:1).

Blake's dazzling sentences about contraries and contrarieties in *The Marriage of Heaven and Hell* seem to have a sexual component that gives authentic human meaning to his opposition of attraction and repulsion, reason and energy, love and hate, contraries that he finds necessary to human existence and without which no progression is possible. Even his famous words the *prolific* and the *devourer* seem to me to refer, respectively, to the male and female of the species in their most fundamental physical roles. Since women necessarily figure in Johnson's views of love, marriage, and even friendship, it is not irrelevant to ask whether his contraries have any ingredient of sexuality in them. There can, I think, be no doubt about the robust, perhaps even clamorous, physicality of Samuel Johnson; and many—perhaps most— of his uses of *imagination* in his prayers and meditations have a sexual content. Their cumulative effect suggests inescapably that his private being was constantly invaded, if not by overt incitements to lasciviousness, then certainly by sensual imagery welling up from within.[18]

The public Johnson is quite different, and there must be few great English authors who are so persistently modest as he, even to the point of evasiveness.[19] Nevertheless, the evidence is insistent that the Johnsonian *concordia discors* would be incomplete—perhaps woefully incomplete—without the presence of sexuality, without interaction between the "two great Sexes [that] animate the World" (*Paradise Lost,* 8:151). Consider *Rambler* no. 99, an essay devoted to the general human community but also to the private communities of human friendship and love. The essay discusses and praises the love of all mankind equally, love which Johnson regards as our bounden duty; he also discusses the private, unequal, individual loves which would be impossible without our passions. This essay Johnson introduces with a long paragraph on what he calls the "cogent principle of instinct," which refers to the need for sexual gratification that man shares with the animals. Johnson on this subject is rare enough to quote in full:

> It has been ordained by providence, for the conservation of order in the immense variety of nature, and for the regular propagation of the several classes of life with which the elements are peopled, that every creature should be drawn by some secret attraction to those of his own kind; and that not only the gentle and domestick animals which naturally unite into companies, or cohabit by pairs, should continue faithful to their species; but even those ravenous and ferocious savages which Aristotle observes never to be gregarious, should range mountains and desarts in search of one another, rather than pollute the world with a monstrous birth. (4:164–65)

The concluding reference to interspecies bestiality is interesting and surprising; but the main point, I repeat, is that Johnson chooses to introduce his discussion of all kinds of human benevolence, tenderness, kindness, and love with a passage on the universal sexuality of nature.

The passage just quoted and the essay it introduces make it clear that for Johnson the deepest human relationships are somehow related to fundamental human physicality, but these statements do not justify our considering sexuality as a human difference or even interpreting the "secret attraction" of all nature to be the result of contrast. But other essays do, by strong implication, suggest the necessity of sexual differentiation. Tranquilla rejects one of her earlier suitors (a man educated in all the "softness of effeminacy") because she soon discovered "that Venustulus had the cowardice as well as elegance of a female" (*Rambler* no. 119; 4:272). And in a parallel passage, Tranquilla's future huband, Hymenaeus, also turns away from a potential mate, Camilla, precisely because she had made too many "advances to the borders of virility." His—and others'—reactions to the manly Camilla are strong:

> But man, ungrateful man, instead of springing forward to meet her, shrunk back at her approach. She was persecuted by the ladies as a deserter, and at best received by the men only as a fugitive. I, for my part, amused myself a while with her fopperies, but novelty soon gave way to detestation, for nothing out of the common order of nature can be long borne. I had no inclination to a wife who had the ruggedness of man without his force, and the ignorance of woman without her softness. (*Rambler* no. 115; 4:250)

I have earlier speculated that Johnson wanted women to overcome their ignorance so that they would be fully capable of the friendship he regarded as absolutely requisite to successful marriage; but he certainly never wanted them to desert their softness. It is highly significant that both his female and male correspondents on love and marriage reject excessive similitude between the sexes. One must conclude, I think, that the spice of the Johnsonian *concordia discors* depended on sexual differentiation and all that that implies.

Perhaps such differences (minus the contamination of mischievous historical stereotypes) lie at the very root of marital happiness, but others like them must also have been regarded as requisite to friendship. Johnson's love of zestful contrast was surely satisfied by his circle of friends, with figures so different from him as Topham Beauclerk, Oliver Goldsmith, Edmund Burke, John Taylor, or John Hawkins.

Johnson's manly lady Camilla says that "she could not but forgive the Turks for their suspecting [women] to want souls" (ibid., p. 249). Her reference to Turkish prejudice sends the mind back to Johnson's play *Irene,* which embodies two relationships that are set off in strikingly dramatic and intellectual contrast—first, the love between Irene and the infidel Mahomet and, second, the love between the Christian Greeks, Aspasia and Demetrius, the first relationship faithless and evil and the second an example of heroic goodness. Let us consider these relationships in the light of *concordia discors,* which at least two passages in the play specifically recall. The prologue brings out the contrarieties inherent in virtue itself:

> Learn here how Heav'n supports the virtuous mind,
> Daring, tho' calm; and vigorous, tho' resign'd.[20]

And Cali Bassa, the sixty-year-old First Vizier, who is ready to be treasonable toward his young ruler Mahomet in order to allow the Christians to escape but who dies in the attempt, brings out the contrarieties inherent in the ideal political state, which is "Unbroken as the sacred chain of Nature,/That links the jarring elements in peace" (1.2.63–64). The deeper *concordia discors* that exists—or ought to exist—in human relationships will emerge as we consider the views of love, women, and friendship held (1) by the Turks, (2) by the apostate Christian, and (3) by the faithful Christians.

(1) The ruler Mahomet calls the idea of a heavenly reward for women a "vain rapture," since for him they possess "inferiour natures" and are formed as sexual creatures solely for the purpose of giving earthly delight. There is no "future paradise" for them, and they end their brief careers in "total death." Only man is sovereign, and only he must therefore worry about futurity (2.7.15, 17, 19). Quite apart from what all this says about the Muslim religion, such cruel and categorical views demonstrate that in Johnson's view the relation of Irene and the Arab ruler, though it might be propelled by lust, cannot possibly possess even a tincture of true friendship.

(2) Irene, the apostate, who is willing to reject her religion both for her personal comfort and also for the possible earthly salvation of

her people, rejects out of hand her sovereign lover's view of her sex. She finds instead that nature has "profusely pour'd her bounties on woman," and she even claims a female share in "the comprehensive thought, / Th' enlivening wit, the penetrating reason" that men can possess (2.7.25, 55–56). Although her subsequent behavior is despicable and leads to her execution at the command of her lover, we must recognize that her views are superior even to those of Cali, who believes that woman is addicted to "softness" and "sorrow," qualities which he calls "unprofitable, peaceful, female virtues!" (3.1.11, 12). But quite apart from her subsequent faithless behavior, Irene's view of love and joy is much too simple to satisfy Samuel Johnson. In a moonlit scene toward the end of the play, a scene that Johnson describes in verse of considerable beauty, Irene recalls Eden and Eve and finds in untested purity and in "elemental joy" the "smile of unoffended Heav'n" (5.2.8, 9). Such "elemental" and Edenic virtues Johnson must surely find inadequate. Equipped with only these, Irene not surprisingly yields easily to temptation. By nature she may be more inadequate than evil, but her inadequacy is profoundly debilitating. She remains incapable of the *concordia discors* that is present in the deepest human relationships.

(3) But the ideal lovers, Aspasia and Demetrius, are fully capable of that. Rewarded with escape and safety and, by implication, a future that fulfills their relationships, they are given lines in the play that embody Johnson's richest insights. The good, pious, beautiful, and loving Aspasia is the *raisonneuse* of the play, superior to Irene by virtue of her severer morality, her uncompromising devotion to her faith, and her unclouded realism, which permits her to expose the illusions, the sentimental half-truths, and the obfuscating rhetoric of Irene. Her heroic virtue makes her understand that in moments of crisis one must seize the flaming sword of wrath and not allow it to sleep in one's hand, even though the risk of action may be physical torture and death. But for all her heroic virtue, Aspasia is deeply and unmistakably a woman. The infidel Abdalla is inflamed to lust by her very presence, and she herself is deeply in love with Demetrius, the Christian hero.

He is as heroic as she, motivated by honor, loyalty, religion. But of him it can also be said that "the pow'rful voice of love inflames" him (2.4.19), and when he and Aspasia meet we learn that he is not only noble and loving but that his very patriotism is energized by his passion: "New force, new courage, from each [loving] glance I gain" (3.11.21). Although the lovers stand on the brink of a destruction from which they are spared, Johnson does not allow their physical danger to mute their physical passion. Aspasia confesses to being "lost in a wild perplexity of joy," and Demetrius describes his emotions as an "ecstacy of love" and "pure affection" (3.10.14, 15). As these lovers look ahead to the issue of their religious fidelity, they foresee a culture which will be characterized by "soft Leisure" and a "Peace propitious," while eloquence and poetry resume their ancient empires. But "the Western World" will also have room for "fond desire" and "the yielding heart," and its culture will make secure the happiness of "the fair and learn'd" (4.1.112–23).

How shall we describe the contrasting elements of *concordia discors* in this, the noblest of all human relationships? The answer is obvious, though only implied in Johnson's play. Individually and together, Aspasia and Demetrius embody both austere, martial virtue and also soft, yielding, heart-melting love. Johnson has found inadequate the ancient topos of Hercules at the Crossroads between virtue and vice, so beloved by the eighteenth century. He does not identify virtue with Minerva alone nor vice with Venus, and man does not have to choose one or the other. Hercules' choice is a false one; and the new Christian hero, who was becoming prominent in English culture under the sponsorship of Dryden, Steele, Rowe, and Richardson, was at once heroic and loving, at once martial and marriageable. A new *concordia discors* arises in uniting what had been immemorially separated. A Christianized Athena and a Christianized Aphrodite were uniting to produce what was called obsessively "the great soul," "the noble soul." Aspasia in the play is one of these, fully aware that in order to achieve this new kind of synthesis, woman must no longer be trained in dependence, folly, affectation, and "habitual cowardice" (2.1.33). The new woman must rise to the challenge of Dryden and take her place alongside man as a heroic heroine in love.

It is difficult to think of qualities more likely to fly apart than hard military virtue and soft tender love. It measures Johnson's commitment to a fruitful fusion of opposites that he makes the attempt to unite them early in his life, if not with full dramatic success, then surely with a clear and resolute mind. *Irene* may not be salvageable for the stage, but it ought to be respected as a noble expression of Johnson's deepest insight into the *concordia discors* of human relationships.

The most striking parallel in Johnson's works to the fusion of opposites we have been discussing is his conception of wit, the most subtle and sophisticated of his many critical principles. There is, however, an important difference between the fusion that takes place in friendship or love and the "combination of dissimilar images or the discovery of occult resemblances in things apparently unlike" in poetry.[21] The union of likeness and difference in human relationships Johnson called *concordia discors*; the union of the natural and the new, the familiar and the unfamiliar in wit he called *discordia concors*. The difference is suggestive. In the first concord is the substantive, in the second discord. It is as though Johnson is saying that in human life the virtues of similarity are fundamental and can indeed be made generative and productive by human difference; but the foundation must always be conformity of idea, taste, habit, and inclination. In literature or art, where the imagination enables the writer to convey to his reader the "energies of passion,"[22] one can give greater rein to variety, dissimilarity, and the crowding in of diverse and novel impressions. In unions of love and friendship, the "effervescence of contrary qualities" must be "gentle" (*Rambler* no. 167; 5:124). But in the domain of literature, where originality, animation, variety, and imaginative energy are abiding *desiderata*, the emphasis can sometimes fall on the *discordia*, though of course we must remember that union in either life or art implies control and order.

Johnson strikes one as being in many respects closer to Coleridge, who followed him, than to any critic of life or art who preceded him. Johnson would perhaps not have understood the Coleridgean notion that the poet in "ideal perfection" destroys in order to fuse and make new, since Johnson's conception of the imagination still regarded it as a combining and not a destroying or even creative force. For Johnson nature must always retain its original integrity, unsullied by artistic form, which always must lead the mind back to it. But apart from this, Johnson would have appreciated fully Coleridge's call for a union in art of the general and concrete, the idea and the image, the individual and the representative, the novel and the familiar (*Biographia literaria,* end of chap. 14). And in the *concordia discors* of life, he would have welcomed the Romantic fusion of judgment and enthusiasm, emotion and order. But we should not end by separating too rigidly the affectionate unions of life from the imaginative unions of art. In art the mind of the reader or spectator is forever moving between the representation and its natural original. Only that poetry is finally worthy which succeeds "in representing or moving the affections."[23] For this reason the *concordia discors* of life is inextricably bound to the *discordia concors* of art, and Johnson has the honor of anticipating the Wordsworthian ideal of pleasure, which unites art—even metrical art—and life—even sexuality.[24] This ideal is one

which the mind derives from the perception of similitude in dissimilitude. This principle is the great spring of the activity of our minds, and their chief feeder. From this principle the direction of the sexual appetite, and all the passions connected with it, take their origin: it is the life of our ordinary conversation; and upon the accuracy with which similitude in dissimilitude, and dissimilitude in similitude are perceived, depend our taste and our moral feelings. (*Preface to Lyrical Ballads,* 1800)

7
Samuel Johnson among the Deconstructionists

*H*arold Bloom has called Samuel John-
son "the greatest critic in the language,"[1] unexpectedly high praise that
tempts me to wonder how—and indeed if—the precursor might have
returned the ephebe's compliment. Such bold fancying leads on to
heady ambition. Could it possibly enlighten or amuse us to extend the
inquiry beyond Bloom to Geoffrey Hartman (like Bloom, "barely a
deconstructionist") and then to Jacques Derrida, Paul de Man, and J.
Hillis Miller, whom Hartman has called "boa-deconstructors, merciless
and consequent"?[2] And also to their followers, associates, and predecessors? I withdraw at once from one of the comparisons hinted at: I
simply do not dare juxtapose Johnson and Derrida. If the only slight
immodesties of Fielding and Sterne provoked such epithets as these—
"blockhead," "barren rascal," "sad stuff," "nothing odd will do long"[3]—
one recoils from contemplating what the following "Derridadaisms"
(Hartman again) would surely have evoked: "the phallus is a 'privileged
signifier' "[4] and "it is difficult [in certain conditions] to separate writing
from onanism."[5] And what new gesture or action might Johnson make
or take to reassert the reality that exists off the printed page were he
to encounter what has become virtually the epigraph of current literary speculation: *il n'y a pas de hors texte?*

139

Of course, *any* attempt to imagine what Johnson, his contemporaries, or his predecessors could have said about our own seething and
teeming hermeneutic culture might be totally aborted if we did the
sensible thing and looked at his *Dictionary* of 1755 with the vocabulary
of the 1980s in mind. The gulf does at first seem to be unbridgeable—
between the Johnsonian then and the Derridean now. The word I just
used, *hermeneutic,* does not appear. There is neither *deconstruction*
nor *displacement* of any kind, neither *textuality* nor *intertextuality*;
there is no *adequation,* no *logocentrism,* no *marginality,* no *undecidability.* *Hermetic* meant only "chymical," and Johnson would not have
permitted us to *reify* or *valorize.* If you *elided* something in Johnson's
England, you cut it in pieces; and the *Dictionary* is of no use in trying
to understand the notion that "Heidegger's Being . . . *elides* with Derrida's pharmakon." When you *inscribed,* you literally wrote on something or you marked something with letters, but you were given no
sanction whatever for permitting "the play of difference [to] inscribe
itself in the text."[6]

But just as I was about to close Johnson's linguistic leaves and shut
the door on this kind of inquiry, my eye fell on *precursor,* which Johnson
defines as "forerunner; harbinger" and illustrates with this teasingly
(Harold) Bloomian sentence from Pope: "Thomas Burnet [son of the
Bishop and a contemporary literary enemy of the poet] played the *precursor* to the coming of Homer in his [Burnet's] Homerides." My mind
leapt at once to *The Anxiety of Influence* (p. 148), where we are told
that for a startled moment it is possible to believe that a later poet has
been imitated by his ancestor in a revisionary process known as *apophrades,* or the return of the dead. Needless to say, *apophrades* does
not exist in Johnson; but *belated,* a more famous "Bloomism," of course
does. It is defined in a way that would not be displeasing, I think, to
the author of *A Map of Misreading,* who displays the dark and bewildering agony of arriving too late on the literary scene. For Johnson, to
be *belated* was literally to be "benighted," as was Milton's "belated"
peasant in *Paradise Lost,* who watched the midnight revels of faery
elves in a forest. Such mad or playful derangements of chronology as
these I have introduced may tease us out of thought as doth eternity
and should be indulged not one second longer than playfulness remains

sane. And yet even so learned and sensible a scholar as Garry Wills, writing a nationally syndicated newspaper column for 13 April 1984, becomes synchronic when cold realism would have insisted that he be diachronic. He writes, "The best judgment on Richard M. Nixon's appearance on 'CBS News' is contained in this magnificent sentence." After quoting it in full—and no one could dispute its appropriateness as well as its magnificence—Wills says, "That sentence is by Samuel Johnson, but the subject is clearly Richard M. Nixon," and he then reveals that he has been quoting *The Rambler.**

Have I seemed to verge on parody? If so, I apologize for raising false hopes. That literary form is quite beyond my powers: I do not know how to tell the truth but tell it slant, as Emily Dickinson urges us to do. Besides, I am quite serious in inviting you to consider the possibility that the lover and frequent user of *sesquipedalia verba* whom I am attempting to honor by placing him in unfamiliar company would have been challenged to put to the test of hard thought the new and sometimes outlandish linguistic formulations we encounter daily. I also suggest that Johnson would have contemplated the present critical scene with an unquenchable fascination not unmixed with horror. It is altogether likely that the criticism of the 1980s would have evoked in him a rich and complex emotion not entirely unlike the post-Burkean, Romantic sublime, a concept which he himself used, though with reservations.

A considerable power in Harold Bloom's criticism is that it forces us to engage in battle with our predecessors, and it is a pity that so few contemporary critics have seen fit to wrestle with Johnson. It was not so earlier in this century. For T. S. Eliot, Johnson stood with Dryden and Coleridge as the greatest trio of critics in English; more than that,

---

*"Those, indeed, who can see only external facts, may look upon him with abhorrence, but when he calls himself to his own tribunal, he finds every fault, if not absolutely effaced, yet so much palliated by the goodness of his intention, and the cogency of the motive, that very little guilt or turpitude remains; and when he takes a survey of the whole complication of his character, he discovers so many latent excellencies, so many virtues that want but an opportunity to exert themselves in act, and so many kind wishes for universal happiness, that he looks on himself as suffering unjustly under the infamy of single failings, while the general temper of his mind is unknown or unregarded."[7]

Eliot always felt Johnson to be a presence who at the very least had to be placed hierarchically. Lytton Strachey believed that Johnson's judgments were "never right," yet he could not ignore them since they were always "subtle, or solid, or bold." And more than one New Critic, trying to rehabilitate Donne and the Metaphysicals, tested his strength against the author of the Life of Cowley and came out of the fray admiring the adversary he had felt impelled to analyze in detail.[8] Such confrontation seems not to take place now. When Johnson is quoted, he is quoted as an aphorist or a verbal miniaturist. Or he is seen swimming along in the current critical stream only occasionally distinguished from his fellows of the finny tribe. Thus Frank Lentricchia says that Hirsch is "epistemologically more lugubrious even than Samuel Johnson," whose criticism is regarded less as thought than self-revelation. But Johnson's criticism, it is conceded, is likely to interest us longer than that of Stanley Fish.[9]

Even the categories that are sometimes imposed on the present welter do not seem to have a place for Johnson. J. Hillis Miller distinguishes canny from uncanny critics. The thought of the uncanny (Paul de Man, Derrida) leads to aporia, the alogical, the absurd, ultimately to impasse; and of course Johnson has no place there. But he does not seem to belong in the company of Socrates and the Socratics either, Miller's canny critics. These have "the unshakable faith that thought, using the thread of logic, can penetrate the deepest abysses of being" and come back with ordered meaning.[10] To such meditations Johnson believed humanity to be unequal: ambitious cosmological systems, he said, are "equally hidden from learning and from ignorance."[11]

We may now have come to the reason why most contemporary critics keep a respectful distance from a great predecessor. They fear *the kick*—that decisive Johnsonian act which, addressing a boulder, establishes a hard and inescapable reality outside mind, outside text, outside language itself. They would be uncomfortable moving from *écriture* and *parole*, from the text and the purely professional literary community, to life and society. It seems unlikely that they will soon desert the risky but glamorous enterprise of helping Western culture attain what Valéry regarded as its destiny—that is, achieving a "rien infiniment riche."[12] It might indeed prove to be rather dull to stand with Johnson by the stream of actuality, watching "with great diligence, the operations of human nature" and tracing "the effects of opinion, humor, interest, and passion."[13] René Wellek—in his recent charge that Deconstruction may yet destroy literary culture because it fails to value the transactions of mind with nature—does not seek the help of Johnson, perhaps because he still wishes to dissociate himself from what he may continue to regard as a crude mimetic literalism. And yet his conclusion is profoundly Johnsonian: "Denying the self and minimizing the perceptual life of man, the theory [of Deconstruction] deliberately refuses to acknowledge that the relation of mind and world is more basic than language."[14]

It would seem that a totally unnavigable sea separates Johnson from the likes of the late Paul de Man. How dare I suggest, then, that there are areas of temperamental sympathy and of philosophical coincidence between an author who marched under the banner of an assertive external nature and those who hoist the flag of mental and linguistic primacy and determinism? The reason, all too briefly put, is that Johnson was no more a mental than he was a moral snob; he was in fact capable of astonishing acts of intellectual as well as personal charity. Besides, I take considerable Boswellian pleasure in bringing him to dinner here with contemporary equivalents of Jack Wilkes, Malebranche, Descartes, Berkeley, or even Hume. Needless to say, the parallels I draw will have to be loose, and I intend no comparative judgments of intellectual worth or achievement.

Johnson was of course far from being an agnostic, a skeptic, a rebel, or a destroyer of convention. But the bent of his mind toward reducing, revising, displacing, or altering mental structures too easily established cannot be overestimated. "Every thing, which Hume has advanced against Christianity," he said, "had passed through my mind long before he wrote."[15] And in our day, when indeterminacy and undecidability are exalted, it is well to note that Johnson respected the flux, complexity, and psychological disruptiveness of language so much that he was sometimes uncomfortable even with definition, which he once said he regarded as outside "the province of man":

> The works and operations of nature are too great in their extent, or too much diffused in their relations, and the performances of art too inconstant and uncertain, to be reduced to any determinate idea....

> Definitions have been no less difficult or uncertain in criticism
> than in law. Imagination ... has always endeavoured to baffle the
> logician, to perplex the confines of distinction, and burst the inclo-
> sures of regularity.[16]

Johnson, one feels sure, was constantly tempted to unravel the skein of
his own and his culture's weaving. Up to a point, and within limits that
I hardly need to define, he may be regarded as one of the most original
and persistent deconstructionists in our language.

In two areas of thought the affinities of spirit between the older
critic and our own contemporaries seem to me to be suggestive and
noteworthy. One concerns the appropriate relation of criticism to creation, and the other concerns the language proper to "critic learning."
In confronting each of these we experience that double motion of early
negation and ultimate affirmation—a "binary" movement of the mind,
as current jargon would have it—that every student of Johnson has
come to expect. Therefore, before we arrive at a sympathy we must
confront a disparity of views. But we must resist the easy temptation
to erect that disparity into a permanent hostility about the issue being
discussed.

One striking feature of current critical thought is its tendency to
take itself very seriously and to regard its concerns as culturally and
politically influential. Thus Philip Rahv and Frank Kermode see a connection between modernist spatial aesthetics and the rise of fascism;[17]
presumably the exposure of such dangerous literary pictorialism would
have to be considered a major political rescue. Internally, within the
domain of literature itself, criticism no longer desires to be considered
an emergent class propelled upward by the assistance of affirmative
action. It asks full equality and proclaims itself willing to submit itself
to the analytical tests and evaluative judgments hitherto given only to
great poetry and fiction. This thrust of upward mobility has led to
dismay in both philosophical and creative circles. John R. Searle finds
the current critical bounciness reduced to absurdity by the view that
"the prime creative task has now passed from the literary artist to the
critic."[18] Saul Bellow thinks that deconstructing professors now control
departments of English and philosophy. Even worse! Bellow continues:

> In the name of "deconstruction," [younger academics] have taken
> over . . . literature itself, operating in the cockpit side by side with
> Shakespeare, Milton, etc., as copilots. These academics—good God!
> Suppose that a dwarf sitting in Shakespeare's lap were to imagine
> that he was piloting the great Shakespearean jet![19]

In response to such claims, if indeed they have been made, and to such
conquests, if indeed they have been won, Johnson would of course
have emitted a long, withdrawing, deconstructing roar of his own.

Johnson regularly denigrated, or at least tended to downgrade, his
own intellectual enterprises. A lexicographer, as we all know, is a
"harmless drudge." Grammatical pedantry is an unhappily inescapable
fate: "No man forgets his original trade: the rights of nations, and of
kings, sink into questions of grammar, if grammarians discuss them."
Scholars should be the satellites of their authors, realizing that their
concerns are usually "of very small importance; they involve neither
property nor liberty; nor favour the interest of sect or party." Even
malicious judgment does little "real mischief. No genius was ever blasted
by the breath of criticks."[20]

But the more closely we examine such denigrations, the more
keenly we sense that if they were not in fact insincere, they were often
playful, sometimes uttered with the intention of disarming opponents
or anticipating objections. In other words, Johnson, to use a favorite
current term, was being proleptical. And we soon come to see that it
was the steady and central aim of his learned prose to exalt learned
commentary. As a learned commentator himself he was sickened by
cant about the dull duty of an editor, and he boldly exalted conjectural
criticism above even the most comprehensive mental powers. Although
he sometimes, to be sure, used the word *genius* to mean only mental
inclination, he often applied it in its most exalted sense ("a mind of
large general powers") to the works of the learned as well as to imaginative creation. It was therefore just and fully Johnsonian that Boswell's
uncle should apply to Johnson himself the word *genius* when he referred to the lexicographer's scholarly achievements, calling him "a
robust genius, born to grapple with whole libraries." And in the famous
critical sentences I now quote, Johnson refers primarily not to poetry

at all but to scholarship: "No man ever yet became great by imitation. Whatever hopes for the veneration of mankind must have invention in the design or the execution; either the effect must itself be new, or the means by which it is produced."[21]

The reason Johnson steadfastly refused to separate *belles* from other *lettres* is that he stood proudly in the venerable tradition that united them. In his Dictionary he defined literature as "learning" and learning as "literature." He would surely have embraced Geoffrey Hartman's opinion that "criticism is part of the world of letters, and has its own mixed philosophical and literary, reflective and figural strength."[22] It would have been easily conceivable to him that learning and criticism were entirely capable of producing a worthy copilot for Shakespeare. For the very greatest scholars and the very greatest critics are creators, uniting imagination with reason, knowledge of men and nature with knowledge of books—in the same way that the very greatest poets do. No artificial barriers separate the thinker from the poet. Mental energy can flow into and out of all genres, all forms, in prose and poetry alike, to and fro between the visual and the verbal, between the imaginative and the ratiocinative.

For this reason it is fully consistent of Johnson to prefer rashness to cowardice even in scholarship (for scholarship read also criticism, the essay, philosophy, the *causerie*): "Presumption will be easily corrected. Every experiment will teach caution.... It is the advantage of vehemence and activity, that they are always hastening to their own reformation." He also censured timidity: "there is ... some danger lest timorous prudence should be inculcated, till courage and enterprize are wholly repressed." We pinch ourselves. Is Johnson talking to teachers, scholars, and moralists and not to poets? He is. And his call for imaginative alacrity in science, natural and otherwise—for vehemence, activity, courage, and enterprise—is itself a creative challenge to learned and expository utterance, for he condenses his ideas (as, say, a great playwright might) into memorable proverb and brilliant trope:

> It may be laid down as an axiom, that it is more easy to take away superfluities than to supply defects.... We know that a few strokes

of the axe will lop a cedar; but what arts of cultivation can elevate a shrub?[23]

    If the example of Johnson is allowed to be instructive, we will of course not rush mindlessly to the judgment and analysis of all that pours from our learned presses. But we will have faith in the ideal that critical scholarship at its best can in its own way rival any other form of expression and thought. And we must surely applaud Geoffrey Hartman for saying that criticism has had a "colorful past," that that past ought to be exemplary, that the attempt to fuse creation and criticism is a worthy modern enterprise necessary to success in both science and the arts, that an essay can be "an intellectual poem" which requires rigorous analysis, and that criticism should be conceived "as within literature, not outside of it looking in."[24]

    The other area in which the critical art of Johnson can be assimilated to contemporary avant-garde criticism concerns vocabulary and style. The very suggestion of affinity here will arouse initial suspicion, perhaps dismay. Johnson, who boasted to Boswell that "he had not taken upon him to add more than four or five words to the English language, of his own formation" (_Life,_ 1:221), frowned on the immodest coinage of new words or the use of old words in unestablished and fantastical senses. In our own day one extremely influential critic has minted or imported such imposing and unassimilable terms as these: _clinamen, tessera, askesis, daemonization, gilgul, zimzum._ Johnson attacked in plain Anglo-Saxon English the habit of "using big words for little matters," which Boswell translated into Latinate diction, deploring the "practice of using words of disproportionate magnitude" (_Life,_ 1:471). In his famous Preface and Notes Johnson employed the following epithets to castigate even Shakespeare (how many of them could justly be applied to the vocabulary that today emanates from Paris or New Haven?): _harsh, ill-sorted, strained, strange, contrived, laboured, ludicrous, farfetched and ineffective, forced and unnatural, fantastically perplexed, unendurable._ Were a modern Johnson inclined to personify a contemporary critic, he would have to swell the Lilliputian Dick Minim to a Brobdingnagian—a Riccardus Maximus, say, a very large critic, great by walking on linguistic tiptoe, achieving a strutting dignity by an ever-enlarging sesquipedalianism. Some of us, retiring in total defeat from the verbal density of an article in *Clio* or *Glyph,* must have surely thought of Johnson's definition of "terrifick" diction—"a style by which the most evident truths are so obscured that they can no longer be perceived, and the most familiar propositions so disguised that they cannot be known." Or of what he called the "repulsive" style: "its natural effect is to drive away the reader." Or at least of the "bugbear" manner: it "has more terror than danger, and will appear less formidable, as it is more nearly approached."[25]

To stop here in our discussion of critical vocabulary and say "there's an end on't" would be to do both Johnson and our contemporaries a grave injustice. Johnson's "small" critics were just that—canting, superficial coxcombs, who disturbed the world by buzzing such omnibus teatable words as "Taste and Grace, Purity and Delicacy" or such foppish coffeehouse simplicities as "manly," "dry," "stiff," or "flimzy." No serious academic critic of today is brushed by that kind of frippery, for the best possess subtle minds full of philosophical, scientific, linguistic, historical, and aesthetic data from many languages and many cultures. Johnson found it to be "invariably true, that learning was never decried by any learned man." If he derided "terrifick" or "bugbear" language, he was a friend to "terms of art," to the language of science and education; and he did not gainsay the right of a learned discipline to create the words it needs: "words are only hard to those who do not understand them," he said, "and the critick ought always to enquire, whether he is incommoded by the fault of the writer, or by his own."[26]

Pedantry is of course a repellent weakness that can cause dismay and hostility, but Johnson defined it as "the *unseasonable* ostentation of learning." Learning in fit season he treated with respect, and he gladly admitted new professional and intellectual terms into both his *Dictionary* and his own vocabulary, often on the basis of only a single authority. He even boasted: "I have much augmented the vocabulary of English."[27]

I earlier mentioned several contemporary critical terms that are not to be found in the great compendium of 1755. A revision in 1984 based on the Johnsonian principles I have just invoked would undoubtedly include them, even the uncouth and whimsical. Johnson said about the policy governing his selection for the *Dictionary*: "I have not rejected any [learned terms] by design, merely because they were unnecessary or exuberant";[28] and the fellows and faculties of the School of Criticism and Theory should be informed that Johnson did include the following: *originary, prolepsis, paradigm, tropical* (from *trope*), *textuary, misprision, signifier,* and the verb, *to privilege*. There is no *ambivalence,* but *ambiguity* is amply defined and richly illustrated. *Narratology* does not exist, but *narrify* does. There is no *nihilism,* but there is *nihility.* And the absence of *diachronic* is partly compensated by the presence of *synchronism* and the *synchronical.* Thus if we had only Johnson the lexicographer to guide us, our generation would not have to walk in total darkness, one reason being that both he and many moderns have drunk from the same wells of classical, religious, rhetorical, moral, and critical learning.

If I have been right up to this point, a Samuel Johnson *redivivus* (1) might conceivably have crushed some currently influential critics for having committed the shameful act of "imposing words" (the "daughters of earth") for ideas (clear mental images) or for things (the "sons of heaven");[29] or (2) he would have applauded the contemporary ambition to make criticism and scholarship imaginatively creative and mentally energetic, enthusiastically giving the enterprise a wide scope to invent and use fully and freely its own terms of art, many of which may ultimately enrich our store of useful intellectual weapons. In an essay that has been a tissue of might-be's and would-be's and of speculations necessarily somewhat fantastic, it may be permissible to imagine further, and finally, what category and what judgment an intellectually brilliant, learned, and widely influential movement like the present one would have elicited in a powerful, analytical, and judicial mind like Johnson's. He would, I believe, have created for the Deconstructionists and their closest allies a category called Metaphysical Criticism. The following sentences from the Life of Cowley about their poetical ancestors in the seventeenth century possess, for me at least, an illuminating pertinence. The first of these sentences is applicable to living critics only in their worst moments, which (alas) exist and exist vividly and which therefore tend to vitiate one of their own central aims, namely, to explore the visionary and the sublime in our tradition, the farthest reaches of human wit and intellectual aspiration in the Western world:

> What they [the seventeenth-century Metaphysicals] wanted ... of the sublime, they endeavoured to supply by hyperbole; their amplification had no limits; they left not only reason but fancy behind them; and produced combinations ... that not only could not be credited, but could not be imagined.[30]

An earlier sentence points to a tendency of the contemporary mind not often enough resisted, a tendency peculiarly characteristic of the new Metaphysicals: "Their attempts were always analytick; they broke every image into fragments."[31]

The concessions I now quote are as fully deserved by our contemporaries as by their poetical forbears. The first, excessively harsh in its opening clause and also in its last phrase, points to a delight in learning and in verbal playfulness that today enlivens much of the best critical utterance:

> ... in the mass of materials which ingenious absurdity has thrown together, genuine wit and useful knowledge may be sometimes found buried, perhaps, in grossness of expression.

Yet Johnson provides the grounds for a kind of minimal approval of what currently and compellingly challenges so much academic attention:

> To write on their plan it was ... necessary to read and think.
>
> *   *   *
>
> ... their acuteness often surprises.
>
> *   *   *
>
> ... they ... sometimes struck out unexpected truth.[32]

I may seem, grudgingly, to have opened only very small doors, but entrances do not always prepare us for what lies within. It is too early to know whether current criticism will produce the prose equivalent of a John Donne. Perhaps not. No one wants another Cleveland[33] in any genre or form. But to be an Abraham Cowley would be far from an ignoble destiny—we certainly cannot fully understand the later seventeenth century or its transition to the eighteenth without him. And as our century dies into the next, we and our descendants will need all the illumination we can get, even from those who may fall short of greatness. Greatness should of course not be glibly assessed or confined only to belletristic creators. We have seen that Johnson, who perceived the imagination fermenting in distinguished learned enterprises, refused to partition the intensely thinking mind, and I have praised those in our day who do not want criticism to stand outside the gates of the literary city, alone and palely loitering. Still, it will not do to end without a dash of good Johnsonian sense, and it may be salutary, even though a bit deflating, to remember this as we labor on in our library twilights: "He that merely makes a book from other books may be useful, but can scarcely be great."[34]

8

Gray's Sensibility

"*Ah, tell them* they are men!" is Gray's sigh as he sees "the little victims" at play on the fields of Eton, "regardless of their doom."[1] "Teach me to . . . know myself a Man" is Gray's prayer for himself at the end of the "Ode to Adversity." Before being anything else Gray desired to be a loving, forgiving, generous, self-scanning human being, and deeper than his humanism is his humanity.

To be a man, however, is, with fatal inevitability, to be melancholy. To lose youthful innocence means to be ambushed by a "murth'rous band" of misfortune and passion. Being a man brings eschatology into the living present, for man is doomed well before the Last Judgment, and he goes through the Great Tribulation on this side of the River Jordan. To be a man is to be condemned to pain, the pain of the passions—tender, hideous, social, private, running the entire Burkean range from the pathetic to the sublime or even the gamut of the century itself, from the social tear of Shaftesbury to Samuel Johnson's solemn and austere realism. The doom is as universal as it is inescapable:

> To each his sufferings: all are men,
> Condemned alike to groan;
> The tender for another's pain,
> Th' unfeeling for his own.
> ("Eton," lines 91–94)

Amazingly, this pessimistic definition of man was written when Gray was between twenty-five and twenty-six years of age, a few months before he confided to West (who was soon to die) that he suffered from white melancholy (with its attendant insipidity and ennui). He could describe that condition as "a good easy sort of a state" only because the black melancholy came intermittently. The dark, hideous mood, which he "now and then felt," came often enough for him to cry out, "from this the Lord deliver us!"[2]

Viewing Gray's life in perspective whole, we must conclude that he did not suffer from two illnesses, leucocholy (chronic and white) and melancholy (black and occasional), but from only one, of which the white was the temporary remission of the black. If we apply Freud's distinction[3] to Gray, we must say that his was melancholia, not grief; for it was a fixed condition, "deep" in the fullest modern sense, a "doom" because it was so persistent and because it arose inexorably and mysteriously from the deep well of the unconscious. It was also a doom because it tortured him into a state of dejection that inhibited his activity and poisoned his quiet. Fixed and permanent, though with blessed remissions, Gray's passions were also hot and searing—a fact that his proverbial silence and sadness, as of a man in grief, his compulsive neatness, his finicky meticulousness, and his quirkish fears (like the fear of fire) should not be allowed to obscure. We must not assume that because the outer man was retiring, the inner man was not intense or that his emotional life was tepid or starved. Judging from the emotion expressed in the poetry and in the greatest of the sad letters, there was that within which passed show. The true man was Gray Agonistes, and the true poetry was carved in a language where emotions press powerfully against cool lapidary statement. The young poet writes compulsively of the "pangs of Passion," of "fury Passions" called "the vultures of the mind." These include "pining Love," "Jealousy with rankling tooth," "Envy wan," and "grim-visaged comfortless Despair." They can be regarded as primarily private, but they have social consequences that make the human environment painful, as Infamy grins and Shame skulks ("Eton," lines 61–80).

Black melancholy was so "frightful"—the word is Gray's (*Corres.,* 1:209)—that it might have had two issues, "moody Madness laughing

wild / Amid severest woe" or self-inflicted death ("Eton," lines 79–80).
Gray might have stood in the line of Romantic suicides. In the *Elegy*
he is half in love with easeful death. Of the Welsh poet, who plunges
from a high mountain to endless night, shouting, "To triumph, and to
die, are mine," Gray said, "I felt myself the Bard."[4] Writing to West,
whose death was imminent, he confessed, "I converse, as usual, with
none but the dead: They are my old friends, and almost make me long
to be with them" (*Corres.*, 1:202).

Gray might have joined his beloved dead by an unnatural act had
it not been for his intellectual and artistic interests—the notebook
jottings as well as the letters, the bibliographical lists as well as the
poetic lines. It is precisely because *sensibility* is a term broad enough
to include all these interests and dispositions that I have preferred it
in my title to *melancholy*, even though melancholy is the more basic
and potent word. But melancholy is too private and too isolated a
condition adequately to describe the Gray of the humanist tradition,
and we must use the broader and milder term sensibility, however
much it may suggest fashionable posturing and the drenched
handkerchief.

But is sensibility, after all, so tame a word? In *Sense and Sensibility*
Jane Austen uses it to describe a disruptive passion that could easily
have led to death,[5] and in *Northanger Abbey* she associates it with the
"luxury of a raised, restless, and frightened imagination."[6] In the *Mysteries of Udolpho* Mrs. Radcliffe has the father warn the heroine of the
very real dangers of heightened sensibility.[7] In *Rambler* no. 28 Johnson
mentions sensibility along with "perturbation."

Sensibility, then, can refer to powerful feeling, to melancholy, both
the white and the black. But it does connect the individual to the world
of travel, books, pictures, and poems. It is in fact a link between these
realms of taste and the deep passions. Sensibility unites, as melancholy
alone does not, the Gray of private suffering and the Gray who loved
the pictorial and the picturesque, valleys and mountains, and landscapes that he called "the *savage*, the *rude*, and the *tremendous*"
(*Corres.*, 2:586).

The relation between Gray's influential public taste and his individual feelings can be viewed in two ways. (1) The poetic, scholarly,

and intellectual interests are suffused with Gray's own sensibilities. Mountains he finds ecstatic because he himself knows or desires ecstasy. (We must assume throughout that Gray used language sincerely and precisely.) (2) Gray's intellectual interests are socially and personally accepted substitutes for the more dangerous personal passions, which may not be fully understood and are neither mastered nor suppressed. To the first of these alternatives—that his researches, say, into newer sources of sensibility are directly caused by his emotional condition and reflect it—Gray seems to give some support: "It is indeed for want of spirits, as you suspect, that my studies lie among the Cathedrals, and the Tombs, and the Ruins. To think . . . has been the chief amusement of my days; and when I would not, or cannot think, I dream" (*Corres.,* 2:565, 566). If he dreams and thinks of medieval remains, well and good. He is illustrating a venerable belief, as old as it is simple, that the artistic and intellectual preoccupations are sincere and reveal the man— a belief affirmed by Burke, Johnson, Tolstoy, I. A. Richards, Fielding, and Aristotle, to name a few.[8] Gray's mountains are pregnant with religion and poetry because Gray's own soul is.

If, however, the man of taste dreams of other things as he studies his ruins, he invokes the second view—that the changing objects of his shifting sensibility are *indirectly* related to the man and that they are the calm and manageable substitutes for potentially disruptive passions. That belief may be less persuasive, and Freud may offend where Fielding pleases. Still, a direct line or nerve from Gray's heart to his writing hand or walking feet may in fact be too strait and narrow a way to permit us to see all that needs to be seen. And it is at least an attractive hypothesis that travel may be a psychologically necessary substitute for travail and that some of Gray's poetry is as much a covering cloak as a revelation.

Ian Jack has persuasively argued that sensibility struggles with stoicism as the *Elegy* takes its final shape, and that sensibility prevails.[9] But stoicism keeps returning—necessarily, one feels—as though disciplined virtue had to be applied like a cold compress to the burning brow of sensibility. Consder one of the most revelatory letters in all of Gray, a letter to the young Bonstetten that includes a passage about Plato (*Corres.,* 3:1117–19). Charles Victor de Bonstetten had come to Gray already in love with dark forests, mountain ascents, the cry of eagles in lonely places, and the horror of birds of prey screeching in the fastnesses. His taste did not need to be formed, and in their many soirees together the middle-aged poet may have been pleased to see in the young Swiss the triumph of his own newer sensibilities. But at the same time there is a return to the Gray of the stoicism of the 1740s, and the circumstances appear to be dramatic. The fifty-three-year-old poet has been overmastered by a passion that is driving him past the line of decorum to the brink of madness. At that point the poet decides that the young man's morals need forming, and the ideal man of the *Republic* is introduced in the middle of a letter that begins and ends in passion. The first paragraph discloses a man on the rack, even his frail body sympathizing with the unquiet of his mind: "I am grown old in the compass of less than three weeks. . . . I did not conceive till now . . . what it was to lose you [he has learned that Bonstetten must leave England], nor felt the solitude and insipidity of my own condition, before I possess'd the happiness of your friendship." The last paragraph of the letter is similarly a cry of the heart: Gray wants the young man, about to be exposed to Continental and urban gaieties, to "shew me your heart simply and without the shadow of disguise, and leave me to weep over it." Between these tortured paragraphs Gray transcribes from his own notebook Plato's description in the *Republic* of a "Genius truly inclined to Philosophy" and sets up as a model to the young man a mind gentle, vivacious, magnanimous and a character that loves truth, probity, and justice. Undoubtedly, of the several virtues Plato recommends it is moderation and temperance that Gray wishes most to enforce on the young friend who had so discomposed his spirits—that quality in the soul of a good man that keeps him but "little inclined to sensual pleasures." Gray is in such anguish that it is difficult to regard the teaching of sensual discipline as merely disinterested instruction. A week later in a letter to Bonstetten in which he quotes Nicholls, whose mind Gray had years before similarly attempted to form, the poet reveals the source of his suffering about Bonstetten: it is that the boy will be exposed to "every danger and seduction," subject to the "allurements of painted Women . . . or the vulgar caresses of prostitute beauty, the property of all," the body and mind turned over to "folly, idleness, disease, and vain remorse" (*Corres.*, 3:1128). In brief, Gray is jealous, sexually jealous. I realize I have risked placing his sermon on stoic virtue under a cloud. But it is a risk one must take. Let the candid reader confront the disciplined ideal of the *Republic* in the midst of these torturing passions and then try to escape the implications of that juxtaposition, which incidentally is Gray's, not mine.[10]

The earlier letter to Bonstetten contains this sentence: "If you have ever met with the portrait sketch'd out by Plato, you will know it again: for my part (to my sorrow) I have had that happiness: I see the principal features, and I foresee the dangers with a trembling anxiety." One pauses at the word *trembling*. Is not Gray confronting his own condition and applying Plato as much to it as to Bonstetten's? Both men need stoical ice. The phrase "trembling anxiety" in the letter takes us back to the "trembling hope" of the *Elegy*:

> No farther seek his merits to disclose,
> Or draw his frailties from their dread abode,
> (There they alike in trembling hope repose)
> The bosom of his Father and his God.
>
> (lines 125–28)

In both the late letter and the earlier poem "frailties" and "trembling" are associated. Is it possible that before the Epitaph had achieved its Parian perfection the same fires had burned in the poet's heart that were to burn again toward the end of his life, almost causing its extinction?

Hope "trembles" in the *Elegy* because of guilt and the prospect of Judgment.* Anxiety "trembles" in the late letter because of amorous jealousy. Sensibility may have trembled all through Gray's life as a result of intense friendships, which can be regarded as the matrix for the triumphs alike of his taste and poetic genius. It is necessary to utter a truism: poetic expression is complexly caused, and causative emotions

---

*I have no wish to deny the biblical resonance in the *Elegy*. Paul tells the Philippians to "work out your own salvation with fear and trembling" (Phil. 2:12). But Gray's sensibility as I am defining it here, which by the standards of his own day would have been considered worse than "frailty," must have given urgency to religious fear.

become inextricably involved in language, image, landscape, topos, icon, and traditions of seeing, knowing, believing, and speaking. But, still, the deepest source of true artistic passion is human passion. Even though the manner is cool, and the passions are capitalized and personified conventionally, Gray the passionate friend guides the hand of Gray the young poet in the early odes.

If it is true that friendship formed the gestalt of Gray as man and poet from the very beginning of his career, many traditional views will have to be revised. Bonstetten himself was surely wrong when he said that Gray had never loved, and Roger Martin, that fine scholar, when he calls Bonstetten Gray's "premier amour."[11] We cannot possibly find Lord David Cecil's terminology and tone adequate when he calls Gray a "confirmed celibate" worried that Bonstetten will go off to revolting sexuality.[12] And Ketton-Cremer may be missing the central drama in Gray's life when he says that the young Swiss aroused in him such emotions as he "had never experienced before, emotions obsessive and overwhelming" (*Gray,* p. 251). The probabilities, from what we know about the friendship with West and what we do not know about the friendship with Walpole, are that Gray's emotions were even then overwhelming and obsessive. The hectic months with Bonstetten constitute the last in a series of attachments that make conventional views of Gray flat and unconvincing. To view the essential and memorable Gray as a shy fastidious bachelor, his heart, however, not totally invulnerable, there being one woman in his life, a woman whose charms may have endangered his quiet briefly, and there being also that awful late flare-up of incomprehensible emotions never before experienced—all this is to carry respectability and reticence too far. It was hardly thus that Gray knew himself a man.

As we have said, Bonstetten's comment that Gray had never loved is totally wrong, unless perchance he means that as an adult Gray had never loved a woman. So understood, the young and somewhat preposterous visitor to Cambridge provides us an insight among others that cannot be ignored. Bonstetten reports that Gray teased out of the young man a full account of his life but that the older man in his turn was totally reticent about his past, between which and the present there yawned "un abîme infranchissable." Whenever Bonstetten touched on Gray's past, dark clouds arose to cover it. Bonstetten, who perceived that melancholy lay at the heart of Gray's character, said of it: "cette mélancholie n'est qu'un besoin non-satisfait de la sensibilité" (*Gray,* p. 253). Bonstetten's is perhaps the most penetrating brief comment on Gray ever made: *sensibilité* is love, and love never fully satisfied cast a pall over the man's spirits.

The clouds that the young man could not dispel from Gray's past we cannot dispel either. But, with the benefit of modern insights into the psyche, we can look a little farther than some critics have. Gray's father was a cruel man, perhaps an alcoholic, who kicked, punched, and cursed his wife.[13] The legacy of the father was one of angry quarrels, vile scenes of verbal and physical violence. On a sensitive boy the effects must have been devastating. As Brydges said in 1834, "the misfortunes of his infancy dwelt like a nightmare on his heart."[14] Certainly one important wound was inflicted by the lack of a father who could have provided a model for the boy's own future manhood. From such circumstances one expects that the mother will be excessively loved, and Mason said that Gray "seldom mentioned his Mother without a sigh" (*Corres.,* 3:926, n. 3). Early, Gray feared the loss of her as a trauma in which he could not see "the least Shadow of comfort" (*Corres.,* 1:67). Later, in 1766, he confesses he had kept the loss of his mother green for over thirteen years—"every day I live it sinks deeper into my heart" (*Corres.,* 3:926). Upon his death he joined his mother in the tomb at Stoke Poges, and the anticipation of that final resting place must have been a kind of comforting ritual, since he urged on his younger friend Nicholls precisely the same kind of burial.[15]

Those are egregiously wrong who think that Miss Speed was the only woman in Gray's life—on two counts: his mother occupied that position and Miss Speed he never really treated as a woman. In very strange language to address to a friend, Gray announced what he chose to regard as a discovery made late in life—"a thing very little known, which is, that in one's whole life one can never have any more than a single Mother. You may think this is obvious, & (what you call) a trite observation. You are a green Gossling!"[16] Certainly so powerful a maternal orientation as that neither Miss Speed nor any woman could reverse. We owe much to Miss Speed, but no love poetry, not even poetry of feeling. To her wit and sprightliness we are indebted for comparable qualities in Gray—notably that exquisite *vers de société,* "A Long Story." And when the lady finally did marry, Gray writes one of his driest, wryest, and sharpest vignettes: "she is a prodigious fine Lady, & a Catholic . . . not fatter than she was: she had a cage of foreign birds & a piping Bullfinch at her elbow, two little Dogs on her cushion in her lap, a Cockatoo on her shoulder, & a slight suspicion of Rouge on her cheeks" (*Corres.,* 3:923). Really wonderful stuff, but like the charming verses it is born of total emotional security. Gray was never in the remotest danger. He was fully free to be Robin Goodfellow.

Gray early describes himself as a "solitary fly" whose "joys no glittering female meets" ("Ode on the Spring," 2:44, 45). That fly possessed a sting, not only for women but for marriage. Very young, the poet was somewhat curious about union between the sexes. Middle-aged petulance, bordering on cruelty, replaced that curiosity. When Mason thought of getting married, Gray asked him about his intended: "Has she a nose?" (*Corres.,* 2:821). Was he perchance wondering if the female was like one of Hogarth's syphilitics, *sans* that protuberance? Or was he merely wondering if hers was aquiline and aristocratic?

A pattern appears to be emerging: the late-life passion for a young man; an excessive love of his mother; fear of the father; a witty passionless heterosexual friendship; and possibly a coldhearted impoliteness in contemplating the marriage of one of his friends. These details, tending as they do to organize themselves into a gestalt, constitute an illuminating biographical supplement to the psychology of Gray as he expressed it in a Latin poem, addressed to West and begun in Florence shortly before, after, or during the breach with Walpole.[17] That didactic poem discusses the senses, and its most interesting and substantial verse paragraph is devoted to the sense of touch. To that sense—quite remarkably—is given the priority usually accorded the sight: it plays the leading role in our sensuous life, coming first and leading the lesser crowd. As first born, it has the rights of primogeniture and asserts a wider sway than the others, not being subject to normal restrictions. Living in the warp and woof of the skin, it is widely diffused through the whole body. Its life begins prenatally in the womb, and birth is a trauma. For then come pain, trembling, savage fury. Touch in Gray's

Latin verse is a stunning parallel to the torturing passions of the early odes, those passions that define manhood as a doom. It is an equally stunning description of pregenital, pancorporal sexuality, the physical love of boyhood, the kind preferred by those who shun normal adult responsibilities and attach themselves to an earlier, a more manageable, and what is regarded as a more pleasurable stage.

The poem on touch may have been written between the ship-wrecked friendship with Walpole and the deeply renewed friendship with West. The surviving evidence permits no one to call these and other friendships of Gray overtly homosexual.[18] But no one who wishes to master the master traits of the poet's life and literary expression— or indeed who wishes to be an honest biographer—can ignore their human intensity. The friendships, together with the beautiful and subtle letters they produced and the poems they ultimately induced, form an unassailable integrity.

The relations with Walpole began in the prelapsarian Eton, upon which the somewhat older poet looked back in the mood of Adam after the Expulsion. The friendship continued at Cambridge with banter, verbal love-play, high spirits, and wit. It was smashed on the Continent, for reasons one can imagine but cannot know certainly. It was at length restored to a relationship of dignity that reopened cautiously and coolly and that ended in respect and even affability—always, however, a sobering contrast to the fevers, palpitations, and racy informalities of the true and early friendship. It was that earlier phase—late Eton, Cambridge, and early Continent—that bore literary and intellectual fruit. The language of Gray's letters to Walpole is a marvel of flexible, colloquial writing, moving from the rhythms of excited and fluttery love-speech to double entendre and parody, mocking Restoration literary poses and even heroic and biblical style. The whole spirit of the young man was involved in this friendship, which provided bright relief from the drunken, illiterate, dull, loutish circles at Cambridge. Walpole's announced visit to the University produced "great extasie" in Gray, "Convulsions of Joy," in fact (*Corres.*, 1:13). Gray longed for the minister's son and showed a fretful jealousy toward Ashton. There is a bit of flutter about what to do with the letters—should Gray keep them (absolutely private of course) or should he burn them? Let Walpole decide.

One letter takes notice of a love affair that Walpole appears to have half confided to Gray: "I confess," Gray replied, "I am amazed: of all likely things this is the last I should have believed would come to pass." He refers to this affair as "the new study you have taken a likeing to" and calls it "the most excellent of all sciences." Then comes a most revealing passage, full of psychological implications and with who knows how much intended or unintended double meaning:

> would you believe it, 'tis the very thing I would wish to apply to myself? ay! as simple as I stand here: but then the Apparatus necessary to it costs so much; nay, part of it is wholly out of one's power to procure; and then who should pare one, & burnish one? for they would have more trouble & fuss with me, than Cinderaxa's sisters had with their feet, to make 'em fit for the little glass Slipper: oh yes! to be sure one must be lick'd; now to lick oneself I take to be altogether impracticable, & to ask another to lick one, would not be quite so civil; Bear I was born, & bear, I believe, I'm like to remain: consequently a little ungainly in my fondnesses, but I'll be bold to say, you shan't in a hurry meet with a more loving poor animal, than
> your faithful Creature
Bruin. (*Corres.,* 1:79–80)

Why did the boys fall into parody? Were they simply high-spirited about language, determined to show their virtuosity—much to the delectation of posterity? Or did a high-flown, mock-heroic style permit confidences without embarrassment and a role-playing which in the raw would have been painful? Adopting the manner of *The Turkish Spy,* Gray sighs: "When the Dew of the morning is upon me, thy Image is before mine eyes." Again, "thou art sweet in my thoughts as the Pine-apple of Damascus to the tast." Again, "Be thou unto me, as Mohammed to Ajesha"—that is, as the Prophet was to his wife (*Corres.,* 1:14, 15).

The intense friendship with West that immediately followed the rupture with Walpole did not lead to the kind of verbal love-play that recalls and mocks the Song of Songs. In the period of Walpole's dominance the letters to and from West were strained or perfunctory. Relaxing somewhat during the Grand Tour, they became, after the breach with Walpole, profound and moving, touching on the great issues of life, death, and mental health, to say nothing of the technical poetic interests shared by two young writers. Suffused with melancholy sentiment and even thoughts of suicide, they almost seem inexorably to move to the climax that so disrupted the whole inner being of Gray, casting a shadow before it happened, the death of West.

Vastly more influential than any literary model, aesthetic configuration, or cultural trend, more intimately related to his mind and heart than the trial and sentencing of the rebel Scottish lords in London, the friendship with West was the soil from which the *Elegy* grew, a traditional view that needs reviving.* But in an even longer perspective— for poetic causes are not necessarily immediate, since human beings never really forget deep experiences but use them even after the lapse of time and memory—we ought to regard both the friendships, with West and Walpole, as the matrix of the poem. Both engaged the deepest recesses of Gray's heart. Both had their joys, but these, to use Gray's poetic phrases, were "imperfect Joys," "fearful joy."[20] Both moved from calm to turmoil and then from agitation to a profound desire for peace and even death. Both the young friends had "died," Walpole as a friend and West as a creature of dust. Both deaths blighted hopes that had been green and tender, both left love unfulfilled. Doubtless both relations were streaked with guilt and potential danger. And of both it can be said that high though the youths had mounted in delight, in their dejection they did sink as low—with fears, fancies, dim sadness, and blind thoughts:

> We Poets in our youth begin in gladness;
> But thereof come in the end despondency and madness.[21]

If the youthful friendships of Gray are the ultimate causes of the *Elegy,* we must surely find unpersuasive Ketton-Cremer's view that

---

*I take this opportunity to abjure my earlier view, expressed in *The Sister Arts,* that the Epitaph of the *Elegy* is intended primarily to commemorate the dead village poet. I then wrote under the influence of a pictorialist model; I am now writing with more dynamically psychological and less purely aesthetic views of poetic art, and hence believe that the Epitaph refers primarily and most profoundly, though perhaps indirectly, to Gray himself.[19]

the poet at the climax of the final version of the poem is the "complete antithesis" of the author, a vision "conjured up by the swain" in language that is theatrical (*Gray*, p. 101). In fact, both the later Christian and sentimental ending and the earlier stoical conclusion are exquisitely sober renditions of Gray's own experience in passionate friendship—experience refined, to be sure, by thought, literary example, austere taste, and the passage of time. Even the rejected lines of the original ending, which everyone praises as more controlled and "classical" than the later, are suffused with recollections of suffering and loss. The cry for calm is in low accents, rising from the ground, but it is piercing. The poet really longs for a death-in-life, the "cool and silent" death of "ev'ry fierce tumultuous Passion," of "anxious Cares & endless Wishes." When applied to the losses Gray suffered in his early friendships, the language is hauntingly precise. And so is the language of the Epitaph. The Swain's sight of the poet is Gray's vision of himself. Even minor details are parallel. The Swain saw the poet stretch his listless length under a beech at noontide poring upon the brook that babbled by. Gray in his letters confesses that he could "grow to the Trunk" of a tree (also a beech) contemplating a natural scene (*Corres.*, 1:47, 48). From his Spring-like relations with Walpole and from his friendship with West, so autumnal, so red-leafed for men so young, imagine what exact analogues Gray might have drawn to these phrases in the *Elegy*: "wayward fancies," "forlorn," "crazed with care," "crossed in hopeless love." Far from being overly dramatic, such language must be regarded as a sober and understated description of the poet's own friendships in their moments of greatest intensity. And the following famous sentences, which have been smoothed into proverbs, imply possessiveness and exclusiveness both toward the beloved partner and toward the emotions aroused: "He gained from Heaven (*'twas all he wished*) a friend. . . . And Melancholy marked him *for her own.*"[22]

Unlike the wound of Philoctetes, Gray's was a guilty one—or so he regarded it—and it did not permit him often to draw his bow. But when he did, the strength of his arm and the accuracy of his aim are owing to his suffering. He arouses an echo in every bosom because in his best serious poetry he knew himself a man. At the heart of his humanity was his sensibility; at the heart of his sensibility was his melancholy; at the heart of his melancholy—to continue opening this Chinese nest of boxes—lay his friendships, enlivening at first but finally inhibited; and at the heart of each hopeless love frustrating its fulfillment was.... But who can go deeper? Who can say what he saw within as he dreamed of some kind of union in mind and body that the evidence suggests his nature deeply craved? Did he see his mother? Or his mother and his father (unreal and idealized) together and in love? Or did he see other successful lovers in the serene and perfect joy he never knew? Traveling in Italy, Gray was wont to set down subjects for paintings that he had never seen executed.[23] Perhaps in dreaming about some of these unrealized subjects he revealed his own deepest self. One of them that he himself would have liked to do had he been an artist Blake realized triumphantly in illustrating Milton, the two angels Ithuriel and Zephon lighting their own way into the bower of bliss where Adam and Eve lay.[24] Where in such a picture would Gray's artistic triumph have lain? In rendering the accomplished bliss of our first parents? Or, if he painted, as he wrote, from his own experience, might it not have been in portraying the two angels viewing but never achieving bliss?

Gray petitioned the great stoical and Christian goddess Adversity to teach him "Exact my own defects to scan" ("Adversity," line 47). Perhaps somewhat too boldly we have snatched Gray's private and privileged self-examination from his hands and looked unceremoniously at his suffering heart. We may indeed have violated his own injunction, not to "draw his frailties from their dread abode." We can only hope that forgiveness is owing affectionate curiosity, a deep sympathy for the man's torturing passions, a modern's tolerance of what once was called aberration, enormous respect for his personal and artistic controls, and gratitude for the thin but golden poetic achievements.

The order and beauty of the early odes and the *Elegy* bear to the early friendships the same relation that the created universe bears to chaos. Gray's chaos may have been without form but it was not void, for on it the poet could breathe the creating word. The good estate of Gray's poetry was blessed with rich black soil, his sensibility—in the fullest sense of that weighty eighteenth-century term. Gray did not achieve the ideal of Samuel Johnson—"the solitude of adversity without its melancholy, its instructions without its censures, and its sensibility without its perturbations."[25] In fact, Gray's adversity is compounded of melancholy, censure, and perturbation. The compensation was that he achieved "Thoughts that breathe and words that burn" (*Progress of Poetry,* line 110). And the procedure we have followed, of trying to imagine the passion that lay behind the words, will, it is hoped, serve the humanistic tradition better than the censoring scissors of William Mason, who sacrificed the humanity of the poet to a false ideal of chilling and inhuman respectability, from which too much of the race and vigor of the poet's life was omitted.[26]

9

Pictures to the Heart:
The Psychological Picturesque
in Ann Radcliffe's
The Mysteries of Udolpho

*T**he term pictorial* is often used as a synonym for graphic, visual, scenic, or sensuous. In his analysis of renditions of reality in Western literature, Erich Auerbach is concerned with the pictorial in this sense, making it the source of important literary value. Failure for him is to be "dry and unvisualized," while success lies in being sensory and pictorial. To write with circumstantial detail is to write "plastically"; the graphic manner floods a work with "a clear and equal light," leaving nothing mysterious in the background.[1] What Auerbach praises is the ancient rhetorical value called *enargeia*—that is, clarity, palpability, a living daylight freshness and fullness of vivid detail.[2]

For many works in the Western tradition the term *pictorial* as defined is not adequate to the visual richness and variety that one finds; and one must have resort to the ungainly but useful word *pictorialist,* which evokes the tradition of literary pictorialism and such specific conventions as the description of an art object real or imaginary; the "quotation" of particular works of graphic art or the reflection of easily identifiable schools of art; ways of seeing trained by visual models in tapestry, sculpture, painting, or the cinema; methods of proceeding and ordering that suggest spatial rather than temporal art. For almost two millennia now—from Homer to Yeats—these Sister Arts conventions have persisted in poetry, providing even within the visual matrix abundant opportunity for imitation and adaptation, convention and revolt.[3]

Pictorialist novels also exist. These have not been much studied, except in notable isolated instances, and little has been said about the tradition, if one in fact exists apart from that associated with the ancient admonition *ut pictura poesis* (as a picture, so a poem). The Pilgrim's Progress of antiquity, the *Tablet* (or *Tabula*) of Cebes of Thebes, is pictorialist in the sense that it begins by introducing the reader to an allegorical picture and proceeds by describing its every section and detail.[4] Similarly, Longus' *Daphnis and Chloe* presents at the outset a large landscape painting from which the action of the novel seems to derive.[5] In the *New Arcadia* Sidney's vision of persons and scenes is stylized into picture and statue, and the action often proceeds in a series of tableaux. In the prose of Laurence Sterne the "attitude" of an individual character is likewise often statuesque or pictorial, sometimes suggesting a specific source in the visual arts: "My father instantly exchanged the attitude he was in, for that in which *Socrates* is so finely painted by Raffael in his school of *Athens.*"[6] In *The Marble Faun* Hawthorne loads every rift with iconic ore: the faun itself by Praxiteles, the statue of the pope in Perugia, and paintings by Guido Reni—all of them symbolic equivalents of human characters or the chief purveyors of meaning and value.[7] George Eliot's novels form a tissue of traditional pictorialist conventions as these had been modified by Hazlitt and the Romantics—traditions that she in her turn adapted to her needs as a Victorian author.[8] Henry James often disposes his scenes like pictures in a gallery or tapestries on a wall, and in chapter 30 of *The Ambassadors* Strether, on an excursion into the French countryside, enters, as it were, a canvas of Lambinet; and the ensuing scene is composed as a series of impressionist paintings.[9] Some of the outdoor scenes of *Women in Love* suggest, as D. H. Lawrence says, the picnics of Watteau and also, as he does not say, the ferns, fronds, and petals on water of Claude Monet. Finally, Nathanael West makes a painting by one of his characters, Tod's apocalyptic *Burning of Los Angeles,* central to the meaning and movement of *The Day of the Locust.* The painting appears at the Day-of-Wrath climax as well as at the beginning, and not only frames the action but insinuates it.[10]

To this partial list of pictorialist novels must be added Mrs. Ann Radcliffe's *The Mysteries of Udolpho* (1794), a work which marked the apogee of the Romantic gothic novel and which held the throbbing attention of more than one generation of young readers.[11] About the picture making in this novel two essential points need to be made. The first is that to Radcliffe's pictorialism the then-fashionable contemporary term *picturesque* can be applied. The other is that, by subtle but persistent metaphorical substitutions, Radcliffe extends her pictures into the heart and spirit of man—an extension that Longus, other writers of Greek romance, Sidney, and writers in the tradition of emblematic and allegorical visualization were unable to make. Hence the phrase of the title of this chapter: "the psychological picturesque."

The picturesque anticipated Ann Radcliffe by only a few years; but when it came into her hands, it bore the weighty sanctions of Edmund Burke, of some of the greatest landscapists of Western culture, of exciting novelistic experiments, and of a contemporary set of enthusiastic aestheticians. The story has often been told of how various ingredients came together to form the pre-Romantic picturesque: the grand sublime of terror that Burke had distinguished from the soft beauty of tenderness, the savage and irregular landscapes of Salvator that contrasted with the delicate landscapes of Claude, the obsessive love of Alpine scenery, and a quickened appreciation of Oriental and Hebrew imagery.[12] Radcliffe's rendition of the historical picturesque is precise and nuanced. She understands both the sublime of religious awe and the sublime of natural fear in the present of physical danger. And her beauty has all the largeness of Claude's vistas in tender lights and the intimacies of cottage and fishing hut expressed by contemporary water colorists—a beauty that soothes the mind and ministers to the affectionate sensibilities. To the Salvatorian sublime and Claudian beauty only a few more pictorial strains need to be added for a full understanding of Radcliffe's picturesque: the fluttering and exotic beauty of Guardi's and Canaletto's Venice; the Magnasco-like chiaroscuro of the gypsy scenes; the disturbing effect of Piranesi's grotesquely imagined interiors in the dark corridors, grating gates, and bloodstained steps of

Part Two

French and Italian castles; and the traces of the "dark pencil" of Domenichino, whom the author invokes by name, on the dark, torchlit chapel interior where the mild face of a venerable monk, his features revealed by his pulled-back cowl, contrasts with the fierce features and wild dress of the condottieri.

These are the colors of Mrs. Radcliffe's pictorial palette, which brought her the rewards of immediate fame. This "great impresario of beauty, wonder, and terror"[13] riveted the attention of her own and succeeding generations of readers. Sir Walter Scott reports that "the volumes flew, and were sometimes torn from hand to hand," and Joseph Warton was surely not the only one whom *The Mysteries of Udolpho* kept from sleep.[14] How shall one explain the spell of this "enchantress"?[15] Surely it was not only the imagined danger of distant places that thrilled her readers. Nor, it seems, would the pictorialist skill alone— what Cazamian praises as the variety, the wealth of coloring, and the charm of her pictures, a talent hitherto unequaled in the English novel[16]—have fastened the reader to those many pages of extended description that our own age finds languid. Nor could it have been the supernatural, which the author almost always in the course of the novel explains in natural terms once an educated character has had time to get in all the facts and refute the ignorant servants. The appeal must have lain in the immediate and intimate suggestiveness, for Mrs. Radcliffe was one of the most deeply penetrating authors ever to have unfolded a slow-moving plot through several volumes.

Many critics have made hints about the hints of Mrs. Radcliffe, implying that her many-layered suggestiveness has its roots deep in our nature and arouses resonances of feeling much deeper than superficial titillation. Catherine Morland turns from immediate concerns in Bath to "the luxury of a raised, restless, and frightened imagination over the pages of Udolpho" (*Northanger Abbey*, chap. 7), and these strong and weighty adjectives of Jane Austen should give pause to those who think that this novel merely makes fun of Mrs. Radcliffe's melodrama. Others have noted that Mrs. Radcliffe's heroines have an almost morbid craving for fear and that her adventures have a dreamlike quality that reveals a mind tremblingly alive to imaginative fear.[17] Even within the novel there is some awareness that an emotional life quickened by the picturesque can be dangerous. Emily's father warns her that excessive sensibility is to be feared, and Radcliffe herself, believing that terror can be wholesome and "expand the soul and awaken the faculties," was careful, like Coleridge after her, to keep terror from becoming an annihilating, freezing horror.[18]

Where shall we locate the fear and terror of her novel, emotions which can, as Hazlitt says, make "the nerves thrill with fond hopes and fears"[19] and which witness to a power of evocation greater than that of any of her countrymen? Her power arouses that part of the civilized psyche where sexual love and sexual encounters are anticipated but never formulated in direct and unequivocal terms or images. To accept this view one must be sympathetic to the notion that profoundly suggestive pictures can be socially or morally acceptable substitutes for forbidden feelings or wishes. Literature of course abounds in examples of pictures as substitutes for real people or for real experience. In Sidney's *New Arcadia* they often take the place of a person, of a loved and lost husband or friend,[20] as is also true in Chekhov's "The Bear," in which a grieving Russian lady caresses her late husband's portrait.

Radcliffe's substitutions are less for what is loved and lost than for what is loved and hoped for. Her heroines usually dally with larger pictures than miniatures, but the suggestions are insistent that the sublime-beautiful landscapes are an anticipation of the rewards that came to Pygmalion, who embraced his statue. The bedchambers, often in an older and isolated part of the castle, with secret entrances, sliding panels, steps leading to deep unexplored recesses, have overtones of sexual danger which, had these been totally displeasing, would have made all life and motion cease. "To the warm imagination, the forms," to quote Radcliffe's own language, "which float half-veiled in darkness afford a higher delight than the most distinct scenery the Sun can show."[21] Such a statement, taken alone, reformulates one quality in the Burkean sublime. But, placed in a Radcliffian context of "warm imagination," that "half-veiled delight" may sometimes be viewed as being as impatient of the "Busie old foole, unruly Sunne" as ever Jack Donne was—and for Donne's reasons.

Radcliffe was much more than a formulary novelist illustrating Burke's distinction between the sublime and the beautiful[22] and merely alternating between Salvatorian danger and Claudian repose.[23] Although she does provide these fashionable alternations, she essentially unites what Burke and his followers had put asunder. Extremes do not always meet, of course, and it would do the melodrama disservice if on one level we did not keep the black villainous Italians, the Montonis and the Orsinos, worlds apart from the good white French, the St. Auberts and the Villerois. But the really interesting zone in the *Mysteries of Udolpho* is that protoerogenous zone where terror and delectation meet, namely, the heart of the heroine. *Sensibility* is the historical word for the inward psychological response to the external picturesque of interreacting terror and beauty—a word that Jane Austen uses unmistakably for sexual love.[24]

Radcliffe almost, in fact, makes explicit the association of pictorialized landscape and love-experience. Valancourt, Emily's lover, first flits unseen but not unnoticed (as poet, lute player, and harmless thief) in a favorite setting near the family home on the edge of the Pyrenees. On the first journey he materializes mysteriously on the road and accompanies the party, it now being perfectly clear that the taste for wild sublimity is a shared one. Even in the sinister abode of the evil Montoni in the Apennines the love-feelings are by no means dissipated, since that formidable pile possesses the "gothic greatness" of a "gloomy and sublime object" and produces "melancholy awe" in Emily—precisely the emotion that Emily shares with her lover, a sure sign that they belong together.[25] After the return to France, Valancourt appears in a delicious southern French vintage; and again, near the climax at the place of first meeting, his mysterious presence is felt and stirs deep chords of fear as well as trembling anticipation. (For one thing his identity is not at once known: is he a robber or the lover or possibly, in a psychophysical sense, both?) It is the cumulative effect of just such juxtapositions as these that make one feel that the sensuous in Mrs. Radcliffe is also the sensual, or at least anticipates the sensual. The sublime/beautiful, dangerous/safe, savage/mild, wild/cultivated alternations and fusions of the pictures suggest love-play and love-experience—an earnest of the full physical and sexual inheritance that physical union will bring.

Prose fiction has often, to use Johnson's phrase, created "pictures to the mind."[26] The ethical and moral emblems of Radcliffe are conventional and superficial, but those of Sidney, Richardson, and others are weighty and impressive, whether they are the ideal representations of *la belle nature* or the grotesque of evil and distorted nature. Verbal pictures have also been—particularly in the romances—supernatural or magical or superstitious, but Radcliffe tends to explain them away. Even deeper than either the ethical or the religious, the moral or the mysterious, are the psychological pictures, pictures to the heart, dream-like pictures that arise from the inner man and either disturb or animate the conventions. The nerve of Mrs. Radcliffe's literary eye extends deep within her being, with the result that the mountain ways of Gascony and the winding corridors of a castle in the Apennines carry their suggestions to the untrodden passes of the human heart and body.[27]

10

Byron's Songs of Innocence: The Poems to Thyrza

*T**he published poems** which are the subject of this chapter number approximately seventeen. They were written over a ten-year period (1806–16), four before and the rest after the death of the person addressed. The premortem poems all appeared in 1806–7 in miscellaneous places. At least five stanzas in *Childe Harold's Pilgrimage* are addressed to the memory of the departed friend, and six separate poems either were once part of the first or second edition of *Childe Harold* or bore some relation to that long poem. The three or four poems that close the canon include one in 1815, which appeared in *Hebrew Melodies,* and also two or three poems of 1815–16 which bear the title "Stanzas for Music," an appropriate denomination, as we shall see.[1] Although the name "Thyrza"[2] is not used in all or even most of these poems, it becomes clear after study that the primary bond of union between them is that the same person is being addressed. The poems themselves are all characterized by an unrelieved seriousness of tone in which musical imagery and musical effects tend to predominate. The stanzaic forms, the meters, the rhythms, and the rhymes are extremely simple and obvious, coming very close to ballad meter, usually being some variant of that poetic form. The manner of address is sincere and direct, the vocabulary severe and spare. And the verse embodies qualities not always characteristic of Byron, an almost total absence of histrionics and a total lack of hysteria. Nor is the mood darkened by what we have come to know as Byronism, guilt-obsessed loneliness. These poems are indeed what our title calls them, songs of innocence, singularly free of any sense of physical filthiness, irrevocable damnation, or human alienation. One must concede at the outset that the poems are uneven in quality: some, especially the earlier ones, are flat and conventional, while others can stand among the best lyrics Byron ever wrote. When read in roughly chronological order, the poems reveal growth in depth and power, providing insights into the way deeply felt experience becomes embodied in the permanent forms of art.

Who Thyrza actually was—or whether the person addressed was an imaginary being—has been much discussed; and many earlier editions of the poems of Byron inform the reader that the poet was successful in keeping the secret during his lifetime, eluding the curiosity of readers and the research of scholars. But all that is now changed, thanks largely to a manuscript note by Ernest Hartley Coleridge, which appears in the copy of Thomas Moore's life of Byron now in the Osborn Collection at Yale. The note corrects Lord Lovelace: he, along with many others, believed Thyrza was a girl who died about the time Byron landed in England in 1811 and whose tresses he continued to wear. These, it was thought, he showed to Lady Byron, who understood that they belonged to the female subject of the lyrics. E. H. Coleridge's clarifying and definitive comment is as follows:

> Lord Lovelace's rambling and meaningless Thyrza-note was designed
> to Combat a theory of mine (and the Athenaeum's long ago)—ob-
> viously the true one—that Thyrza and Edleston were one and the
> same person. I maintained and maintain that Byron's feelings on this
> point were entirely to his credit, and that Lord Lovelace wilfully or
> stupidly misunderstood the whole incident. E.H.C.[3]

All scholars now accept this identification.

We are not without information regarding the person identified. John Edleston was a boy two years the poet's junior who sang in the choir of Trinity College, Cambridge, and whom Byron met in October 1805, soon after he arrived at the university. The young man was of humble birth; he presented, in January 1806 or later, a cornelian to the poet, perhaps as a token of gratitude for having been saved by Byron from drowning. Some evidence suggests that the poet helped the young man financially to such an extent that Byron was led into deep debt—a fact that may account for the somber cast of his mood at that time. But somber or not, the poet's feelings developed into what he called love—a "violent, though *pure*, love and passion." So intimate did the affair become that Byron on 23 February 1807 had to "keep the subject of my 'Cornelian' a *Secret.*" Byron was attracted by the young man's voice, countenance, manner—and deeply sympathized with his financial needs. Their almost constant association seems to have led to dalliance as well as discussion of Edleston's future as a partner in a London mercantile house, in which Byron decided to support him. The most striking quality of the friendship was its rapturous release from psychological pain. When the two were together, Byron felt joy in the intimacy; when they separated, his mind became "a *Chaos* of *hope & Sorrow.*"[4]

But separate they did and must. Byron embarked on a two-year tour of the Continent—travels that bore voluminous and revolutionary literary fruit and that did not bring him back to England until June 1811. He returned from considerable suffering abroad—as well as from exhilarating adventure; but the deep gloom that now depressed his spirits was quite unlike anything he had known before. In his homeland he suffered the loss of five friends and a mother. Although all these friends had been beloved, Byron grieved for none more deeply than John Edleston, about whose death he had heard from the boy's sister some months after it had occurred in May 1811. The grief overwhelmed his spirits at first and then, along with recollections of the living intimacy, entered deep into his psyche, where it became a kind of Byronic spot of time. It was, when conscious and perhaps also when unconscious, a focused center not of mystical exaltation but of combined friendship and loss, of combined love and purity—a kind of passionate innocence not easily come by and never again recovered or repeated.[5]

Leslie Marchand is quite right in calling the attachment to Edleston "probably the deepest, sincerest, and most unqualified of any in his life."[6] The two-year separation during Byron's travels had not dimmed the memories of the intimate ecstasies, and now the premature death stirred the poet into a series of poetic utterances that exceed in number and quality those made during the young man's lifetime.

Professor Marchand has also said that the Thyrza poems have never been considered as a whole or been accorded the evaluative criticism they deserve.[7] It is to that challenge that the present chapter attempts to rise—an attempt that cannot be separated from a study of the poet's sensibility, which for Byron was always the immediate and effectual cause of the verse. Since he looked into his heart and wrote, and since interior experience was always clamoring to get out in the form of verbal expression, no interpreter of the lyrics can ignore his life and his feeling.

On 22 June 1813 Byron wrote to Thomas Moore, "I don't know what to say about 'friendship.' I never was in friendship but once, in my nineteenth year, and then it gave me as much trouble as love."[8] The poet unquestionably refers to the Edleston affair. And since, as we have said, we are concerned with "sincere" poems, we necessarily turn to the sensibility that stimulated their coming into being. What, then, was the state of Byron's spirits when he first met the young chorister at Cambridge? It cannot be too strongly emphasized that he was already sexually experienced, having been titillated by a wanton maidservant (who combined Scottish piety and low habits) to an unconscionably early and perhaps sordid loss of sexual innocence. It is also true—and we are now on an entirely different plane—that he had been in love with his beautiful cousin, Margaret Parker, whose early death he mourned, and that at eighteen he had loved Mary Chaworth, who married another—a loss that he mourned long and embodied in his intermittently ardent and beautiful poem of 1816 entitled "The Dream" ("Our life is Twofold . . ."). Two emotions may have early emerged from his *affaires de coeur* (and *de corps*): physical disgust at Shelleyan nympholepsy,[9] revulsion at whoredom—and a consequent striving after unattainable purity. At Harrow he had added the dimension of "passionate friendship" and "affectionate camaraderie." But about these last there is no evidence of an accompanying sense of evil or shame, a sense that seems to have been reserved for some kinds of heterosexual love.

The evidence of the Thyrza poems seems to enforce the view that Byron carried to his Cambridge friendship an aura of sweet and lingering innocence, a gentle contrast to the heartier and headier dissipations of the bottle and the brothel, which also continued at Cambridge. Such venereal and bacchic pleasures—with perhaps laudanum thrown in for good measure—were not allowed to poison the male friendships, including the most passionate—perhaps the only passionate one. It may be hard for some to believe that an ecstatic friendship which apparently involved some physical contact (though how much we of course do not know) could breathe an odor of angelic sanctity. But apparently for the experienced Byron, whom contemporary morality would have called degenerate, precisely that was the case. Flitting from girl to girl in transient affairs smelt of corruption. The friendship with Edleston represented moral nobility and emotions as close as Byron ever came to religious exaltation.[10]

When on 30 June 1809 Byron sailed from Falmouth for the memorable *Wanderjahre* on the Continent, he was "tolerably sick of vice which I have tried in its agreeable varieties."[11] On his return he was doubtless even sicker of heterosexual dissoluteness and carnality.[12] And when, after his return, he confronted the loss of his mother and of several dear school companions, he thought with especial poignance about the loss of Edleston and began idealizing a friendship that had been at once passionate and pure. Surely one reason Byron came to believe—and there is a long tradition behind such a view—that friendship was superior to love was this: that it could not result in marriage. Between men there was no way of kneading "two virtuous souls for life / Into that moral centaur, man and wife."[13] But though the relations with Edleston did not result in a waste of shame, they did cost an expense of spirit. Byron had to turn, as was his wont, to poetry for mental and spiritual relief—the only reason, he once said, that he ever wrote.

When we confront the poems, we must provide for each of them—or at least for each appropriate grouping of them—the proper literary ambience. Before he wrote his first Thyrza poem, Byron had had a short but prolific career as a teenage poet. Many poems from 1802 on are dedicated to girls and concern the subject of love. They are heavily and obviously rhythmic, flat and one-dimensional in meaning; and their range of mood spans cynicism and sentiment, conventional attitudes about death and a few anticipations of the Byronic humor that is to come. These anticipations strike one with greater force than the somewhat surprising recollection of Crashaw in one of the poems "To Caroline." Byronic verse tends to yield easily to the lilt of feminine rhymes and literary allusion—

> Why should you weep, like Lydia Languish,
> And fret with self-created anguish?
> ("To a Lady": "These locks, which fondly . . .")

The only reason for pausing to notice the invasion of the early love poetry by the mercurial lightness of the *Don Juan* tone is that this quality is so conspicuously—and, one would guess, so purposefully—absent from the Thyrza series, which is governed by the unrelenting seriousness that may have characterized Byron's mood during his friendship with Edleston.

Although it has a few feminine rhymes, the first poem to Edleston ("The Cornelian": "No specious splendour . . ."), so entitled because of the boy's gift of a heart-shaped stone to the poet, is a sentimental poem—in both important eighteenth-century meanings of that adjective. The tear dropped on the blushing gem sanctifies both stone and tear—"And, ever since, *I've lov'd a tear.*" But besides the fashionable and saccharine appeal to the *coeur sensible,* the poem is sentimental in the sense of expressing moral sentence—here the Romantic notion that flowers raised in "Nature's wild luxuriance" bloom with greater beauty than sheltered plants. The poem is flawed, particularly in its excessively conceited last stanza. But containing at least two lines of extreme Wordsworthian simplicity, it represents an advance over what Byron had been doing—an advance continued in "Pignus Amoris" ("As by the fix'd decrees . . ."), the next Thyrza poem, which refers to that pledge of love, the cornelian, and expresses, in simple octosyllabic lines rhymed *a b a b,* the ideal of sincere, open, and innocent love. Without a trace of coyness or false adulation—the poet celebrates the joy of being loved for oneself alone—love here stands naked and even a touch selfish, without Petrarchan excrescence of any kind, virtually without imagery, and certainly with no trace of the dark tensions of guilt. Indeed, the pleasure is unalloyed with baseness, life is without crime, and "Innocence resides with Joy"—sentiments that scarcely justify G. Wilson Knight in his suggestion that the homoerotic passion expressed in these poems was regarded as sinful.[14]

The "Form," the "voice," and the "blushes" join with the "seraph choir" to make to "Stanzas to Jessy" ("There is a mystic thread . . .") a Thyrza poem—for this complex of imagery is the kind that the Edleston magnet draws to itself. The poem ends platonically as two souls flow into one. But before that conventional climax is reached, the poem comes close to suggesting that the relationship, though guiltless, has not been entirely platonic: lip is pressed to lip and bosoms pillow aching heads. But the spirit of innocence is not evaporated in this preliminary, boyish, unconsummated kind of dalliance that strikingly recalls the delicate eroticism of the enormously influential Rousseau. If the "Jessy" poem ends platonically, "The Adieu" ("Adieu, thou Hill!") ends religiously, as if to enforce upon us the realization that the Thyrza sensibility is never far from religious hope, here expressed by one who believes he will soon die. Byron, about to travel, bids farewell to more than his Cambridge "Friend" and the "gentle love" he embodies. In fact, only the seventh stanza is directly addressed to Edleston—a verse that takes on a special quality of purity of body and mind when placed in the context of the young Byron's already turbulent eroticism:

> And thou, my Friend! whose gentle love
>   Yet thrills my bosom's chords,
> How much thy friendship was above
>   Description's power of words!
> Still near my breast thy gift I wear,
> Which sparkled once with Feeling's tear,
>   Of love the pure, the sacred gem:
> In that dear moment quite forgot;
> Our souls were equal, and our lot
>   Let Pride alone condemn!

The sentiments of equality, purity, tenderness, and gentleness in love make this poem the farewell of a Man of Feeling. Such was the contemporary idiom in which Byron first couched the most heart-penetrating friendship he was ever to know.

Then Thyrza died, and oh! the difference to Byron. The loss represented a fall from what we have described as passionate innocence or sensual chastity, a love enjoyed that may never have been consummated. Without abandoning the ideal of severe simplicity that had hitherto guided him in these poems, Byron now darkens and deepens the tonality and produces poetry of more compelling urgency. But not at once. When Thyrza, the "more than friend," enters some five stanzas of *Childe Harold,*[15] he inspires rhetoric rather than art, albeit a rhetoric that remains straightforward and heartfelt. The stanzas have biographical and psychological interest, suggesting that of all the friends Byron had lost in so short a space (and one must include his mother) only Thyrza remains an unsullied—perhaps even untouchable—recollection of pure devotion and love. Edleston, entering the deepest mind of the poet, is beginning to glow with an idealism against which the world's slow stains and rapid sins can be forever contrasted. Thyrza has become a haven of calm, subsisting at the heart of endless agitation.

A cluster of poems, the earliest written in 1811 and all published in the first or second editions of *Childe Harold* in 1812, may be said to spring from grief that is still green. The octosyllabic lines, the prevailing *a b a b* rhymes, the simple imagery of voice and form, the cornelian (that *pignus amoris*), and "refined and guiltless" emotions—all these link this cluster with the poems written at Cambridge. Except that now all is lost, and perhaps for the first time Byron is truly *bent* in grief. Loss and a growing sense of the world's evil moved Blake to sing Songs of Experience; Byron continues to sing Songs of Innocence. The first of these, directly addressed "To Thyrza" ("Without a stone to mark the spot"), ends in a mood of quiet—even quietistic—submission and prayer. Agitation about the world is implicit ("I would not wish thee here again") but subdued. But agitation replaces calm in "Away, away, ye notes of woe!" as pain clamorously drowns out prayer. The reader's interest quickens because Byron, the world-weary traveller, becomes a presence, though not an overwhelming one, in the poetry.

Self-contemplation becomes unbearable to him, and his personal anguish has cosmic overtones, because a mysterious "heav'n is veil'd in wrath." This shift from the recollected Edleston (a singer who has produced aural imagery in the verse) to the cosmically deserted Byron is exquisitely accompanied by a shift to visual imagery. Thyrza is now

> A star that trembled o'er the deep.

But as the imagery shifts, the doom is mitigated by the recollection that the star beamed tenderness, the very image and sentiment Byron expressed for an innocent heterosexual love that he had lost when Mary Chaworth married another ("The Dream": "Our life is twofold").

Three poems ("One struggle more," "Euthanasia," and "And thou art dead") should be considered together, even though one of them may technically not belong to the series. All are concerned with death, two somewhat conventionally, the third in a moving though extremely chaste climax. In "One struggle more, and I am free," the poet refers to the cornelian that had played such an important symbolic role in the relation of the loving friends. But Byron feels it necessary to conceal his beloved's sex by referring to "*her* grave" (emphasis added). This bit of evasion, fully justified in many poetical circumstances, here tends to veil the naked sincerity we have come to expect in these lyrics. It takes its toll in this particular utterance, which becomes conventionally Anacreontic, as the poet calls for the wine of forgetfulness. But the poem does have two redeeming lines, among the most piercing that Byron ever wrote: "Though pleasure fires the madd'ning soul, / The heart,— the heart is lonely still!"

"Euthanasia" ("When Time, or soon or late"), which is not a Thyrza poem in topic, tone, or imagery, is closely related because it envisages the poet's own death, perhaps a response to the continuing contemplation of his friend's. It begins by longing for death's "dreamless sleep" and ends by asserting, " 'Tis something better not to be." The gentle nihilism here expressed faintly recalls Swift contemplating his own death and includes a flick at women that is untypical of the series to Thyrza—however much antifeminism there may be elsewhere in Byron.

In "And thou art dead, as young and fair" the series reaches its emotional climax. The gentle self-regarding nihilism of "Euthanasia" is now richer, and the poet has, as in the tradition of the pastoral elegy, achieved a kind of reconciliation to his loss. Above life and even above death, above change and even above immortality, the choirboy is now, as it were, a dreamless Nothing. In a poem that is metrically and stanzaically the most complex of the series, Byron gives us a memorable phrase in referring to Edleston's as "thy buried love." But the word *buried* can also refer to the poet's own recollection, which is sinking deeper and deeper into the unconscious mind. Though the living years are best, they are gone, and one must inevitably turn to what lies underneath earthly and psychological surfaces. Such is Byron's unadorned way of telling us that general *Angst* has now replaced living love and of invoking, without any touches of self-glorification or self-pity, that tortured and alienated spirit of his. This poem is, metrically and thematically, a climactic literary response to the poet's great grief. Art is in the process of taking over, and a chastened and controlled poetry is becoming the correlative of a "love where Death has set his seal."

In one sense the series may now be said to have ended. But there remains an artistic afterglow—the emotion being recollected in a harmonious kind of tranquility like distant music on waters or like broken fragments of a once-loved reality. "If sometimes in the haunts of men" presents two choices—that of gradual forgetting (the haunts of men can be drowned in the bowl of forgetfulness) or that of loving recollection now made tender with irretrievable loss. Byron chooses the latter—a selection of solitary life and thought over social dissipation. That choice he makes because Thyrza had been the one and only person really to love him—a theme of the earliest utterance and undoubtedly a reality of the relationship that made it unique for Byron. In a slight two-stanza poem "On a Cornelian Heart Which Was Broken" ("Ill-fated Heart!") Byron still is haunted by the gift given him by Edleston, that pledge of love that had been the theme of more than one of the premortem poems. And one of the *Hebrew Melodies* ("Oh! snatched away in beauty's bloom") is an exquisite classical elegy, showing that aesthetic distance is setting in. He modifies, with controlled grace, a commonplace used by Dryden in one of his most moving but also most controlled classical imitations, as he hopes that a rose-bearing turf and not a heavy tomb will rest on the remains of his beloved.[16]

Thyrza usually invoked musical imagery, and it is fitting that three of the four poems entitled "Stanzas for Music" belong to what we have referred to as the poetic afterglow of the loss. Since they are not obviously a part of the main series, something of subjective judgment inevitably enters our relating them to the Thyrza sequence. But without them—or so it seems to one interpreter—a rich delicacy would be lost: indeed, one of the climaxes—the artistic one—would be missed entirely. The poem beginning "There's not a joy the world can give" is inspired by the Duke of Dorset, another friend of Byron's Harrow years who had died. But unless the ear is entirely deceptive—and if our sensitivity to Thyrza tone and imagery can be trusted—it is the Cambridge choirboy's all but invisible presence that adds to this poem the warmth and originality that the other poems to Dorset lack. A septenary line is here preserved from lilt and lullaby in order to express genuine pathos. When Byron writes, " 'Tis not on youth's smooth cheek the blush alone, which fades so fast," one thinks of Edleston, not Dorset; and the unadorned cry of the closing stanza invokes the overwhelming Thyrza experience:

> Oh could I feel as I have felt,—or be what I have been,
> Or weep as I could once have wept, o'er many a vanished scene.

Another of the "Stanzas for Music" embodies in its first lines a recollection more appropriate to Thyrza than to any one else:

> Bright be the place of thy soul!
> No lovelier spirit than thine.

The conventional "Light be the turf of thy tomb!" is here repeated and slightly varied, though somehow its present association with religious optimism and vague, somewhat sentimental theology makes it less impressive. Still, the lightening delicacy of the tone shows us a diminished suffering. The poet is apparently escaping a continuing involvement of spirit that would have left less room for disciplined elegiac art.

Such art is attained in the last of the "Stanzas for Music" (written on 28 March 1816). No external fact and no internal image compellingly links this utterance of haunting poetic beauty with the Thyrza series. But critical intuition does, leading one to believe that it is the Thyrza friendship which indeed transcends the magic of all of "Beauty's daughters" and that the sweet voice now heard on the waters is a transmutation of the Cambridge chorister's voice heard at Trinity College. If this instinct is to be trusted, then in this poem a deeply felt experience and an even more deeply felt loss are translated first into nature's nocturnal round and then into a lyric expression as delicate and lovely as anything Byron ever wrote. Since it is difficult to think of an early life experience that more surely deserves such a climax than the affair with Edleston, one hopes that the Thyrza canon closes with this short, two-stanza poem:

1.

There be none of Beauty's daughters
  With a magic like thee;
And like music on the waters
  Is thy sweet voice to me:
When, as if its sound were causing
The charmed ocean's pausing,
The waves lie still and gleaming,
And the lulled winds seem dreaming.

2.

And the midnight moon is weaving
  Her bright chain o'er the deep;
Whose breast is gently heaving,
  As an infant's asleep:
So the spirit bows before thee,
To listen and adore thee;
With a full but soft emotion,
Like the swell of Summer's ocean.

Everyone agrees that Byron's poetry, whether calm or anguished, was self-expressive, written for the relief of suffering or even of excessively painful joy. The canon of work so abundant and varied as Byron's shows that at different times and for different purposes he was guided by a variety of poetical models and ideals. What ideal governed the Thyrza poems? It could not have consisted of the criteria that Northrop Frye invokes in censuring the Byronic lyric for lacking ambiguity, irony, intensity, and vividness—"the words and images being vague to the point of abstraction."[17] At his weakest the lyricist deserves Frye's lash. But at his best he ought to be judged by other standards than those requiring many-layered richness; in fact his achievement ought to be measured against the ideal he set for himself in the amorous lyrics. Early in his career he wrote:

> Fictions and dreams inspire the bard
> > Who rolls the epic song;
> Friendship and Truth be my reward—
> > To me no bays belong; . . .
> Simple and young, I dare not feign;
> Mine be the rude yet heartfelt strain, . . .
> ("L'Amitié est L'Amour Sans Ailes": "Why should my anxious breast")

That ideal of unfeigned simplicity persists—even as late as the fifth canto of *Don Juan,* where the first two stanzas are devoted to "amatory poets" and their "liquid lines mellifluously bland" and to a rejection of the Ovidian, Petrarchan, and Platonic traditions in amorous verse. (He calls Petrarch "the Platonic pimp of all posterity"—and so fells two of his poetic enemies with one blow.)

> I therefore do denounce all amorous writing,
> > Except in such a way as not to attract;
> Plain—simple—short, and by no means inviting,
> > But with a moral to each error tack'd,
> Form'd rather for instructing than delighting,
> > And with all passions in their turn attack'd.
> > > (5.2)

One cannot take too seriously the moral profession; but "plain—simple—short" are adjectives that epitomize the Byronic manner in the Thyrza poems. They also describe the neoclassical ideal for short lyrical verse, exemplified in the dicta of Dryden, Dennis, Fielding, Hume, and Johnson, who provides what could have been a motto for Byron, "He that professes love ought to feel its power."[18]

About Byron's lyrics in general, T. S. Eliot is abruptly dismissive: "With most of his shorter poems, one feels that he was doing something that Tom Moore could do as well or better."[19] Using a criterion of impersonality for the lyric that he was later to disown by writing highly confessional religious poetry, and perhaps anticipating Frye's requirements of multivalent richness, Eliot has reached for the wrong critical tools. But his mention of Moore does raise a name which belongs in the Byronic context, however much the Irish bard may have been surpassed by the English peer. In the volume of melodious amatory verse Moore pretended to have collected, *The Poetical Works of the late Thomas Little,* the use of the octosyllabic line, the tender and sentimental themes, the simple rhyme scheme, the relatively few allusions (and these often religious), and now and then the sweet lilt of the feminine rhymes—all these qualities do anticipate the Thyrza lyrics.[20] But in assessing poetic values Eliot's quick equation of Moore and Byron is simply unjust to the Edleston verses: the easy, gentle Moore lacks the authentic and serious personal emotion that suffuses the chaste and inevitable simplicity of Byron's lyrical voice.

It is not surprising that poems so simple and personal as Byron's to Thyrza should tend to elude the critical grasp. Judged, as they most certainly should be, by the ideal of lyrical simplicity, they must be allowed to escape the censure that they lack richness of resonance and the complexity of ambiguity. Sincerity, directness, depth of feeling, piercing lines and stanzas, and growing subtlety and strength they do possess. But they lack the variety of metrical and verbal nuance which Wordsworth's comparable poems to Lucy possess, nor do they reach Wordsworthian depths of psychological desire, controlling philosophical naturalism, or overarching mystery—qualities that make of Lucy an authentic Coleridgean symbol. Somewhat below, then, the greatest of the shorter Romantic lyrics, Byron's series remains well above the conventional flatness to which Eliot wished to reduce Byronic lyricism. The Thyrza poems do not possess what Goethe isolated as *Manfred's* great quality—"the gloomy heat of an unbounded and exuberant despair."[21] But they can be said to have achieved the less paradoxical and less ambiguous virtues this chapter has invoked. Any worthy and ample anthology of shorter Romantic lyrics would contain many of them, and a good anthology of shorter English lyrics selected from all periods would include four or five of those written after the death of Edleston, when Byron's feelings took on a distance congenial to echoing beauty. One animating life runs through all these poems, even the less successful ones. Something unique in tone, imagery, or form will tell the reader he is in the presence of the acute sensibility that Edleston aroused in Byron. And that impression of unifying energy attests both to the authenticity of the feeling and the authority of the art.

11

William Blake: Christ's Body

In 1798, in a moment of angry and radical protest, Blake affirmed his belief in the Bible and professed himself a Christian.[1] That belief appears virtually everywhere in his poetry, except perhaps in his first work, the unillustrated *Poetical Sketches*. In *Innocence* Christ is immanent in nature and appears as child, shepherd, lamb, and lion. In *Experience* and the Lambeth prophecies Jesus is implicitly present as a revolutionary hero, as Orcan energy, or as a phase of historical consciousness. In the "terrific parts" of the later prophecies, properly called Christian, the historical Jesus and the mythical Christ are both prominent. And in many of the late personal lyrics and prose declarations Jesus is often at the center of devotional attention. It is with the later work that this chapter is primarily concerned.

Blake was that rarest of phenomena in English art, a Christian painter. Christian themes, remarkably scarce in English art even in its earlier periods, abound in Blake, who was born in a century when in European art generally there was an absence of religious feeling.[2] Romantic painting did, to be sure, return to religious themes, but these were often "transformed" into secular substitutes. The traditional Lamentation and the expiration of a saint, for example, reappeared in Romantic art as domestic and ostensibly secular deathbed scenes in which the deceased on his bed was surrounded by a mourning family—a theme present also in Blake.[3] The greatest of the Romantic painters,

Goya, did paint Christ—but infrequently compared to Blake. Goya's Christ usually appears in flickering lights and shadows, his body or his face obscured, a mysterious force that generates its own kind of power but one that lacks a palpable presence.[4]

What Goya's Christ lacks Blake's possesses fully, a human body. And in this respect it is the Englishman and not the Spaniard who is closer to the central Christian tradition. For, although the interpretations have varied enormously through the centuries, the language of the Bible proclaims loudly that Jesus possessed and possesses a body. It is called a "temple," as is the body of his followers, for in his role as Redeemer he is also "the Savior of the Body." In his death he "bare our sins in his body." Sacramentally, his body is broken again and again in the Mass, and Christians are mystically regarded as the several members of his one body. There are in Pauline theology two bodies, the natural one, which is sown in corruption, and the spiritual or glorious body, which rises from the dead.[5]

The biblical expressions of the preceding paragraph reappear often in Blake, sometimes in the kind of pious ejaculation characteristic of dissenting Christians through the centuries and sometimes in shockingly bold interpretations of orthodox doctrine. From the revised *Vala* until the last letters, Blake quotes, echoes, amplifies, and revises the resounding scriptural utterances about Jesus' body, while in his paintings, from the hundreds of illustrations of Young's *Night Thoughts* in the nineties to the last great Dante illustrations, the person of Christ is an unmistakable physical being. For our discussion of this important theme in word and design we may choose as an epigraph the following sentence, engraved on the *Laocoön* plate about 1820:

> The Eternal Body of Man is The Imagination,
> >God himself
> that is
> >The Divine Body } . . . [Yeshua] Jesus: we are his Members
> > > > > > > (E., p. 273)

This sentence, which runs like a border on the left-hand side of the plate, reveals metaphorically the circular motion that many of Blake's designs literally possess. It moves from man to imagination to God to Christ and back to man again. One can enter the sentence, as it were, at any point and come out with all elements present, each assimilated with the others. The nouns being all nominative, they remain unaffected by the simple copulative verb: God is Christ, Christ is Imagination, Imagination is Man. One may put these noble nouns in any other order one chooses—the important fact remains that all are equal and each ends up becoming the other. This process takes place without loss of identity, for each entity possesses a body, the pivotal and uniting concept in the declaration. Just as there are three bodies (Laocoön's and his two sons') on the plate[6] that bears this engraved sentence, so there are three bodies in the sentence: man's, Christ's, and God's. The *primus inter pares* is that of Christ, since it mediates between God and man. It is Jesus' body that redeems man and God alike, both man's art and man's mind. With equal justification it could be argued that man is the first among equals, since it is his image that Christ assumes in revealing the essence of God. God says to Christ in the *Everlasting Gospel*:

> Thou art a Man God is no more
> Thy own Humanity learn to adore
> (E., p. 520)

But then Blake, as if to upset either of the priorities just mentioned, gives bolder lettering to *Imagination* than to any other word in the sentence we have chosen as our epigraph, warning us that Jesus must also be viewed psychologically and artistically.

The Man Jesus: A Context for Blake

The central Christian paradox, that Jesus was at once very man and very God, has encouraged radically antithetical beliefs about his person during the Christian centuries. Blake, with unmistakable and reiterated force, emphasizes the human. He endows the historical Jesus with a "vegetable" body like our own.

It would be difficult to exaggerate the disconcerting originality of Blake's portrayal of the physical humanity of "the man Christ Jesus"

(1 Tim. 2:5). But his character of Christ does not stand alone. It is not unrelated to the revolutionary attempts of some of his English contemporaries to displace the divine figure enshrined in the churches. Paine was one of these, and Blake in that angry moment alluded to at the outset found it possible to see in Paine's work the inspiration of the Holy Ghost and to find him a truer Christian than his indignant and frightened episcopal adversary.[7] But Paine's "Religion of Humanity"[8] is, in the last analysis, timid and imaginatively thin and did not command Blake's respect for long. While Paine saw in religion "a law and a tye to all able minds," Blake found that the "religion of Jesus was a perfect law of liberty."[9] Although Paine grudgingly conceded that the story of Christ was "the least hurtful part" of the Bible, Jesus remained essentially inaccessible to modern man—the "Christian church [having] sprung out of the tail of heathen mythology." Paine's Jesus was a "virtuous and an amiable man," to be sure, an admirable preacher of benevolence; but he lacked the energy that animates Blake's portrayal. In Paine there was too much of the bland Shaftesbury or the smiling, cynical Voltaire to nourish for very long the mind of a man who loved the Bible and adored Christ.[10]

It is different with Joseph Priestley. His pages have been called "uninspired and uninspiring,"[11] but his view of Christ was anything but arid. And Blake must have admired his courageous defiance of many establishments as he attempted to free the Church of the corruption of historical Christianity. There are of course differences between the two reformers, the chief being that Priestley, a Unitarian, stresses the superiority of God the Father while Blake's Christ regularly tends to replace the Father until he has been truly softened into a loving and forgiving Jehovah. But the similarities are more important than the differences, and one finds in the polemical learning and homiletical eloquence of Priestley much that was congenial to Blake. Priestley, regarded by his foes as a dangerous heretic, wanted desperately to live within the faith, professing himself a Christian both among the freethinkers of Paris and the ecclesiastics, Roman and Anglican, of his own country. He attacked the orthodox views of Jesus' divinity and came to disbelieve in his miraculous conception. He derided the view of Jesus as a "superangelic spirit or the *Arian logos*," as an offspring of that

"Platonic nous" that entered Christianity with the Gnostics and persisted among the theologians of the eighteenth century. Priestley wanted a man of flesh and blood, not a Jesus who was "one of the *aeons*," a being so depersonalized that he "ate and drank in a peculiar manner, not voiding excrements." Priestley found the doctrine of the substitutionary atonement of Christ a "gross misrepresentation of the character and moral government of God," a doctrine "greatly disfiguring and depraving" the "scheme of Christianity." On the positive side, he, like Blake, placed Jesus well above the noblest of the ancients, Socrates; he accepted as necessary and crucial the belief in Jesus' resurrection and the immortality of the human spirit—"a prospect which nothing but the gospel can give us." He had faith that the kingdom of Christ would one day embrace all mankind and extend to the end of time. He found, even in a superstitious period like the Middle Ages, the salutary sweetness of individual piety and belief in a personal Christ. He believed that Jesus was blasphemed more by Christian corruption and the hideous cruelties of religion than by almost anything else. To the author of "The Grey Monk" and the prose passages in *Jerusalem* all this must have seemed to restore salt to preaching that had lost its savor. For Blake was also a confessed soldier of Christ, fighting corruptions in Christianity and cruelties in all religions and attempting to restore belief in *"this simple humanity of* Jesus," Priestley's obsessively recurring phrase.[12]

A subtler and grander Christ than one could expect from the polemical prose of a dissenting preacher and chemist was Blake's heritage from that great Christian reformer, John Milton. How Blake softened and humanized the austere and sublime religion of Milton in the linear delicacies and the chromatic harmonies of his water-color illustrations has been described elsewhere.[13] But there was enough of the loving human Jesus in Milton's prose and poetry to warrant considering that poet an important source of stimulation for Blake's more insistently human Savior. In *Paradise Lost* (1.4) the first mention of Christ refers to him as the "one greater Man," the new Adam who will regain the "blissful Seat" (1.5) lost at the Fall; but it is perhaps "th' exalted man" of *Paradise Regained* (1.36) who is Blake's nearest prototype. In response to this poem Blake created nine separate portrayals of Christ;

in response to *Paradise Lost,* he created five.[14] Milton's Christ in *Paradise Regained* is in "youths full flowr" (1.67), a man of "deep thoughts" (1.190), who "into himself descended" (2.111). As a youth he had burned with heroic ambition to save his people from the Roman yoke, and, abjuring violence, he had tried to fight for equity and freedom with "winning words" that would make "perswasion do the work of fear" (1.221–2)—a promise of Mental Fight and Intellectual Battle that Blake must have cherished. Blake, however, goes beyond even the Milton of *Paradise Regained* in humanizing the Son of God, whose central characteristic in the earlier poet remains filial piety and obedience. Blake's Christ seems to undergo a deeper sensual temptation than Milton's stoical, heroic God-man. In "The Banquet Temptation" (fig. 9) Blake tempts Christ with much more than the "pompous Delicacies" (2.390) of food and drink that the fasting Son of Man had rejected in Milton. Blake's Christ recoils, openmouthed—as though both tempted and repelled in horror—at the women the artist has drawn—women who can best be described in the words of that "dissolutest Spirit that fell," Belial: they are "expert in amorous Arts," "skill'd to retire, and in retiring draw / Hearts after them." They are capable of "draw[ing] out" the "manliest . . . brest" with "credulous desire" and "voluptuous hope" (2.150,161–7). That kind of temptation Belial had desired but Satan and Milton had rejected as unworthy of Christ and doomed to failure. But Milton's description of the rejected temptation stimulated Blake to confront Christ with the alluring and swelling curves of seductive* women and so humanize the scene much beyond what Milton would have regarded as appropriate. For Blake's Christ, possessing a body whose flesh is apparent under the flimsy dress he wears, is tempted by female blandishments; but Milton's is at this point tempted only by food on a "stately board" near which stands a chaste and orderly array of solemn youths, Diana's nymphs, and ladies fairer than "Fairy Damsels" (2.350–61).

Thus Milton, for all the heroic humanity of his Christ, cannot be

---

*The three standing figures (see fig. 9) whom Christ repulses suggest the classical Three Graces, but the scaly Satanic vest of the foremost strongly hints at danger in their allure. Blake elsewhere found the classical sinister, though sometimes beguiling.

Fig. 9. William Blake, *The Banquet Temptation*,
illustration to Milton's *Paradise Regained*. Water color.
Fitzwilliam Museum, Cambridge.

Fig. 10. Michelangelo, *The Resurrection of Christ*
(detail). Black chalk. British Museum,
Department of Prints and Drawings.

said to anticipate fully the extremely physical Christ of Blake's vision. Only Michelangelo can be said to have done that. Nowhere in the antecedent tradition is there a Christ closer to Blake's than his. In the Tondo Doni at the Uffizi, Florence, the child Jesus is a nude, dark-haired little Italian boy. The nude Christ-child in Bruges has chubby legs and thighs and unusually large testicles. Even in the last Crucifixions, a spiritual vision if there was one in art, where Christ's body is less physically assertive than usual, a real physical presence is still communicated. In the *Pietà* of the Vatican the dead body is handsome, its flesh supple and yielding.

In his portrayals of the risen Christ Michelangelo also anticipates Blake, for the fiery glory of resurrection has not consumed the flesh or the form. In *The Risen Christ,* a statue in Santa Maria sopra Minerva, Rome, the body is nude, the musculature is prominent but more delicate than that of Christ's body in the *Last Judgment* on the Sistine walls, which is also emphatically human. The face of the statue is Grecian, though lightly bearded; the nose delicate, the eyes pensive, the hair soft and curly, the genitals unconcealed. One of the most remarkable of Michelangelo's achievements in linear art is his study, now in the British Museum (fig. 10), in which Christ rises effortlessly, almost soaringly, from the tomb in the kind of inspired levitation with which Blake often endows Redeemer and redeemed.[15] Both artists were led to show the power of line over matter by the thought of resurrection.

Blake's "Vegetated" Christ

Blake's belief in the human body of Christ has its lighter and darker side. The example of Michelangelo leads naturally to the congenial aspect. In Blake's paintings the child Jesus, curly-headed, his male member visible, sleeps as the mother hushes the young Baptist. The boy in the house of the carpenter recalls the Poet of Innocence, holding in his hand, however, the compass and the rule, iconic signs of future ominous import that may foreshadow Experience.[16] The man Jesus appears to be especially close to poets, infants, mothers, and lovers. As the Good Samaritan in the Young illustrations, he ministers to a wounded traveler lying partially nude under a tree, a figure who of course stands for suffering Man but who also may recall the Poet. Even when bearing the scroll of judgment Christ is described by Blake as representing the "Eternal Creation flowing from the Divine Humanity in Jesus" (E., p. 554). He stands in a cluster of grapes (that symbol of physical love), as lovers kiss and a mother nurses a child (fig. 11). He reclines at a table laden with vine and fruits, an "omnipotently kind" Jesus who "takes His Delights among the Sons of Men." He, not God, creates Eve under a crescent moon and so institutes Beulah (fig. 12).[17]

A good summary emblem of Blake's human Christ of mild, gentle, and sexually fertile manhood is the Christ who baptizes. A reddish-haired Jesus attracts the gaze of a young Poet who looks fixedly at him. Beside the Poet are babes and children, mothers and old people, some of them nude or nearly so. Three or four couples are near or at the age of sexual awareness, into which Christ seems to be baptizing some of the young.[18]

Sexuality in Blake is seldom without a darker side, and Christ, who possesses a "vegetable" body, cannot escape the terror and the tragedy of physical life. In a tempera of 1825, the Mother weeps, her halo is ominously spiked; behind her the night is dark, and the sky contains only pale golden stars. The child's eyes are red-rimmed at the bottom, and his whole coloring and mien suggest darkness. This holy pair does not reassure us; the picture is far from comforting.[19]

Now and then the gentle Jesus of Blake's paintings may seem to verge on sentimentality. But taken as a whole his portrait of the man Jesus is far from sentimental or simple, darkened as it is with ambiguity and conflict. In a watercolor, "Christ taking Leave of His Mother," John shows the tender emotion, not Mary, whose tearless eyes stare and whose face wears an expression of harshness and distance.[20] In the concluding line of "To Tirzah" Blake echoes Jesus' rejection of his mother, "Woman, what have I to do with thee?" (John 2:4 and E., p. 30). It is part of the unpleasant task of Los the poet and his wife Enitharmon to "draw" the Lamb of God "into a mortal form" so that he "may be devoted to Destruction from his mothers womb." By his "Maternal Birth" he becomes the "Evil-One," or Satan; he takes on the "Satanic Body of Holiness" and as a "Vegetated Christ" becomes a blasphemy.[21]

Jesus inherited his maternal humanity by the normal natural act, not by supernatural impregnation. He was conceived in adultery—an

Fig. 11. Blake, Design for Young's *Night Thoughts*, No. 512. Water color. British Museum, Department of Prints and Drawings.

Fig. 12. Blake, *Creation of Eve*, illustration to Milton's *Paradise Lost*. Water color on paper. Courtesy Museum of Fine Arts, Boston.

act that Mary herself admitted and that Joseph did not deny but forgave (*Jer,* 61). The body that thus originated in a secret act of sin was most certainly endowed with sexual appetite, and the bold and conventionally impious question of the *Everlasting Gospel* (E., pp. 521–23), "Was Jesus Chaste?" must, like all the other questions that introduce the several sections of that powerful and angry poem, be answered negatively. Jesus had assumed a body that felt "the passions that with Sinners deal" (E., p. 877). And Blake must surely have disagreed with those who "say he never fell" (ibid.). It is probable that the one who selected publicans and harlots (the biblical *sinner* becomes *harlot* in Blake) for his company literally entered the Magdalen's "dark Hell" and literally dwelled in her "burning bosom" (E., p. 522). Even in so frank a poem as this Blake does not directly say that Jesus sympathized with Mary to the extent of sharing her physical passion; but it is consistent with his whole doctrine of incarnation and of the divine participation in the human that he should have entertained that notion. The "shadowy Man" (the anti-Man Satan, a fiend of righteousness, the new Urizen) threatens Jesus with the "festering Venoms bright" of venereal infection and with other diseases by means of which he "binds" the "Mental Powers" (ibid.). (The last clause, incidentally, shows that Blake understood what a mischievous and poisonous deterrent to pleasure and to the sensual imagination the fear of infection could be. He also saw that sexual fears and hesitations inhibit *all* mental life.)

The veil of Blake's myth only barely conceals his entertainment of the notion that the vegetated body of Jesus knew passion or desire and that in his maternal humanity he may indeed have experienced the sufferings that often attend the indulgence of sexual appetite. He is said to have been born "in the Robes of Luvah," the Zoa of physical passion. Disease forms a "Body of Death around the Lamb / Of God, to destroy Jerusalem, & to devour the body of Albion." And the clouds of Ololon "folded" around Jesus' limbs "as a Garment dipped in blood," the last being a phrase that invokes the passionate Zoa, Luvah.[22]

There is, therefore, much to put off on the Cross and in the tomb. In the magnificent watercolor that illustrates Michael's prophecy of the crucifixion in *Paradise Lost,* Book xii (fig. 13), the Orcan sexual serpent is nailed to the Cross along with the body of Christ, and at its foot lie

dead the bodies of Urizen, or death, and Vala-Rahab, fallen sexual nature, she too a "Mother of the Body of Death" (*Jer.* 62.13; E., p. 213).

What reconciled Blake to so radically literal an interpretation of
the physicality of Jesus as that we have been discussing? He seems to
have believed in the value of a spiritual *difficulté vaincue*—that is, the
deeper the bog, the more heroic the rescue; the graver the sin, the
more glorious the redemption; the greater the participation, the profounder the sympathy. Blake apparently craved an experienced rather
than an innocent savior. Forgiveness, always difficult, becomes truly
sublime when it first understands and then pardons the guilt of sexual
infidelity. Crime statistics keep showing that the sins of the flesh are
among those most difficult to forgive. And so it is precisely at the point
where mercy meets bodily sin that the spirit of Jesus is most fully
revealed.

> O holy Generation! [*Image*] of regeneration!
> O point of mutual forgiveness between Enemies!
> Birthplace of the Lamb of God incomprehensible!
> (*Jer.*, 7.65–67; E., p. 150)

We have seen that Blake regarded the "Birthplace of the Lamb of God"
as an adulterous bed. That point alone is not significant. The redemptive
fact is that the magnificent forgiveness offered Mary by Joseph released
her from crippling fear, causing her to flow "like a River of / Many
Streams in the Arms of Joseph." And her new joy seems somehow
commensurate with the gravity of her fault: ". . . if I were pure, never
could I taste the sweets / Of the Forgive[ness] of Sins"; "If I were Pure
I should never / Have known Thee" (*Jer.*, 61.11–12, 28–30, 44–45; E.,
pp. 211–12).

Being born of Mary, Jesus came of a physical line that included
that prostitutor of natural sexuality, Rahab (*Jer.*, 62.10; E., p. 213). The
result was that his natural body, capable of all the naturally innocent
Beulah joys, also had its unpleasant clayey side. Blake dramatically
makes the possession of a sexually sinful body a precondition of a
glorious, sinless body—even for Christ. Blake certainly risked the censure implied in Paul's question, "Shall we continue in sin, that grace

Fig. 13. Blake, *Prophecy of the Crucifixion*, illustration to Milton's *Paradise Lost*. Pen and water color. Courtesy Museum of Fine Arts, Boston.

may abound?" (Rom. 6:1). The least calculating of men, Blake would scarcely have plotted in cold blood a sin-grace sequence. But sin was obviously deep in the human physical condition, and the death and resurrection of one whose body was compounded of clay did release an abundance of grace. So Blake sang a Hallelujah Chorus on the Fortunate Incarnation:

> He died as a Reprobate. he was Punish'd as a Transgressor!
> Glory! Glory! Glory! to the Holy Lamb of God
> (*Milton* 13{14}.27–8; E., 107)

The Resurrected Body

Since the death of Jesus purged away his mire and dross, the adoration of a physical Jesus is idolatrous cadaver-worship.

> He took on Sin in the Virgins Womb
> And put it off on the Cross & Tomb
> To be Worshipd by the Church of Rome
> (*Everlasting Gospel*, "Was Jesus Gentle,"
> lines 55–57 [E., p. 524])

A resurrection is clearly necessary, and to Blake Jesus' acquisition of a new body was an especially precious belief. It supported his conviction that "Mind & Imagination" were living realities that transcended "Mortal & Perishing Nature" and constituted "the Divine bosom into which we shall all go after the death of the Vegetated body." It is touching to read the last letters of the aged Blake as he is about to assume what he called "our Eternal or Imaginative Bodies." These bodies, constituting "The Real Man" or the "Imagination," can predate death and grow "stronger & stronger as this foolish Body decays." And in that conviction Blake will follow his friend Flaxman into "his Own Eternal House . . . Into the Mind, in which every one is King & Priest. . . ." All these quintessentially Blakean phrases express a fervent personal faith, and there is testimony that Blake attained in his later years a kind of radiant sainthood.[23]

Blake's personal faith is serene, but it remains a faith and not a philosophy. Neither he nor the apostle Paul explains what a spiritual, eternal, or resurrected body is. But unlike Paul, Blake *portrayed* the risen Christ, and he may be said to have brought life and immortality to light in his art.

The primary fact about the resurrected Christ is that he still possesses a body. And that body remains in appearance very much what it was before the crucifixion and resurrection. Jesus is still blond, bearded, his cheeks red or pink, his demeanor tender and mild, his face and figure handsome, as the flowing garment he continues to wear follows the contours of his muscular body. He remains, except for a few scenes which are bathed in mysterious light, a clear and well-outlined human being, fully corporeal. One characteristic, already alluded to, seems to have become more prominent—that wonderful, gravity-defying lightness of movement, as Christ springs up, swirling with the clouds or flames, cutting a swath of human radiance as he rises (see fig. 14). His hands are now nail-pierced; his eyes are touched with wonder and suffering and sometimes appear bold and decisive. This figure is the harbinger of all the resurrections Blake as a Christian poet of love and hope has sung about—of the earth that "shall arise and seek," of the youth and the pale virgin who "arise from their graves and aspire," of the nations and peoples, who, when the "grave is burst," "spring like redeemed captives."[24]

Michelangelo may, as we have suggested, have taught Blake how to draw the movements of a resurrected body. But another artist, not hitherto mentioned, may have created subtler examples of a physical-spiritual body streaming mildness and glory, a body that is spiritual without being vaporously unsubstantial and that is physical without being gross or earthbound. That artist is Fra Angelico, who, according to Samuel Palmer, provided Blake with an "ideal home"—that is, with a resting place for his imagination. For, said Palmer, it was on this artist's memory that Blake, who "fervently loved early art," dwelt "with peculiar affection."[25] If in Milton we see a Christ in whom the fullness of the Godhead dwells bodily—a being of power, justice, and righteous anger as well as mercy—in Fra Angelico we see a Christ full of grace and truth. As a child he is blond, fair, sweet, tender, sometimes extending his hand in blessing, sometimes instructing. The body that is taken from the Cross is still delicately handsome, the hair soft and

Fig. 14. Blake, Design for Young's *Night Thoughts*, frontispiece. Water color. British Museum, Department of Prints and Drawings.

tender, falling in long curls, the eyes clear even in death. In the *Noli me Tangere* at San Marco, Florence, the resurrected Christ remains blond and lightly bearded and the curly hair has been straightened. Lacking the curvaceous body beneath light clothing that Blake's Christs often have, Fra Angelico's here possesses an almost translucent quality, an air of delicate and transcendental sadness. The body, though substantial, seems barely to touch the ground. In *The Entombment* now in Munich the dead body of Christ appears to be standing with very little help. Although it is in *rigor mortis,* the persisting life principle seems to be expressed by the fact that one man can lift it without strain.[26] Fra Angelico must have struck the poet-painter as one who had solved the problem of how to paint a resurrected body—of how to etherealize it without robbing it of substance.

Not all of Blake's Christs are individual beings whose physical humanity is paramount. Sometimes they are bathed in supernal light: Christ is born, is adored by the Magi, and prays on his bed as divine radiance lights the scenes.[27] Or Christ appears in allegory or emblem as the mediator between God and Man, as a personification of Mercy, or as a king who sits stiffly on a throne, attempting with one hand to put on the girdle of strength.[28] Or Christ may appear in "Judgments" or "Epitomes" along with almost hundreds of other bodies in comprehensive expressions of the whole truth about human destiny, large and complex works of art designed to express the "Eternal Vision or Imagination of All that Exists."[29]

Identification with the Glorious Body of Jesus

To "internalize" an ideal—such is the modern way of describing the psychological process by which an admired person comes to fructify the inner life. Blake described it more poetically and humanly: the reader or spectator enters "into these Images in his Imagination, approaching them on the Fiery Chariot of his Contemplative Thought" and then making a "Friend & Companion of one of these Images of wonder." If we can do that, Blake says, then we too arise from our graves and "meet the Lord in the Air."[30] Blake's language is biblical, and of course the process of identification with Christ has always been regarded by the Church as the essence of conversion. Blake engraved on one of the climactic plates (17) of his *Job*—that great story of the salvation of both God and Man—some ten verses from the Gospel of John, chapter 14: these verses present the ideal of union in love between God, Christ, and the believer—he in us and we in him. Blake had come to admire those Christians—Saint Teresa, Madame Guyon, Fénélon, and Wesley—who preached a gospel of pure love, pure because it was total and interior and ran counter to external formalities.[31]

There is considerable evidence that Blake renewed, perhaps more than once, his spiritual contact with Christ in moments of exalted and intense dedication.[32] Those moments are illuminated by the four designs we shall now study, ranging in time from the early 1790s to the last years of his life.

1. *The Frontispiece to* Experience

It does not seem to have been noticed that Christ appears on the frontispiece of the *Songs of Experience* (fig. 15). The halo in some copies has been ignored because we have not understood the baffling arrangement of the two figures. The design becomes clear if we see it as a version of the story of Saint Christopher bearing the child Jesus. That legend, extremely popular throughout the centuries, Blake could have encountered in many paintings, engravings, stained-glass windows, frescoes, and statues. Mrs. Jameson said in 1848 that figures of Saint Christopher were "very common" on the walls of old English churches,[33] and the saint bearing the Christ-child was painted or engraved by Mantegna, Pollaiuolo, Altdorfer, Dürer, Van Eyck, and Rubens. One of the closest to Blake's frontispiece is the painting by Hans Memling that appears on one of the outside wings of a triptych (fig. 16).[34] The saint, who stands on a rock in a free-flowing mantle, is not the dark and grizzled giant often portrayed, but a more delicate man of Christ-like appearance.

As always, Blake adapts the legend to his own purposes. The shepherd advances from Innocence to the frontier of Experience, marked by the suggestion of water in the lower left-hand corner. The child is sometimes haloed but always winged—the divine joy of Innocence that has been revived in all of us by hearing the Piper's song and that must now be borne from Innocence into Experience by the Bard. The child

Fig. 15. Blake, *Songs of Experience*, frontispiece, copy E. Relief etching with pen and water color. Henry E. Huntington Library and Art Gallery, San Marino, California.

Fig. 16. Hans Memling, *Saint Christopher*, from *The Virgin Enthroned with Saints*. Oil. Courtesy of the Trustees, The National Gallery, London.

does not straddle the shoulders, as in most representations of the Saint Christopher story, but sits on the head of his bearer: the artist who later portrayed Milton entering his foot may here be suggesting that Christ must be received intellectually, mentally. It is more likely, however, that Blake wants us to concentrate on the disturbed expression of the shepherd. It may express a deep and unconscious feeling that, although he is a "Christopher" or "Christ-bearer," he is not yet united with his ideal. Jesus is an external burden, not an inner vision.

2. *Christ in the Illustrations to Young's* Night Thoughts

In that large gallery of watercolors created to illustrate the once popular poem of Young, Christ appears again and again in impressive individual drawings and series of drawings that cannot here be studied in detail. He is often the visual counterpart of—one can even say the replacement of—God the Father. For when Young writes "Dread Sire," or "Father of all," Blake portrays Christ gathering the little children to himself; when Young writes of the "Father fond . . . / Of Intellectual Beings," Blake draws a Christ blessing.[35] Christ in the Young series possesses all the human characteristics previously noted as belonging to his earthly ministry, and Blake is now in the 1790s affirming a cheerful cosmology—Christ transcends nature and will conquer death. Two aspects of this Christ throw light on the identification of the poet with his resurrected body. Christ has a special relation to the young Poet, from whom he receives a tribute of verse called "A Miniature of thee," or who appears in the guise of the Prodigal embraced not by a father but by Christ, or who reaches out toward the healing hand extended by Christ. The designs portray Christ and the Poet yearning to come together.[36]

But from some of the profoundest portrayals of Christ in the Young illustrations the Poet is absent. Four of these in a series show Christ attaining the resurrected or spiritual condition that will make the deepest unity possible.[37] In the first Christ stands on a cliff being tempted by a staring, youngish, beardless, blond, roundmouthed Satan, his hair flaming, a creature rude as well as nude. This Satan is a demon that Blake feared, a lawless and merciless power who creates State Religion and many other ills, an enemy who must be subdued. In the next Christ appears with another fearful enemy, Urizen as Death, kneeling abjectly before the "bright Preacher of Life" (*Jer.*, 77.21; E., p. 230), who is stronger than his enemy. In the next, to which we shall return, Christ, in a partial radiance, is emerging from the darkness that surrounds him. And finally the resurrected Jesus appears fully human as he reveals himself to the doubting apostle, Thomas.

The penultimate in this series of four (fig. 17) portrays a Christ who assumes the cruciform position and displays hands that are pierced and torn by nails. The eyes, sad and upward-looking, show the marks of suffering, and the entire countenance is that of one who has known terror. Deep night still surrounds the figure and subdues his radiance. Though transfiguration is not complete, it is being achieved. This Christ is portrayed between the Cross and the tomb; the physical, sexual body is being put off and the resurrected body is being put on. The lower body remains obscured, while the head is irradiated, the hair flaming to each side. The moment is one of psychological tension. On its successful issue depends the salvation—the mental health—of the poet, for it is with the emergent Christ that he will henceforth be identified.

3. *Christ in* The Four Zoas

Christian imagery appears to enter this manuscript in a rush of revision, as Blake moves from *Experience,* where Christ is only implicitly present, to the Christian prophecies, where he stands at the apex of the myth. The Christ with whom we are most concerned here appears in a cluster of three[38] within the manuscript, all of them portraying the risen body. A magnificent Christ in an engraving for the Young series which is here inserted into the manuscript is even more powerful in its rising motion than it was in the watercolor original, where the beard and the radiance are less pronounced and the eyes less bright and piercing. (It appears that it is the *humanity* of the rising Christ which is being more strikingly affirmed in the engraving than in the watercolor.) On the next page, also an engraving imported into the manuscript from the Young series, the risen Christ stands in flames, the nails still in his hands and feet, his eyes mild but troubled as he looks down into a fiery abyss. Finally, at the culmination of Night 8, an original pencil and crayon sketch (fig. 18) is a new inspiration, a profound and moving rendition of the resurrected body. Like Raphael's God,[39] the risen Christ pushes away the clouds. Lightly bearded as Blake's Christ nearly always is, his genitals are obscured by lines and shadows. Does Blake wish to say that the days of the Babylonian sexual captivity are over for Christ and can also be over for man? The eyes bear a more unmistakable message: calm now, they seem to have known turmoil; and if they reveal mercy, it is a mercy that has followed suffering. Distinctly a Christ, this figure may look like Milton, Los, the risen Albion, Blake, or any "Christ-like man"[40] without being the less Christ for that. This masterpiece of few and energetic lines portrays a merciful hero, something quite new to history, available to all as an inner and also an outward-flowing energy.

4. *The Christ of the* Paradiso

In Canto 14 of the *Paradiso* Dante sees both Beatrice and Christ, each enveloped in a light so dazzling that the poet must in the end abandon speech and listen to music. The poet learns that the disembodied spirits he now beholds long for the new bodies and the redeemed organs of sense with which they will be endowed at the general resurrection. For the present the vision can only be a general illumination, an ever-changing play of light and shadow. Christ also apppears in a fountain of light, in which the radiance assumes the form of the Cross. In rendering Dante's vision in an unfinished wash drawing Blake recalls the Cross and retains the light. His Christ stands in a blazing sun, his hair aflame and his arms extended in the cruciform position (fig. 19). But here, as always in Blake, light is only a garment, and the living form is a body. In Dante the spirits look to the future for their glorious bodies. Blake's Jesus already possesses his, and it is the fully human and totally recognizable body that we have come to know. Christ wears a light garment that conceals the genitals but does not cover the navel or obscure his pronounced musculature. The hair is curly, the beard short; and the eyes, like those of the Christs in the Young illustrations and *The Four Zoas,* are eyes that have suffered and known love.

How shall we explain the exaltation and intensity of this drawing, whose every line is instinct with energy? In portraying Christ, Blake had not always achieved so consummate a union of mildness and strength, of mercy and force. Here the vision is personal; and magnetic

Fig. 17. Blake, Design for Young's *Night Thoughts*, No.
264. Water color. British Museum, Department of
Prints and Drawings.

Fig. 18. Blake, Illustration to *The Four Zoas*, Night
VIII, MS, page 116. Pencil drawing and crayon. British
Library, Department of Manuscripts.

lines of identification seem to arise from the Poet at the bottom to his master at the top, for the linear sweep of this design is upward. The garb of Christ near his neck recalls—even reduplicates—the simple dress of the Piper of Innocence. Christ in apotheosis remains what he has always been—the shepherd, the sweet singer of the new Israel, the shoot from the stem of Jesse, a David *redivivus.* But now the intensity is such that one can think only of a consummated spiritual union between the Poet and Christ, that union which the Saint Christopher-like Bard of Experience had not yet achieved and for which the youths of the Young designs yearned. To return to one of the equations of our epigraph, the Imagination *is* Yeshua, Jesus.

We should not be surprised by the audacity of this identification. Union with Christ is the consummation of the Christian dream, and Blake has prepared us for it. A series of other identifications move toward this climax. In a poetical epistle to Butts in 1802 Blake describes an encounter with Los, who flamed in his path as a real sun. The great Zoa of the Poetic Imagination, said Blake, flamed in the poet's path while "the bows of *my* Mind & the Arrows of Thought" glow, and breathe an ardor that seems to heat even the sun.[41] That experience is recalled at least twice in *Milton.* On one plate Los steps from the sun just behind Blake, who is putting on his sandal and who looks back at the fiery man behind him (fig. 20). The language interprets the scene; Los, says Blake,

> ... kissed me and wished me health,
> And I became One Man with him arising in my strength:
> ... Los had enterd into my soul:
> ... I arose in fury & strength.
>
> (22[24].11–14.; E, 117)

Blake's union with Los is only an earnest of the even greater union with Christ, whose "Divine Appearance *was* the likeness & similitude of Los."[42] When in the moment of great artistic and prophetic inspiration Blake says that he became "One Man" with Los, he is virtually saying that he became Christ, who is often called One Man, the authenticator and supporter of all artistic form, the breath and finer spirit of all prophecy. . .

Fig. 19. Blake, *Dante Adoring Christ*,
illustration to Dante's *Paradiso*. Pencil with
pen and water color. National Gallery of
Victoria, Melbourne. Felton Bequest, 1920.

Fig. 20. Blake, *Milton*, copy A, plate 21. Relief
etching with water color. British Museum,
Department of Prints and Drawings.

We are now at the glowing core of Blake's vision,* and we must be careful to be precise. Blake's sense of identification with Christ is profound, and he must surely have felt that he had in vision attained that "Eden" in which Jesus lives "in us, and we in him . . . in perfect harmony," since he hopes that his reader will with him become "wholly One in Jesus our Lord."[43] But however intense the identification, individuality is never lost. It would be ironic if the Christ who preserved the "Eternal Individuality" of the sleeping Albion should allow it to be weakened when the Eternal Man awakens to vision (*Jer.,* 48.3; E., p. 196). But of course Blakean identification always keeps identity intact. In the portrayal of Dante's vision (fig. 19) the Poet stands before Christ open-armed and receptive but as a distinct and separate identity. It is so also when Adam stands before the crucified Christ (fig. 13) or when Albion contemplates his Lord on the cross (*Jer.,* pl. 76).

Thus of Blake's climactic portrayal of Christ we may use the term *identification* but not *absorption,* which tends to blur outline and lineament. Union, yes; fusion, no. Christian oneness, yes; mystical, Neoplatonic, Oriental, Gnostic unity, no. From that kind of vagueness and insubstantiality Blake was preserved by his conception of the body of Christ. A body may be attracted to another body, but it is also the nature of a body to resist absorption and to keep some kind of distance.

It was surely his unwavering commitment to a physical Christ that underlay his conception of essential artistic form as human and bodily. We do well, therefore, not to confuse his idea with that of the Romantic naturalists, for whom form is organic as a plant or a vegetable is organic. Blake's form is organic, to be sure, but as a man is organic. And Blake's larger forms are conceived of as purely human reduplication and extension. The lineaments in Blake's forms "tend & seek with love & sympathy" the "Divine Humanity." When individual forms are fruitful and multiply, they constitute a family, One Family, which is another name for Christ—a family united in love and benevolence, joy and

---

*The reader, in case he missed or has forgotten the earlier discussion of this plate in the Preface, is referred to p. xvi. The suggestion of the homoerotic may confuse the discussion, but it may also explain in part—though in part only—the intensity of this vision.

sorrow, as brothers, sisters, sons, fathers, and friends are united in a human community.[44]

Blake's belief in the one family of man united in benevolence and brotherhood may suggest Shaftesbury and the Latitudinarian divines of the eighteenth century. But for Blake these thinkers must have seemed to produce only "Swelld & bloated General Forms," a phrase that not unjustly characterizes the mental forms and the prose style of the third Earl, whose hymn to nature celebrates a being who is "boundless, unsearchable, impenetrable." Pope, who in *An Essay on Man* never once mentions Christ directly, says that God "loves from Whole to Parts" but man "Must rise from Individual to the Whole. . . . / As the small pebble stirs the peaceful lake."

Blake must have found Pope's spreading circles only another example of deadly abstraction. Closer in time to Blake, Rousseau may have been for a time attractive; but Blake came to believe that the Confessor knew of no way to cast out sin and that the writer who began by calling everyone good by nature ended a friendless creature haunted by evil men. Blake early proclaimed himself of another school, in which particularity and Christianity were united. Lavater wrote that "mankind differs as much in essence as they do in form, limbs, and senses—and only so, and not more." To that sentence Blake responded: "This is true Christian philosophy far above all abstraction." Describing the "Beauty proper for sublime art" (that is, the "idea of intellectual Beauty"), Blake said it consisted of "lineaments, or forms and features that are capable of being the receptacles of intellect." If these words had been written by someone else, Blake would surely have exclaimed in the margin, "A golden sentence. This is our Lord."[45]

12

"What Seems to Be: Is": Blake's Idea of God

*B*lake *is unconventionally* and excitingly religious. Neither orthodox formulation nor liberal-progressive theology comes close to being adequate to his idea of God. His God is not a wholly other, who directs men by laws or motivates them by externally bestowed grace. Nor is he immanent in nature, traditionally the second book of God, whose glory the heavens declare and whose handiwork the firmament shows forth. Nor is he disclosed in the many inherited religious and philosophical paradoxes or antitheses that juxtapose the one and the many, the moved and the unmoved, the general and the specific, essence and accident. None of the foregoing is sufficiently vivid, poetic, intimate, or pluralistic to meet Blake's spiritual needs. What then can God be said to be? Above all else an intellectual achievement, a product of mental fight, of a suffering psyche. He emerges, not in argument or logic but in existential struggle, as a person, sometimes in historical record, more often in vision. No reader should expect to finish this chapter with a clear or precise definition; some sense of what it meant for Blake to believe in God is all that can be asked for.

"Great Eternity": Blake's Heaven

From about 1794, the year in which he may have engraved *The Book of Urizen*, Blake tended to refer to his special version of heaven as Eternity, Great Eternity, or Eden.[1] He continued in letter, lyric, and prophecy to use the traditional term "heaven" in a good sense (a place of beings who surround, support, and inspire his spirit), which we must sharply distinguish from the home of "Angels & weak men,"[2] the conventional heaven of *The Marriage of Heaven and Hell*, where hell is the source of a redemptively purging energy. But in this commentary I lay aside that famous and dazzling inversion, which is also present in the Lambeth prophecies and *The Songs of Experience*, and concentrate on Great Eternity, which is a good, though not a conventionally good, place, the environment of Blake's divine being. *Eternity* and *eternal* are noble biblical words, but they are also noble secular words, used by unbelieving or purely humanistic writers to refer to the transcendent both in this life and sometimes even in the next. Thus Shelley refers to Adonais as a star who "beacons from the abode where the Eternal are." Blake's eternity is both secular and spiritual, artistic and religious; and if the two can in any way be separated, it must be said strongly—and, it would seem in opposition to much contemporary criticism—that the religious is fundamental.

Recognizing that purely moral judgments (as contrasted with religious), along with temporal and spatial conceptions, must be reduced to a minimum, we must nevertheless try to isolate the kind of goodness inherent in this spiritual locality. It is populated by "myriads," who are described as all "the wisdom and joy of Life." It cannot be separated from Eden, where the unity of all the faculties is perfect and brotherhood is universal. It is a place of sweetness and happiness, the "land of life," a place of "warmth" and "perfect harmony." Above all, it is the place of the "Divine Presence," for it is presided over by Christ, who cannot always or fully be distinguished from "the Eternal Father." Paradoxically, it is at the same time a place of limitation: not of evil, to be sure—for so blatant a contradiction could not be tolerated—but of qualities that suggest the purely human, sometimes the human even in its fallen condition. The Eternals can shudder as Los often does, or petrify like Urizen, both of whom are called Eternals. They and their confreres are often afraid of becoming what they behold, and collectively they can groan in deep trouble, like the whole creation in the Bible as it awaits its deliverance. Eternals lament, weep, rage, separate themselves from their environment, or flee into the deep. They are scarcely a body of palm-bearing, harp-playing resurrected saints or angels adoring eternal majesty in order serviceable.[3]

Can these paradoxes and contradictions (if so indeed they are) be resolved? Not surely by conceiving of Blake's Eternity as an enclosed garden with a sky-god viewing it from above and enforcing immutable laws, nor by considering it as in any way static, formal, abstract, geometrical. But if we try to think of it as Blake did and so experience its force, the copresence of these kinds of goodness (mostly joy) and of limitation (mostly purely human) becomes at least understandable. For Eternity is infinite and flexible, a place of movement and energy—a place, in fact, of raging, consuming, warring energies. Its people are "drunk with the Spirit, burning round the Couch of death," a condition of intensity doubtless in part caused by their being in the presence of a threat. But no matter what they do or where they are, the Eternals live in "wild flames," which, however (if I may change or mix metaphors lamentably), move like biblical wheels within wheels—not, as in the world of Locke and Newton, like "wheel without wheel, with cogs tyrannic." Like living forms responding to heat and cold—even like sexual organs in amorous activity—beings in Great Eternity contract and expand. Such visionary motion stands in contrast to the perceptions of a corrupt human society, which are "frozen to unexpansive ... terrors."[4]

So much for what we may call the "climate" of Eternity, its "intellectual pleasures & energies." What about its people and government? It is clearly not a monarchy or an episcopacy; it is without conventional ruler divine or ecclesiastic; God as person or form appears when perceptions contract or expand. If anything, it is a council, Congregational in government, which in its collectivity is called the Divine Imagination—a committee of burning presences who are free to come and go, to divide in opinion from one another, to take separate actions. For example, some choose to "disregard all Mortal Things"; others choose to descend, view mortality more closely, and participate, at the edge of life, in its redemption. Its presences are, in part, Blake's friends and his great predecessors, including Milton, who has lived there about a hundred years and is now driven by his fellow eternals into Blake's earth-hell (Ulro). Another historical person, who has entered Eternity frequently in vision, believes he will also enter it at death, when he goes into "his Own Eternal House . . . into the Mind in which every one is King & Priest."[5] Eternity is a state of mental energy and creation, of heightened self-consciousness, available now to anyone willing to become a prophet; but it is also a postmortem life that continues the strenuous joys that have led to spiritual greatness in time. To and from Eternity not only real people like Milton and Blake come and go, but also reified faculties and cultural forces like the Four Zoas, along with other products of imaginative seeing that have taken on the status of real entities.[6]

The Eternals are capable of actions, of which two are particularly notable, even though somewhat grotesque or awkward in their presentation. One is the erection of a tent or tabernacle with pillars and a curtain to separate and enclose unknown space, an unpleasant but necessary action to prevent the ultimate disaster of formlessness, which to Blake is always "Deep, horrible without End." The other action is the dispatching into history of the guardians of man's form, who, considered in a chronological line, constitute epochs of human religious history. It may seem uncouth to commission *eyes* or to embody them in institutions; but the image came to Blake from his source, where the "eyes of the Lord . . . run to and fro through the whole earth" (Zechariah 4:10). In any case, Blake pours out his most intense dramatic and imagistic energies upon the action of the Eternals in sending forth these "seven Spirits . . . into all the earth" (Revelation 5:6), an action that recalls not only the Bible but the commissioning of Christ by God in *Paradise Lost,* Book 3, and perhaps also the debate among the Four Daughters of God over which divine quality will prevail in dealing with man. Blake's Council of Eternals divides in debate, as the minions of Satan do in Milton's hell. Some, the more adventurous, wish to descend and see for themselves the changes in Albion, both the man and the place. Others opt for inaction; these are more cautious, more exclusive, fearful of birth and death and perhaps also of sexuality, and partial to the equality of Eden to which they are now accustomed. But the bold ones prevail, crying out, "Bring forth all your fires! / So saying, an eternal deed was done: in fiery flames."[7]

Such, then, is Blake's heaven, which is less dramatic than Milton's hell but considerably more interesting than his heaven, with its fixed hierarchies, or Dante's *Paradiso,* with its highly formalized fire and light. The very humanity of Blake's divine place has left its edges loose and its definition contradictory; its very flexibility makes it conceptually elusive. And yet these very qualities guarantee not only its appeal but, for Blake, its redemptive effectuality. His is a very special and virtually unique communion of saints, of the noble living and the noble dead in a state of expanded awareness that thrives upon dynamic change and the interaction of living contraries.

God in History: Urizen the Tyrannical Father

The entrance of the Seven Eyes of God into history was a mixed blessing at best if we except Christ, the seventh and last Eye, and S. Foster Damon has summarized their various failures. The first five need not detain us, since they are remote from Blake and us; they remain unexplored in the prophecies. But the sixth Eye, Jehovah of Israel, the Lawgiver of Sinai, the creator of the patriarchy, impinged on Blake every day of his life; and grave moral and psychological suffering must reside in the fact that Blake had to call him "leprous" and even regard the psychocultural condition over which he presided as "the ancient Leprosy." This Lawgiver-Father is united in Blake's myth with Urizen, the Zoa from whom he is not clearly separated until important revisionary developments in *Jerusalem* and later works remove the leprosy and the tyranny.[8]

Urizen is surely one of the most impressive symbols created in English Romantic poetry—complexly and broadly conceived but always as palpable and solid as he is suggestively multivalent. He is figured forth as an irresistible natural force like winter (snow, cold, hail, darkness, ice, freezing storms are his natural milieu) or as impenetrable matter like rock, brass, and, especially, iron. He is the original solipsist, a tough and unyielding selfhood, whose master trait is a tyrannous will.

His tyranny expresses itself in two related but separable clusters of activity. (1) A personification of the faculty of reason, this Zoa manifests himself in culture as Cartesian or Newtonian, as the *esprit de système,* as the geometer God, as a logocentric maker of legalistic books and tablets, as an abstract logician, analyst, and generalizer, and as an architect who creates impressive but essentially inhuman shapes of metal and stone. (2) He is also the original superego—a *paterfamilias,* king, pope, bishop, priest—the transmitter of religious, social, and national codes. What gives him his essential unity through all these diverse psychological, cultural, and historical manifestations is that he embodies quintessential tyranny, indeed the very tendency itself toward selfish domination; he is maddened by an obsessive desire to be God and proclaim himself as such. Again and again he utters variants of the cry, "Now I am God from Eternity to Eternity," a cry he repeats even when he stands in the midst of his ruined world. That cry is echoed by Los, Tharmas, Vala, Albion, the Spectre of Urthona, and Satan, Urizen's successor in Blake's myth. It cannot be stressed too often that his master trait, the ruling passion that organizes his gestalt, is the will to power— a quality that gives a coherent body, as it were, to this "Schoolmaster of souls," this "great opposer of change," this "dread form of Certainty." And Blake made this quality basic and causal as well as organizing: "A Tyrant is the worst disease & the Cause of all others."[9]

It has long been believed, but not often enough said in our day of understandable timorousness in judging religions, that Urizen is not a parody but a direct representation of what Blake saw as the God of Judaism and Christianity in their codified forms as Mosaic and Pauline inscriptions. The Jesus of ecclesiastical tradition says, "And I say also unto thee, That thou art Peter, and *on this rock* I will build my church" (Matt. 16:18, emphasis added). Urizen says, "Lo! I unfold my darkness: and *on / This rock* place with a strong hand this book / Of eternal brass, written in my solitude" (*Urizen,* 4.31–32 [E., p. 72], emphasis added). He is called "the Mighty Father" (*Four Zoas,* 15.12 [E., p. 309]), he creates iron laws that no one can keep even "one moment," and he curses his children for not keeping them. These allusions to the scriptural God are by no means fortuitous: Blake is taking on the patriarchy at its source. But he also attacks the God of his predecessor Milton, who had called nature the creation of "The Great Work-Maister" God (*Paradise Lost,* 3.696). Blake calls Urizen "the great Workmaster" (*Four Zoas,* 24.5 [E., p. 314]). Urizen, winning a victory over Los, collects himself in "awful pride," attacks the spirit of Jesus as visionary and soft, and proclaims himself "God the terrible destroyer":

> Ten thousand thousand were his hosts of spirits on the wind:
> Ten thousand thousand glittering Chariots shining in the sky:
> They pour upon the golden shore beside the silent ocean.
> Rejoicing in the Victory; & the heavens were filld with blood.
> (*Four Zoas.,* 12.24, 26, 32–35 [E., p. 307])

In *Paradise Lost,* Jesus, riding "the Chariot of Paternal Deitie," attacks his enemies:

> Attended with ten thousand thousand Saints,
> He onward came, farr off his coming shon,
> And twentie thousand (I thir number heard)
> Chariots of God, half on each hand were seen.
> (*Paradise Lost,* 6.750, 767–770)

Unmistakably, Blake views Milton's patriarchal and militaristic Christ as Urizenic, and his own Urizen as an embodiment of supreme paternal power.

Blake once said to Crabb Robinson that he did not believe in God's omnipotence,[10] and he declared in annotating John Caspar Lavater, "No Omnipotence can act against order," and in annotating Swedenborg, "There can be no Good-Will. Will is always Evil" (E., p. 593, 602). Blake rarely regarded the will of God as good. What did he do, then, with these traditional qualities of the Godhead, omnipotence and will? He bestowed them on his Urizen in an imaginative act which proclaimed that just as that unforgettable old man is a creature of the poet's mind, so the patriarchal God is a creation of man's collective mind. For all their strutting pompousities or thundering damnations, both alike are creaturely. The perception of that equation is of ultimate importance to Blake and his critic—in healing his own mind and in giving us a clue to the power of his art.

That power appears very strongly in the visual Urizen. The sharply etched but heavy presence of that anti-man (here we refer of course only to his fallen condition) may be said to give him precisely what he sought, a "solid without fluctuation" (*Urizen.,* 4.11 [E., p. 71]). From our point of view, we have a haunted and haunting image whose intense condensation by artistic means and whose realized powers of formal articulation create for it inescapable psychological and aesthetic space. This imaginative body is a *coincidentia oppositorum* in the fullest Romantic sense, combining authority with sentimental pity, strength with weakness, fallen majesty with hints of future redemption. Rising as a counterrevolutionary figure over the Atlantic; sitting in his vegetable or rocky cave, weeping (see fig. 21); making mystical signs on his metal books; poising himself on rocks with a dark void below; applying his compasses to the creation of the world; touching the first man with clay (see fig. 22); hovering over Job as a nightmare (see fig. 23)—these direct and indirect portrayals of the tyrant oppress the spirit as they make Blake's point about a tryant-deity. Such artistic power in the visual medium must surely owe much to the art of the age as well as to Blake's remote ancestor, Michelangelo:[11] to formidable contemporary images of Saturn, Jupiter, Oedipus, Lear, Laocoön, Ugolino, and Nebuchadnezzar, many of whom Blake himself portrayed as Urizenic. To this powerful antigeriatric current in an age of revolution Blake submitted himself early, and he unflaggingly transmitted its energies until his very last days.[12]

The verbal Urizen is at least as impressive, and he is most fully developed as a mythic actor in the book that bears his name and in *The Four Zoas.* It has sometimes been said that Blake in his late great prophecies tired of his antiman and replaced his evil tyranny with Satan and his redeemable portion with Los.[13] Blake did, to be sure, make some adaptations appropriate to his new attack on Deism and to the direct entrance into his myth of Milton. But if anything is clear it is that Urizen, though not so frequently named or so directly portrayed as before, has not died but lives on as a deeply rooted tendency to tyranny that continues to plague human nature even in post- or antireligious

Fig. 21. Blake, *The Book of Urizen*, copy G, plate 11.
Relief etching with water color. Lessing J. Rosenwald
Collection, Library of Congress, Washington, D.C.

Fig. 22. Blake, *Elohim Creating Adam*. Color print
finished in pen and water color. Tate Gallery, London.

Fig. 23. Blake, *Book of Job*, plate 11.
Engraving on copper. British
Museum, Department of Prints and
Drawings.

cultures. Thus Satan speaks like Urizen ("I am God the judge of all") and, as Los and his consort Enitharmon come to know, actually "*is* Urizen."[14] Thus the "Spectre" of Urthona (an imaginative man's negative double), who is defined as the "Reasoning Power / An Abstract objecting power that Negatives every thing" (*Jer.,* 10.13–14 [E., p. 153]), says in quintessentially Urizenic fashion, "I am God O Sons of men!" (*Jer.,* 54.16 [E., p. 203]). And thus even Vala, Blake's Venus, cries out, "I alone am Beauty," "I am Love" (*Jer.,* 29.48, 52 [E., p. 176]). Vala is here following her acknowledged and unacknowledged master Urizen in the most mischievous of his psychic annexations—the strategy of appropriating individuality and erecting logically analyzed and dialectically separated qualities into tyrannous hypostatizations that eat up the winged joys of life and the minute particulars of art.

Blake's Anxiety

Anything as compelling as a drive toward Urizenic tyranny will inevitably cause anxiety in one who recognizes its presence and realizes its evil potential. And in creating Urizen, Blake writes not as an unconscious transmitter of intuitive insights but as a full-bodied Romantic in the noon blaze of an aroused self-consciousness. Blake attributes anxiety even to the Eternals; it is acutely present in Los, when he is working outside eternity in time, to retain vision in periods of great tribulation. Two passages involving Los define two kinds of psychic anxiety. (1) A fearful Los cries out in *Jerusalem:*

> Yet alas I shall forget Eternity!
> Against the Patriarchal pomp and cruelty, labouring incessant
> I shall become an infant horror.
> (83.3–5 [E., p. 241])

(2) Much earlier, in *The Book of Urizen,*

> Los wept howling around the dark Demon [Urizen]: . . .
> Groaning! gnashing! groaning!
> (6:1, 7:2 [E., pp. 73–74])

Why such anguish? Because imagination feels the pains of separation from reason. More remotely and profoundly, because Urizen now is "Unorganized" (6.8), with only a "fathomless void" (6.5) beneath him; and Los realizes that he, like the fellow immortal whose form he must rescue through creation, can also fall into unbeing. The first passage grows out of a profound fear of becoming what one beholds—that is, of becoming a newly reborn Urizenic man with a tyrannous spirit. The second grows out an even greater fear of the void. This greater fear is harrowingly illustrated in Los's fall, which takes place when he becomes wrathful after his wrenching separation from Urizen and after he has been assigned the task of watching over his fallen companion. His very fury, now objectless, has eaten up all the solidity that once supported him, leaving only a horrid vacuum beneath and around him.

> Falling, falling! Los fell & fell
> Sunk precipitant heavy down down
> Times on times, night on night, day on day
> Truth has bounds. Error none: falling, falling:
> Years on years, and ages on ages
> Still he fell thro' the void, still a void
> Found for falling day & night without end.
> (*Book of Los*, 4.27–33 [E., p. 92])

Harold Bloom has said that a poetic text is "a psychic battlefield upon which authentic forces struggle for the only victory worth winning, the divinating triumph over oblivion."[15] The sentence is fully applicable to Blake if we alter the word "oblivion" to "nonentity." But what is nonentity? It must surely be a form of madness whose exact nature cannot at present be recovered. Quite literally—and Blake was a great literalist of the imagination—Los has lost his reason in the separation from Urizen that tortures him, and now a profound void gapes before him. Was this the "Nervous Fear" Blake confessed to feeling as the "dark horrors" of the American and French revolutions "passed before [his] face?" Are the groanings of Los those "Perils & Darkness" Blake says he himself "traveled thro'" and from which he came out victorious?[16] Doubtless in part, at least. But our aim here is to recover Blake's idea of God, not to psychoanalyze him; and to the fear of the void we shall return in the next section when we try to see how the anxiety of emptiness is cured.

The other fear, expressed in the first passage quoted above, that Los will forget Eternity in his antipatriarchal struggle, is very closely related to our subject—the fear that in creating Urizen he will become his own creature's creature. This fear must have been very real, since Blake regarded the tendency to tyranny as a kind of original sin, present in all of us and perhaps peculiarly clamorous in himself. Generating the debilitating anger we saw in *The Book of Urizen* and *The Book of Los,* and in *The Four Zoas* generating an even more debilitating "furious pride," the struggle against "Patriarchal pomp and cruelty" (*Jer.,* 83.4 [E., p. 241]) leads Los into a vile capitulation to his enemy: "Our God is Urizen the King, King of the Heavenly hosts," he says. "We have no other God but he" (*Four Zoas.,* 48.11, 15–16 [E., p. 332]). This abjectness, this declaration of perverted faith, leads the imaginative artist, who must surely know better and must therefore be full of anxious fear about his degradation, to proclaim his godhood "over all" and even to reduce his own eternal imaginative form of Urthona to a mere "shadow." How close all this was to Blake's own spirit can only be surmised, but surely the expulsion from the psyche of the codified God of Abraham, Isaac, and Jacob and of the institutional Father of our Lord Jesus Christ cannot have been accomplished without an expense of spirit and a waste of shame. Los speaks of "Inspiration deny'd; Genius forbidden by laws of punishment" (*Jer.,* 9.16 [E., p. 152]), showing that patriarchy can enter the very soul of an artist to frustrate his vocation. But the Established God in the soul is a pancultural condition, more broadly conceived than loss of artistic faith; the nadir is recorded by Blake:

To Sin & to hide the Sin in sweet deceit, is lovely!!
To Sin in the open face of day is cruel & Pitiless. But
To record the Sin for a reproach: to let the Sun go down
In a remembrance of the Sin: is a Woe & a Horror!
A brooder of an Evil Day, & a Sun rising in blood.

(*Jer.,* 50.25–29 [E., p. 200])

Here is the heart of Blake's patriarchal anxiety; here Blake weighs fully his own burden of the past.

These then are the two great anxieties of Blake—a fear of the void and a fear of what God the Father Almighty, Maker of Heaven and Earth and Creator of the Western Patriarchy, can do within the soul of man. Is there a connection between the two? There must surely be. Alberto Moravia has one of his characters in *1934* say that an "ambiguous and dissociated condition ... is characteristic of every society based on fear" and that "in a regime of terror it's impossible not only to distinguish truth from falsehood, but also to distinguish the truth of falsehood."[17] In other words, where a tyrannous will prevails in all its whimsicality and unreason, man loses form, distinction, and value. Tyranny creates the void. It is a pity that Blake himself did not explore more fully the relationship between the two great fears of his Los.

Before leaving the fear of an unforgiving, tormenting God, the creator of a fiery hell and of the laws of punishment, it must be emphasized that it is not the power of a really existent, vengeful tyrant in the skies whose judgments Blake fears. He was a man disposed to faith, but he was not superstitious, and he would never have allowed himself to be guided by craven fear. To such a real tyrant he would have cried out with the fiery Orc of his radical political period: "No more I follow, no more obedience pay" (*America,* 11.15 [E., p. 55]). It is rather the devastation wrought by the *idea* of a tyrannical God-Dictator that Blake fears—the damage to the individual and corporate psyche. He also dreads what the very possession of such an idea over so many centuries implies about our nature and about the real danger of a recurring appetite for tyranny. It is not only Christ who is resurrected in Blake; Urizen arises again and again even after, as we have seen, he has lost his name.

Harold Bloom, the most original and brilliant student in our time of poetic sublimity and its relations to anxiety, regularly aestheticizes the fears of poets like Blake. It is not an antecedent God but an antecedent poet who engenders anxiety, particularly if influence has been strong and inescapable. For Bloom the location of the anxiety must largely be a speculative and indirect extrapolation from poetic texts, because he believes that in reality poets "tell continuous lies about their relations to their precursors" and, like all analysts of the mind from Freud on, he regards his poet-patient's resistance to such a theory as evidence for its validity. But do Milton's successors ever betray, directly or indirectly (for all traumatic unworthiness reveals itself somehow), a "sense of trespass" in the presence of their poetic father?[18] (Perhaps William Collins did indeed feel tremblingly unworthy in his relations to Milton.) There is no trace of agon in Wordsworth, even though the later poet does call his predecessor's soul "awful." He corrects the language of *Paradise Lost,* sometimes challenging an idea here and there with all the relaxation of a Samuel Johnson, but he usually confirms Hazlitt's judgment that "Milton is his great idol, and he sometimes dares to compare himself with him." Nor is there any evidence, overt or covert, of personal tension or of a large revisionary enterprise at work in Coleridge's relations to the great poet. Quite the contrary! Coleridge says, "It is very common—very natural—for men to *like* and even admire an exhibition of power very different in kind from any thing of their own. No jealousy arises." And Coleridge is at his ease when he sets about finding in the great-souled Milton illustrations of his own theories of poetry and the imagination.[19] Blake betrays many signs of sharing the hero worship of the Romantics for the great of the past, who were, in his view, the embodiments of the true God—the only truly available revelation outside the mind of the seer himself.

But of course Blake's attitude toward Milton is vastly deeper-going and more strenuously spirit-consuming than that of his fellow Romantics. Because Milton, like Dante, is in part a victim of the God-idea of the patriarchate, he evokes in the bold and ever-challenging Blake a complex and majestic task of revision that stretches the younger poet's spirit to the breaking point. The soul of Milton must be purged—as Blake's own soul must be continually purged—of the murderous notion of a cruel divinity and also of that tyrannous tendency in human nature, the selfhood. But there is no evident jealousy of Milton's power or authority as a poet, no desire to murder the aesthetic father or to become his father's father, no desire to displace his predecessor; there is, rather, an ambition to purge his master's spirit, to soften his acerbity, to unite him with his emanation and so feminize his psyche, and to enlist his mature and unspoiled genius against the common enemy, Urizen. All of which in fact Blake succeeds in doing! He does not misread

Milton—he reads him all too accurately; instead, he revises him—rebuilds him, as Milton himself reconstructs Urizen, removing the clayey dross of the patriarchy and remodeling him in the life-giving red clay (Adam) of the true God.

Can we describe Blake's emotion toward Milton more accurately? It was not Oedipal love-hate but rather profound admiration combined with lamenting tears over a partial betrayal of otherwise shared religious ideals. "Who would not weep if Atticus were he?" Blake must have felt in the presence of patriarchal elements in Milton's thought precisely what he felt whenever and wherever he beheld the tracks of the Urizenic (Satanic) "Wheel of Religion":

> I wept & said. Is this the law of Jesus
> This terrible devouring sword turning every way?
> *(Jer.,* 77.13, 14–15 [E., p. 232])

Thus Bloom, one of the most stimulating of modern critics, seems to have mislocated Blake's *agon,* which arose in a conflict with the God of the patriarchy. But that same critic has perceived, with uncanny insight though without elaboration, that the chariot of fire that Blake himself mounts to wield his bow of burning gold and shoot his arrows of desire, is none other than one of the Old Testament tropes for God, the chariot of Ezekiel, the Merkabah, the very vehicle in which Milton places his Christ.[20] The boldness of Blake's transumption is almost beyond belief, indicating that the cure of his anxiety was as deep-going as his suffering had been intense.

God the Divine Hand and Jehovah the Good Father

Wordsworth wrote,

> . . . my voice proclaims
> How exquisitely the individual Mind . . .
> to the external World
> Is fitted:—and how exquisitely, too—. . .
> The external World is fitted to the Mind.[21]

Blake's high argument is of course different, since the polarities are not the same; but the "fit" is equally exquisite. For God removes effectually and precisely both of the fears described in the preceding section: God the Divine Hand removes the anxiety of emptiness, and Jehovah the good Father removes the anxiety of primal and ever-recurring tyranny, replacing Urizen and annihilating Satan. Blake's God is created within a structure of desire as a projection of our perceptions and as a fulfillment of our needs. He is not a being wholly other, wholly causal, wholly antecedent. He is, in fact, not ontological at all—at least the argument whether he exists does not interest Blake. God belongs magnificently to the environment of integrating energy which is Blake's Great Eternity. We should note in passing that Blake has radically revised yet another great Western doctrine about God, the doctrine of the fitness of ends and means, of divine purpose and natural powers.

The horror of "indefinite space," which, we remember, tortured the Eternals, Urizen, Los, and Blake himself, is erased by the Divine Hand, by God conceived of as limit, as a formal restraint upon both contraction (which would otherwise drive into the concentrated hardness of a cosmic black hole) and opacity (which would otherwise smoke away into airy nothingness). This idea becomes illuminating, though complex, when Los working at his creating forge feels the finger of the Hand Divine over his furnaces, putting a limit to destruction as he uses his divinely given powers which are "fitted [observe again this important theological and Wordsworthian word] to circumscribe this dark Satanic death." Why should Los, just at the moment in which he senses that he is being led by brotherhood and mercy, feel terror at this task? Because he senses that in the act of giving form he crucifies Christ afresh, an action that causes him to undergo in his own spirit the bodily passion of his Lord. For by creating bodies of any kind, Blake-Los is reenacting an incarnation, which inevitably leads to a crucifixion and only then to a resurrection. This chain of salvation, requiring that bodies be put on before they are put off, is one of the very few laws of Blake's cosmos. But certainty of Christlike death, particularly since it can be a redemptive death, does not alone explain the fear; the creator is also "terrifd at the shapes / Enslaved humanity put on."[22]

What Blake calls "organization"* (one of his truly great words and one exactly expressing the healing of a mind that fears the void) is a divine accomplishment which creates a body for Urizen—a process Blake repeated obsessively—and which transforms that body into energetic creativity. The salvation of the wintry old God-man is told fully in *The Four Zoas* and need not be recounted here—his multiple resurrections from his slimy bed into a restored force in the psyche. But its climax does deserve attention. Los had already created Urizen's human, fallen form, which we know so well. Now realizing that he must "modulate" his Orcan fury into which the very idea of Urizen seemed designed to precipitate him, he embraced his own "raging flames" and

> . . . drew them forth out of the depths planting his right foot firm
> Upon the Iron crag of Urizen thence springing up aloft
> Into the heavens of Enitharmon in a mighty circle
> And first he drew a line upon the walls of shining heaven
> And Enitharmon tinctured it with beams of blushing love.
>
> (*Four Zoas,* 90.26, 32–36 [E., p. 370])

Mr. and Mrs. Blake are once more in Great Eternity, together producing illuminations, having sprung up into this realm in a leap firmly supported by Urizenic iron. Los then separates Urizen's true image ("shadow," denoting art) from his warlike patriarchal spectre:

> Startled was Los he found his Enemy Urizen now
> In his hands he wondered that he felt love & not hate
> His whole soul loved him he beheld him an infant
> Lovely breathed from Enitharmon he trembled within himself.
>
> (*Four Zoas,* 90.64–67 [E., p. 371])

---

*Blake preferred this word to "order," which was closely associated with the dark and sickly dens of the Establishment, although he could use "order" in a favorable sense. It was a great evil in Blake's thought to be "disorganized," but to be "organized" was a comparably greater good. To be organized meant to be possessed of minutely articulated parts and to be endowed with living organs. The great Organizer is Christ, and, after him, the poet.

We can now see that the healing of the mind by the Divine Hand was a complex double process. It began by giving Urizen the body of that familiar whitebearded old man, to resist the suctions of the void. It ended by releasing the primal energy of this old man into a resurrected form—that "radiant youth" we see in "naked majesty":

> So Urizen spoke he shook his snows from off his Shoulders & arose
> As on a Pyramid of mist his white robes scattering
> The fleecy white renewd he shook his aged mantles off
> Into the fires Then glorious bright Exulting in his joy
> He sounding rose into the heavens in naked majesty
> in radiant Youth.
>
> (*Four Zoas,* 121.27–32 [E., p. 391])

The paradox of the conquest of fear through form is a deep one, but it is rooted in reality. It is as though one might say: I now realize that what has tortured me for years—and tortured whole cultures for centuries—is a creation of my own mind and of millions like me. I have created the image of that fear as honestly as I can, at whatever cost. I see that it does correspond to what I have feared, and I am free of its terrors, which are now "cathected" to my representation. I am therefore no longer haunted by its freely floating, uncontrolled, demonic energy, and I am now enabled to imagine even the humanly attractive and dynamic form that lay behind what caused my fears and may indeed have given them such potency. For it is apparent that so vigorous and persistent a power as tyranny must have derived from some kind of primal energy. Such is Blake's idea of catharsis, the work of God the Divine Hand.[23]

The other aspect of divine salvation, the salvation from the fear of tyranny in oneself and in society, is the function of the Good Father. It is unnecessary to specify Blake's early, middle, and late alternatives to the bad patriarchy of Jehovah-Urizen, alternatives revealed in his many honorific uses, all through his career, of the word "father" in a good sense and his many portrayals at all periods of benign old men. At no time was Blake without the idea of a good father, even though the concept may have gone partially underground in his revolutionary period. We can therefore absolve Blake of the "psychopathy" that Freud and Alan Harrington have found endemic in modern society, the absence of a superego.[24] Nevertheless, much of Blake's vision is dominated by the cruel father who tortures the mind not least by being an answering image to the inner tendency of human nature to tyrannize. This image must be cast out, and anyone wishing to follow the progress of this purgation should study closely the career in Blake of Jehovah, first the leprous sixth eye of God but finally the Lord Jehovah who creates "merciful Order" (*Jer.,* 49.55 [E., p. 199]) and as Elohim Jehovah proclaims the "Covenant of the Forgiveness of Sins" (*The Ghost of Abel,* 2.24 [E., p. 272]). Once Blake is certain of mercy, he is willing to restore might, omnipotence, law, and will to the divine principle, a fascinating development that must be discussed elsewhere.

One might pause to ask why Blake felt such an urgent need to create in his latest prophetic work a virtually separate ideal of Jehovah and his covenant of mercy. Why would not Christ do, the ever-merciful Lamb of God, the image of the Father and of humanity itself? It may be that Christ had been too intimately associated with Los, with the human imagination, with Blake himself, with youthful energetic humanity. Now that Urizen, the primal old man of history, has himself become a naked youth, a bright preacher of the Everlasting Gospel of life, there is a potential danger of another void. Venerability is lacking. But that quality is restored to human life in Jehovah, the Ancient of Days, healed of his leprosy and now the universal patriarch of a Covenant of Mercy. Jesus can, to be sure, be called "Father & Saviour," but Western man is not fully at ease without Jehovah, the archetypal father.[25]

Three notable visual designs represent the union of mankind with redeemed and restored venerability. On Plate 99 of *Jerusalem* (see fig. 24), God the Father embraces a youthful being (male or female, male-female?) in flames of desire and intellectual energy that recall the flame-plants of the *Songs of Innocence*. The other two appear as illustrations to Dante's *Paradiso*. Both show Saints Peter and James, each bearded but in heartwarming good health and benevolence. In the first (fig. 25), James, a good, sound, decent old man, extends a fraternal hand to a truly merciful Peter, whose eyes stream mercy and whose obvious marks of suffering qualify him to give a blessing. In the second (fig. 26), circling energies of love unite, in overlapping roundels, Dante and Beatrice and a youthful Saint John with the older veterans Peter and James. This is an embrace of Great Eternity where there is no longer patriarchal tyranny nor any generation gap whatever. But the patriarchal beards remain to remind us of what has been, what might have been, and what again might be.

Blake lived through a revolutionary period in which, as Edmund Burke said, "sons ... called for the execution of their parents" and "wretches calling themselves father ... demand[ed] the murder of their sons." Images of castration, mutilation, and cannibalism abundantly mark the relations of fathers and sons. Blake, as we have seen, expressed revolutionary antipaternalism, but he seldom stooped to such violence. He never descended to the brutality of a Goya, to take but one example, whose Saturn has bitten off the head of a mature being, an adolescent or perhaps a man.[26]

Is Blake's meaning illuminated by two great father-creations of our own century? He is surely as realistic as Freud in perceiving the mischief that a tyrannical father can do in the psyche of man, but he is not imprisoned in the Freudian realism that sees identification with the father as usually ambiguous, the boy's imaginative sympathy for the father arising only because he wishes to replace him, to attain ascendancy over him, and then to enjoy "a true object-cathexis toward his mother."[27] Jung believed the figure of the "Wise Old Man" to be archetypal, one of the "organizing dominants" of fourfold consciousness; and the Jungian "anima always stands in the relationship of a daughter to the wise old man." But this figure is only a "fragment of the objective psyche," though an "autonomous entity," who appears in all cultures as someone possessing authority, whether as magician, doctor, priest, teacher, professor, grandfather, or even hobgoblin.[28] Jung's archetypal structure, working itself out from the psyche into culture and deriving historically from a primeval teacher of alchemical secrets, is essentially bland compared to Blake's. It lacks the terror Blake finds in omnipotent Urizenic authority and also lacks the intense love the poet bestows upon the Jehovah of the Covenant, the Jesus of mercy, or the redeemed Heavenly Father. Nor is there in Jung the fierce antitheses of cruel patriarch and embracing father, nor the everlasting tension of warring contrarieties

Fig. 24. Blake, *Jerusalem*, copy F, plate 99. PML, 953. Relief etching, uncolored. The Pierpont Morgan Library, New York.

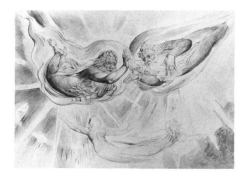

Fig. 25. Blake, Illustration to Dante's *Divine Comedy*, No. 95 *(St. Peter, Beatrice, Dante, with St. James)*. National Gallery of Victoria, Melbourne. Felton Bequest, 1920.

Fig. 26. Blake, Illustration to Dante's *Divine Comedy*, No. 96 *(St. Peter, St. James, Dante, Beatrice with St. John the Evangelist)*. British Museum, Department of Prints and Drawings.

engaged in the mental battle that Blake called the "War & Hunting" of Great Eternity (*Milton,* 34.50; 35:2 [E., pp. 134, 135]). Blake believed that redemptive force fully existed only in a divine being who is "The God *of fire* and Lord *of Love*" (*Jerusalem,* pl. 3, "To the Public" [E., p. 145]).

Conclusion: Regression and Subjectivity?

The most serious charge that can be made against the thought of Blake as it has been presented in this commentary is that it is regressive and entirely subjective. Blake writes after an intense vision,

> I remaind as a Child
> All I ever had known
> Before me bright Shone.[29]

And "return" is everywhere a compulsive imperative; both the lyric and prophetic muses direct this command to the fallen earth, to Jerusalem, and to England itself. But to what are we asked to return? Sometimes to Beulah,[30] that place of pastoral rest between earth and Eden, which Blake mercifully opens to weary earth-travelers and to his knights of mental fight. But most often it is to Eternity that Blake summons us, and can anyone possibly call it a place of narcissistic arrest or infantine peace? Existing in Blake's Eden is rather like what one imagines a great conductor to experience when he is translating *The Rites of Spring* into a performance, churning up a raging energy on which form is being impressed.

Blake's way of destroying error (stop beholding it, and it will burn up) has of course seemed notoriously subjective and easy to some. Subjective it certainly is. But easy? A mind habituated by centuries of powerfully sanctioned beholding is not changed by fiat, and what is to be burned up in the Last Judgment growing out of prophetic vision is a stubborn reality of our culture, however subjectively produced. Centuries of false seeing have been reified into institutions and cultural forms; the idea of God has produced a terribly real and inescapable presence in actual life, as palpable as a mountain, as irresistible as a hurricane.

> ... What seems to Be: Is: To those to whom
> It seems to Be, & is productive of the most dreadful
> Consequences to those to whom it seems to Be: ...
>
> (*Jer.*, 32.51–53 [E., p. 179])

Blake has expressed the weight of this burden marvelously in the drawing already mentioned (see fig. 23), where a heavy, torturing, self-reflective Urizen-Satan haunts Job on his bed.

It is rather easier to believe that a false vision can create a bad culture than that a good vision can create a good culture. But there is no reason why the mind which produces Los and Christ may not be as consequentially powerful as the mind which produces Urizen-Satan. And one must surely allow some kind of existence to the Divine Hand, which through fashioning bodies heals Blake's mind, and to the good Father, who creates a covenant of mercy and forgiveness of sin and so allays Blake's anxieties. It takes at least two to enter into a covenant. The prophet, Blake's Strong Man, not only rages with inspiration; he "marches on in fearless dependence on the divine decrees," and a decree implies somebody at the other end.[31]

And yet this most antinomian of Christians does not permit us to base his belief upon natural, logical, institutional assumptions, or to derive from his fierce dedication an unmistakable sense of ontological being. He rests his case against Bishop Watson entirely on inner certainty, and it is difficult to resist the conviction that in the end Blake's God, as so many have in the past believed, is a structure, a product, a sublime projection of the "Imagination which is spiritual Sensation."[32] It is not quite just to call Blake a man of faith; he is, rather, a man of sight—a seer, in the etymological meaning. And the relationship between what he needs to see for his own mental health and what he in fact ultimately comes to see is so close that it is hard to escape an overwhelming sense of subjectively produced truth. And yet we must remember that *all* affirmations of faith or of vision raise precisely this problem of external objectivity. Samuel Johnson, who tended to regard God as "the great Lawgiver of the universe," a "Creator," and a "Govenour,"[33] may have been projecting his own desire for order and social peace on the entire universe. Freud's brilliant and disturbing analysis of the dynamic relations of belief and desire has enormously extended the bounds of the subjective.

But however rational, empirical, or skeptical an investigator may think he has to be, he can surely never deny the flaming force of Blake's final embrace of the good father, Jehovah, whom he saw as a person. However internal or organic the poet's vision—and it was neither Mosaic nor Pauline but Johannine—it is never abstract, general, or purely mystical, fusing bodiless essences in light and fire. In Blake's vision it is clearly outlined identities that unite, as living lovers with bodies do. Blake saw real people, real forms. And God is one such.

We cannot therefore say that Blake has answered the perhaps unanswerable question of *what* God is. But he tells us *where* God is. He is in the very center of the integrating and integrated psyche; there he lives and moves and has his being. Since we have spent so much time on the idea of a false God, it is not irrelevant to ask in conclusion,

> Where is the Covenant of Priam, the Moral Virtues of the Heathen
> Where is the Tree of Good & Evil that rooted beneath the cruel heel
> Of Albions Spectre the Patriarch Druid! . . .
>
> (*Jer.*, 98.46–48 [E., p. 258])

In other words, where is Urizen? For Blake-Los, he now lives in the "Outward Spheres of Visionary Space and time," remanded to only the "shadows of Possibility." He belongs to "Visions & . . . Prophecy," where we can "Foresee & Avoid" him, though escape from him is by no means certain.[34] To create such a place for him almost cost Blake his humanity. But through that effort the most ancient heavens became fresh and strong.

Notes

CHAPTER 1

1. *Laodamia,* line 65. For an exhaustive bibliography of primary materials related to this word in the eighteenth century and to psychology in general, see David G. Schappert, "Selected Bibliography of Primary Materials," in *Psychology and Literature in the Eighteenth Century,* ed. Christopher Fox (New York: AMS Press, 1987), pp. 303–45.

2. John Dryden, "Sigismonda and Guiscardo" (from Boccaccio), lines 151–52; Alexander Pope, *Windsor Forest,* line 90; Samuel Richardson, *Clarissa* (London: Everyman's Library, 1932), 2:22; Jane Austen, *Northanger Abbey* (Oxford: World's Classics, 1976), p. 262.

3. William Cowper, *The Task,* 4.284–85.

4. *Aeneid* 4.165–72.

5. Dryden's translation (12.967–72) of *Aeneid* 12.665–68. Virgil's use of *conscia virtus* (line 668) should be compared with his use of precisely the same phrase to refer to an inner power that impels the aged Entellus to drive a younger man before him in rekindled strength and fury (5.455).

6. C. S. Lewis, "Conscience and Conscious," chap. 8 of *Studies in Words* (Cambridge, Eng.: Cambridge University Press, 1967), p. 191.

7. Timothy C. Potts, *Conscience in Medieval Philosophy* (Cambridge, Eng.: Cambridge University Press, 1980), p. 4.

8. See Arthur Sherbo's review of my *Sex and Sensibility: Ideal and Erotic Love from Milton to Mozart* (Chicago: University of Chicago Press, 1980) in *Modern Philology* 79 (February 1982): 323–26. Responding to his corrections and suggestions, I have in this chapter attempted a fuller treatment than was possible in my book (Index, s.v. "Conscious") or indeed in Sherbo's review or in his own earlier study of the word as a term of poetic diction. See *English Poetic Diction from Chaucer to Wordsworth* (East Lansing: Michigan State University Press, 1975).

9. See E[dward] P[hillips], *The New World of English Words* (London, 1602, 1706); [Thomas Blount], *Glossographia* (London, 1670); *Glossographia Anglicana Nova* (London, 1707); Nathan Bailey, *Dictionarium Britannicum*

(London, 1730); Thomas Dyche and William Pardon, *A New General English Dictionary* (London, 1744).

10. Donald Greene, *The Age of Exuberance: English Backgrounds to Eighteenth-Century English Literature* (New York: Random House, 1970), pp. 92–100.

11. *Clarissa,* 2:306, 378–79.

12. John Arthos, *The Language of Natural Description in Eighteenth-Century Poetry* (Ann Arbor: University of Michigan Press, 1949), pp. 122–23 and Sherbo, *English Poetic Diction.*

13. "Ode on the Death of a Favorite Cat . . .," line 7: "Her conscious tail her joy declar'd." Geoffrey Tillotson's comment is sensitive but perhaps endows the line with too much loftiness and somberness. "No better word than *conscious* could be applied to the stealthy expressiveness of a cat's tail, but the word was enriched for the reader of 1748 because of the status and colouring of *conscious* amid the poetic diction of a great deal of the world's poetry. Its status had been of the highest, and its colour of the darkest." *Augustan Studies* (London: Athlone Press, 1961), p. 77.

14. Marshall Brown, "The Pre-Romantic Discovery of Consciousness," *Studies in Romanticism* 17 (Fall 1978): 387–412, esp. 398–99.

15. Lewis, *Studies in Words,* p. 207.

16. Johnson, *Dictionary:* "1. Endowed with the power of knowing one's own thoughts and actions. . . . 2. Knowing from memory; having the knowledge of any thing without any new information. . . . 3. Admitted to the knowledge of any thing; with *to.* 4. Bearing witness by conscience to any thing." Thomas Sheridan, *A Complete Dictionary of the English Language,* 2nd ed. (London, 1789): "Endowed with the power of knowing one's own thoughts and actions; knowing from memory; admitted to the knowledge of any thing."

17. David Hume, *An Enquiry concerning the Principles of Morals,* in the *Enquiries,* ed. I. A. Selby-Bigge, rev. P. H. Nidditch, 3rd ed. (Oxford: Clarendon Press, 1975), par. 204 in sec. vii, p. 252. See also the longer discussion "Of Greatness of Mind" in *A Treatise of Human Nature,* ed. Selby-Bigge, rev. Nidditch, 2nd ed. (Oxford: Clarendon Press, 1978), III.iii.ii (pp. 592–602).

18. *Spectator* no. 224, par. 2. The Spectatorial comments on consciousness are close to those of Joseph Butler in his sermon "Upon Self-Deceit" (Sermon 10 of *Fifteen Sermons*): "Truth, and real good sense, and thorough integrity, carry along with them a peculiar consciousness of their own genuineness: there is a feeling belonging to them, which does not accompany their counterfeits. . . ." I quote from W. E. Gladstone's ed. of *The Works* (Oxford: Clarendon Press, 1896), 2:179.

19. Letter to William Hayley, 23 October 1804, in *The Complete Poetry and Prose of William Blake,* ed. David V. Erdman, commentary by Harold

Bloom, newly rev. ed. (Garden City, N.Y.: Anchor Press/Doubleday, 1982), p. 756 (hereafter cited as E.). The friend is one John Hawkins.

20. Blake, Preface to *Milton* (E., p. 95). It might prove fruitful to investigate the use of *conscious* in the literature of dissent to see if there is a specific background to Blake's usage.

21. *A Descriptive Catalogue,* Number V (E., p. 545).

22. "Mary," lines 9–12, from the Pickering Manuscript (E., p. 487).

23. South, Sermon 14 in *Sermons Preached upon Several Occasions* (Philadelphia, 1844), 1:224, 233.

24. The Greek phrases come from the *Odyssey* (6.51, 57). The translation, quoted from Pope's *Odyssey* (6.79–81), is apparently by William Broome. See George Sherburn, *The Early Career of Alexander Pope* (Oxford: Clarendon Press, 1934), p. 260.

25. *Our Mutual Friend,* Book 1, chap. 11.

26. Christopher Ricks, *Keats and Embarrassment* (Oxford: Clarendon Press, 1974), p. 4.

27. See Jean H. Hagstrum, *Sex and Sensibility,* Index, s.v. "Innocence."

28. Pope's *Iliad,* ed. Maynard Mack et al., Twickenham Edition (London and New Haven: Methuen and Yale University Press, 1967), 7:cxlvii, n. 3.

29. *Clarissa,* 2:22.

30. "Quite flatly, the meaning of 'conscious' in Lovelace's letter is 'guilty' ": Sherbo's review (see note 8 above), p. 325.

31. John Locke, *An Essay concerning Human Understanding,* ed. P. H. Nidditch (Oxford: Clarendon Press, 1975), p. 341. I believe it is valid to associate Locke's view of the mind with sensibility, but I recognize that this association rests on a more fundamental matter, Locke's use of consciousness as the criterion of personal identity. For a searching discussion of this belief, the background for it, and the reactions to it, see Christopher Fox, "Locke and the Scriblerians: The Discussion of Identity in Early Eighteenth-Century England," *Eighteenth-Century Studies* 16 (Fall 1982): 1–25. The Lockean definition of the self is not an easy concept to derive from his work. Observe in *Essay,* pp. 2, 24–25, 27, how he wavers between identifying it with substance and saying it comes and goes with consciousness. See the useful article by David P. Behan, "Locke on Persons and Personal Identity" in *Canadian Journal of Philosophy* 9 (1979): 53–75. For a comprehensive and persuasive study of personal identity and consciousness in the early eighteenth century, see Christopher Fox, *Locke and the Scriblerians* (Berkeley: University of California Press, forthcoming).

32. *The Cyclopedia: or Universal Dictionary of Arts, Sciences, and Literature* (Philadelphia, n.d.), vol. 10, n.p., under "Conscience." The 1st ed. appeared in London in 1728.

33. *Clarissa,* 1:460. Clarissa, now a prisoner of Lovelace away from her home, is in mental anguish not only about what she should do next but because Anna Howe has been making imputations of *"latent or unowned inclination"* in Clarissa (1:455).

34. William Empson, *The Structure of Complex Words* (Totowa, N.J.: Rowman and Littlefield, 1979), p. 250.

35. See Sigmund Freud's "The Antithetical Sense of Primal Words" and "The 'Uncanny,'" both of which appear, translated, in *On Creativity and the Unconscious,* ed. Benjamin Nelson (New York: Harper, 1958), pp. 55–62, 122–61.

36. See, for example, J. Hillis Miller, "The Critic as Host," in *Deconstruction and Criticism,* ed. Harold Bloom et al. (New York: Seabury Press, 1979), pp. 217–53.

37. Dryden's dedication to Roger, Earl of Orrery, in his Preface to *The Rival Ladies* (1st sentence). See Lancelot Law Whyte, *The Unconscious before Freud* (New York: Basic Books, 1962), where the Dryden passage is quoted and where other examples are given, notably one by Ralph Cudworth in *The Intellectual System of the Universe* (1678), cited on pp. 95–96. See also Christopher Fox, "Defining Eighteenth-Century Psychology," in *Psychology and Literature,* pp. 14–15.

38. Pope, *Dunciad* (A), lines 53–54. In the Dryden and Pope passages we must leave open the possibility that the authors refer, though with vivid metaphors, merely to the inchoate or unformed.

39. The *Rasselas* quotations come from chap. 48. The examples of Johnson's scientific terminology I have drawn from W. K. Wimsatt, *Philosophic Words* (New Haven: Yale University Press, 1948), appendix A.

40. The quotations from Hume all come from the section entitled "Of Personal Identity" in *Treatise of Human Nature,* I.iv.6 (pp. 251–63).

41. Samuel Taylor Coleridge to Thomas Clarkson, 13 Oct. 1806, in *Collected Letters,* ed. Earl Leslie Griggs (Oxford: Clarendon Press, 1956–), 2:1197.

42. "Of Personal Identity" in *The Whole Works of Joseph Butler* (London, 1852), p. 264. The essay I quote from is the first of two dissertations appended to *The Analogy of Religion.* Christopher Fox has pointed out to me that Butler, Reid, and others who had difficulty in accepting Locke's analysis of the self erroneously saw him as assimilating consciousness and memory, the latter being only a single mode of consciousness, which in its totality constituted the criterion of self-identity. For a criticism of the view that Locke equates consciousness and memory, see Behan, "Locke on Persons" (pp. 54–56).

43. Thomas Reid, *Essays on the Intellectual Powers of Man,* I.i.7, in *Works,* ed. Sir William Hamilton (Edinburgh, 1863), 1:222–23.

44. *Two Dissertations concerning Sense and the Imagination. With an Essay on Consciousness* (London, 1728), p. 147.

45. From the third of "Three Dialogues between Hylas and Philonous" in _The Works of George Berkeley,_ ed. A. A. Luce and T. E. Jessop (London: Nelson, 1949), 2:233–34. See also 2:231.

46. Immanuel Kant, _Critique of Pure Reason,_ trans. Norman Kemp Smith (New York: St. Martin's Press, 1961), p. 136.

47. James Engell, _The Creative Imagination: Enlightenment to Romanticism_ (Cambridge, Mass.: Harvard University Press, 1981), p. 61.

48. The Coleridge quotations all come from the _Biographia Literaria,_ chaps. 12 and 13.

49. See my _Sex and Sensibility,_ pp. 269–70.

50. In _Spectator_ no. 38, par. 4, Steele describes the affectation that arises from "an ill govern'd Consciousness." We can avoid such folly when "our Consciousness turns upon the main Design of Life" (par. 5).

51. The first "Essay upon Epitaphs" in _The Prose Works of William Wordsworth,_ ed. W. J. B. Owen and J. W. Smyser (Oxford: Clarendon Press, 1974), pp. 52–53.

CHAPTER 2

1. Life of Dryden in _Works of Johnson_ (Oxford, 1825), 7:322, 324; Life of Pope in ibid., 8:341; Dryden, _A Discourse concerning the Original and Progress of Satire_ in _Essays of John Dryden,_ ed. W. P. Ker (Oxford: Clarendon Press, 1900), 2:93 (hereafter in this chap. cited as Ker). Benjamin Boyce, _The Character-Sketches in Pope's Poems_ (Durham, N.C.: Duke University Press, 1962).

2. "How _easy_ is it to call rogue and villain, and that wittily! But how _hard_ to make a man appear a fool, a blockhead, or a knave, without using any of those opprobrious terms!" Dryden also discusses how to "spare the grossness of the names, and to do the thing yet more _severely_" (Ker, 2:92–93; emphasis added).

3. _Original and Progress of Satire_ (Ker, 2:108, 113).

4. See Hagstrum, _The Sister Arts_ (Chicago: University of Chicago Press, 1958), pp. 11–12, 121, for a definition and discussion of _enargeia_ as distinguished from _energeia._

5. _Original and Progress_ (Ker, 2:93). Jack Ketch was a notable hangman of the period.

6. Stanza 7: "his/Hand" refers to that of the poet or painter.

7. Earl Miner, "The 'Poetic Picture, Painted Poetry' of _The Last Instructions to a Painter_" in George deF. Lord, ed., _Andrew Marvell: A Collection of Critical Essays_ (Englewood Cliffs, N.J.: Prentice Hall, 1968), p. 171.

8. Lines 942–43. The poem may be read in _Poems on the Affairs of State,_ ed. George deF. Lord (New Haven: Yale University Press, 1963), 1:99–139. This volume and its sequels should be consulted, passim, for evidence of the pictorialism described here (see esp. 1:liii and 3 [ed. Howard H. Schless]: 184). For the genre, see Mary Tom Osborn, *Advice-to-a-Painter Poems, 1653–1856* (Austin, Tex.: University of Texas Press, 1949) and Hagstrum, *Sister Arts,* pp. 120–21.

9. *Mores Hominum, The Manners of Men, Described in Sixteen Satyrs of Juvenal* (London, 1660). This handsome work is a revision by Sir Robert Stapylton himself of the translation and edition of 1647.

10. *Ars Poetica,* lines 661ff. For Dryden's statement and his use of the motto, see *The Poems of John Dryden,* ed. James Kinsley (Oxford: Clarendon Press, 1958), 1:215–16. As an example of the pervasiveness of pictorialism in Dryden, extending even to his translations, see Sue W. Doederlein, "*Ut Pictura Poesis:* Dryden's *Aeneïs* and *Palamon and Arcite,*" *Comparative Literature* 33 (Spring 1981): 156–66.

11. "D——n J——n's Answer" in *The Poems of Jonathan Swift,* ed. Harold Williams (Oxford: Clarendon Press, 1958), pp. 994–95.

12. Quoted from *The Correspondence of Alexander Pope,* ed. George Sherburn (Oxford: Clarendon Press, 1956), 2:142; by Boyce, *Pope,* p. 119.

13. *Last Instructions to a Painter,* lines 885–906, in *Poems on Affairs of State,* 1:136.

14. "Advice to a Painter," lines 7–8 in ibid., 1:214.

15. *Absalom and Achitophel,* lines 596–97.

16. Ibid., part 2, lines 460–61.

17. Pope, *An Epistle to Dr. Arbuthnot,* line 331.

18. Pope, Epistle 1, *To Cobham,* lines 244–45.

19. *Caricature* was defined in the posthumous tenth edition of Johnson's Dictionary (1808) as "exaggerated resemblance in drawing" and in the edition of 1827 as the "representation of a person or circumstance, so as to render the original ridiculous without losing the resemblance." This definition, though known from the Restoration on, does not appear in the earlier editions published in Johnson's lifetime. The term came into the official dictionaries late no doubt because the popularity of visual caricature in England was relatively late. See M. G. Dorothy George, *English Political Caricature to 1792* (Oxford: Clarendon Press, 1959), vol. 1.

20. *Mac Flecknoe,* lines 106ff.

21. *The Dunciad* (A), 1:43ff.

22. *Imitations of English Poets,* "II. Spenser, The Alley," lines 28ff. in Pope, *Minor Poems,* ed. Norman Ault and John Butt (London: Methuen & Co., 1954), p. 44.

23. See Jonathan Swift, *A Tale of a Tub,* ed. A. C. Guthkelch and D. Nichol Smith (Oxford: Clarendon Press, 1920), p. 240.

24. "A Digression concerning Criticks," ibid., pp. 97–99.

25. "On the Irish Bishops," lines 41–44 in *Poems of Swift,* ed. Harold Williams (Oxford: Clarendon Press, 1937), p. 805.

26. "Ode to the King on his Irish Expedition," line 121, ibid., p. 10.

27. See Mario Praz, *Mnemosyne* (Princeton: Princeton University Press, 1970), p. 137.

28. "My Lady's Lamentation and Complaint against the Dean," lines 67–86, *Poems of Swift,* ed. Williams, pp. 853–54.

29. See Hogarth's copy of a caricature by Leonardo in *Characters and Caricatures* in Ronald Paulson, *Hogarth's Graphic Works* (New Haven: Yale University Press, 1965), vol. 1, pl. 174. For Paulson's commentary see ibid., 2:188–89.

30. Praz, *Mnemosyne,* figs. 55, 56.

31. I owe most of these references to Frederick Antal, *Hogarth and His Place in European Art* (London: Routledge & Kegan Paul, 1962), pp. 130–31.

32. *The Rape of the Lock,* 4:49–52.

33. Item 27 in *Musaeum Clausum* in *The Works of Sir Thomas Browne,* ed. Geoffrey Keynes (Chicago: University of Chicago Press, 1964), 3:115–16.

34. Quoted by Benjamin Boyce, *The Polemical Character, 1640–1661* (Lincoln, Neb.: University of Nebraska Press, 1955), pp. 53, 56–57.

35. M. G. Dorothy George, *Hogarth to Cruikshank* (London: Walker, 1967), figs. 13, 119. Pope's head wears the papal crown and Johnson has ass's ears.

36. Pope, *The Art of Sinking in Poetry,* ed. Edna Leake Stevens (New York: King's Crown Press, 1952), p. 28.

37. *The Dunciad* (B), 1:289–90. For Fielding's comments on Heidegger, see *Tom Jones,* book 13, chap. 7.

38. "Tim and the Fables," lines 17–18, in *Poems of Swift,* ed. Williams, p. 783.

39. James Kinsley, "Dryden's Bestiary," *Review of English Studies* 4 (Oct. 1953): 331–36.

40. *Poems of Swift,* ed. Williams, pp. 82–85.

41. *Spectator,* no. 198 (17 October 1711). For Pope's portrait of Cloe, see Epistle 2, *To a Lady. Of the Characters of Women,* lines 157–80. See also pp. 48, 49–50, and 125 in the present volume.

42. Second frontispiece to *Mores Hominum* (1660). Hogarth represents the satirical muses that inspire Samuel Butler as satyrs. See Hogarth's frontispiece to *Hudibras* in Joseph Burke and Colin Campbell, *Hogarth* (London, 1968), pl. 97.

43. Item 27 in *Museum Clausum,* a work originally printed in the *Miscellany Tracts* (1683). Compare Browne's statement in *A Letter to a Friend*: "When Mens Faces are drawn with resemblance to some other Animals, the *Italians* call it to be drawn in *Caricatura*" (*Works of Browne,* ed. Keynes, 1:106).

44. *Christian Morals,* part 3, sec. 14, in *Works of Browne,* ed. Keynes, 1:280.

45. *Sermon against foolish Talking and Jesting,* quoted by [Corbyn Morris], *An Essay towards Fixing the True Standards of Wit* . . . (London, 1744), p. viii. This essay was republished by the Augustan Reprint Society, Series One: *Essays on Wit,* no. 4 (Nov. 1947), with an introduction by James Clifford.

46. Epistle 3, *To Bathurst,* lines 299–305.

47. Quoted by Boyce, *Polemical Character,* p. 55. See also Flecknoe, *A Collection of the Choicest Epigrams and Characters* (1673), p. 1, for a definition of character as distinct from "Pourtract."

48. Nahum Tate complimenting Thomas Flatman. Quoted by William H. Halewood, " 'The Reach of Art' in Augustan Poetic Theory," *Studies in Criticism and Aesthetics, 1660–1800: Essays in Honor of Samuel Holt Monk,* ed. Howard P. Anderson and John S. Shea (Minneapolis: University of Minnesota Press, 1967), p. 193.

49. Samuel Johnson, *Poems,* ed. E. L. McAdam, Jr., vol. 6 of the *Yale Edition of the Complete Works of Samuel Johnson* (New Haven: Yale University Press, 1964), p. 268.

50. *Spectator* no. 555 (6 Dec. 1712).

51. Pierre Legouis, *Andrew Marvell: Poet, Puritan, Patriot* (Oxford: Clarendon Press, 1965), p. 169.

52. Pope, *An Epistle to Dr. Arbuthnot,* lines 211–12.

53. Quoted from *Guardian* no. 4 by Boyce, *Pope,* p. 12.

54. Boyce, *Pope,* p. 41.

55. John Caryll, "The Hypocrite" (1678), lines 64–67 in *Poems on Affairs of State,* ed. Elias F. Mengel, Jr. (1965), 2:106. See K. H. D. Haley, *The First Earl of Shaftesbury* (Oxford: Clarendon Press, 1968), pp. 201–205. See also Robert Voitle, *The Third Earl of Shaftesbury, 1671–1713* (Baton Rouge: Louisiana State University Press, 1984), pp. 5–7.

56. Quoted by Boyce, *Pope,* p. 114.

57. Quoted from Walpole, *Royal and Noble Authors,* by Osmund Airy, ed., Gilbert Burnet's *History of My Own Time,* 2 vols. (Oxford: Clarendon Press, 1897–1902), 1:183, n. 2.

58. Boyce, *Pope,* p. 75.

59. Quoted by J. Jean Hecht, "Eighteenth-Century Graphic Satire on Historical Evidence," *Studies in Burke and His Times* 10 (Spring 1969): 1258–59. For a study of the relationship between the historical Slingsby Bethel and Dryden's Shimei, showing the poet's ability to make an essential art form from a "few shards of Bethel's public life," see Robert W. McHenry, Jr., "Dryden's History: the Case of Slingsby Bethel," *Huntington Library Quarterly* 47 (Autumn 1984): 253–72.

60. Paulson, *Hogarth's Graphic Works,* vol. 2, pl. 178 (pp. 192–93); for commentary, see 1:192–93.

61. *Spectator* no. 537 (15 Nov. 1712). Hughes is thinking of extreme forms of caricature, for he adds the clause: "but in such a Manner as to transform the most agreeable Beauty into the most odious monster." The most violent qualities of emblematic caricature were eliminated from the practice of portrait caricature; this fact did not affect the definitions until much later (see n. 19 above).

62. *Original and Progress of Satire,* in Ker, 2:93.

63. E. H. Gombrich and E. Kris, *Caricature* (Harmondsworth, Eng.: Penguin Books, 1940), pp. 10–15. On Bernini and caricature Filippo Baldinucci wrote in his life of Bernini, which first appeared in 1728: "Effetto di questa franchezza é stato l'aver egli operato singolarmente in quella sorte di disegno, che noi diciamo Caricatura, o di colpi Caricati, deformando per ischerzo à mal modo l'effigie altrui, senza togliere la somiglianza, e la maestà." This comment is very close to that of Hughes (see n. 61, above), but it makes more of keeping the resemblance. See *Delle Notizie de' Professori del Disegno da Cimabue in qua* 20 (Florence, 1774): 132.

64. *Art of Sinking,* ed. Stevens, p. 15.

65. Epistle I, *To Cobham,* lines 178–79, 181.

66. John Evelyn, *Numismata* (London, 1687), p. 225.

67. Lines 150ff.

68. Lines 544ff. Dryden's portrait should be carefully compared with Burnet's prose description and Butler's character of Buckingham. See esp. Samuel Butler, "A Duke of Bucks" in *Characters,* ed. A. R. Waller (Cambridge, Eng.: Cambridge University Press, 1908), pp. 32–33. Butler calls Buckingham's appetite in pleasure "diseased and crazy"; Dryden calls him a "blest madman." Butler comments on his "excess" and "variety"; Dryden calls him "So over Violent, or over Civil, / That every man, with him, was God or Devil." Burnet may be said to have drawn a historical sketch; Butler, who tries to present a "Monster" that "deforms Nature," provides a kind of emblem caricature; Dryden's, the most devastating of all, is a portrait caricature.

69. Epistle 2, *To a Lady. Of the Characters of Women,* lines 69–86.

70. *The Court and Character of King James* (London, 1650), pp. 178–79.

71. *Hudibras,* 1.1.241ff.

72. In the "Argument" of Satire 6 (*Poems of Dryden,* ed. Kinsley, 2:694).

73. Juvenal said that his victims were all dead, their ashes safely "under the Flaminian and the Latin Road" (see Niall Rudd, *Satires of Horace* [Cambridge, Eng.: Cambridge University Press, 1966], p. 260).

74. For a fuller commentary, see Hagstrum, *Sister Arts,* pp. 236–41.

75. On the popular journalistic satire, verbal and visual, that succeeded the work discussed in this chapter and that adapted the emblem to current political and social events, consult Vincent Caretta, *The Snarling Muse: Verbal and Visual Political Satire from Pope to Churchill* (Philadelphia: University of Pennsylvania Press, 1983).

76. *Don Juan,* canto 3, stanza 100.

77. *The Vision of Judgment,* stanza 66.

78. Germane to the discussions in this chapter of history, portraiture, and the association of the visual and verbal arts is Richard Wendorf, *The Elements of Life: Biography and Portrait Painting in Stuart and Georgian England* (Oxford: Clarendon Press, 1989).

CHAPTER 3

1. Philippe Ariès, *L'Enfant et La Vie Familiale sous L'Ancien Régime* (Paris: Editions du Seuil, 1973), pp. 102–104, 137, 141. Cp. the reproduction opp. p. 104 of Holbein, *The Burgomaster and his Family.* A frontally nude small child is represented, as the family and nuns worship the Virgin and the Holy Child. For a stimulating analysis of children in art (with separate sections on girls and boys), see Edgar Wind, *Hume and the Heroic Portrait: Studies in Eighteenth-Century Imagery* (Oxford: Clarendon Press, 1986). Wind's approach is different from mine: he explains the differing emphases and points of view as arising from philosophy or ethical thought (e.g., Hume's and Samuel Johnson's), especially in the contrasts between Gainsborough and Reynolds (pp. 22–28).

2. See also Jane Lane (Elaine [Kidner] Dakers), *Titus Oates* (Westport, Conn.: Greenwood Press, 1971), p. 17.

3. See Leo Steinberg, *The Sexuality of Christ in Renaissance Art and in Modern Oblivion* (New York: Pantheon Books, 1983). Steinberg, in discussing many hitherto unknown and ignored paintings, shows that the humanity of Jesus was in part established by representations of his sexuality as an infant.

4. The passages in Wordsworth on the child are quoted and discussed by Richard Onorato in *The Character of the Poet: Wordsworth in the* Prelude (Princeton: Princeton University Press, 1971), pp. 182–205; by Peter Coveney, *The Image of Childhood* (Baltimore: Penguin Books, 1967), pp. 68–83; and by Adolph Charles Babenroth, *English Childhood* (New York: Columbia University Press, 1922), pp. 299–396.

5. Both the text of the poem and its colored design are reproduced by Geoffrey Keynes in his facsimile ed. of *Songs of Innocence and of Experience* (New York: Orion Press, 1967).

6. *Collected Essays, Journalism and Letters of George Orwell,* ed. Sonia Orwell and Ian Angus (London: Secker & Warburg, 1968), 4:330–69.

7. *The Friend* for 3 August 1809. See earlier discussion on identity in the chapter on *conscious* (pp. 19–22).

8. Wordsworth, "The Kittern and Falling Leaves," beginning "That way look."

9. For a discussion, see Beverly Fields, *Reality's Dark Dream in Coleridge* (Kent, Ohio: Kent State University Press, 1967), pp. 42–43.

10. Wordsworth, 1850 *Prelude,* 2:239–40. As was frequently the case, the wording of the 1805 *Prelude* (2:243–45) is stronger and more passionate: there the babe

> Doth gather passion from his mother's eye.
> Such feelings pass into his torpid life
> Like an awakening breeze, . . .

11. 1850 *Prelude,* 1:635–36.

12. On Wordsworth and his mother, see Onorato, *The Character of the Poet,* pp. 182–205, and Wallace W. Douglas, *Wordsworth: The Construction of a Personality* (Kent, Ohio: Kent State University Press, 1968), pp. 6–10, 65–69.

13. *Image of Childhood,* p. 29.

14. On this and other sentimental novels, see James R. Foster, *History of the Pre-Romantic Novel in England* (New York: Modern Language Assoc. of America, 1949), pp. 169–85. For a defense of the subtlety of *The Man of Feeling* and of the importance of a multileveled reading, see John K. Sheriff, *The Good-Natured Man: The Evolution of a Moral Ideal 1660–1800* (University, Al.: University of Alabama Press, 1982), pp. 82–91. On fine feeling in general, see Janet Todd, *Sensibility: An Introduction* (London: Methuen, 1986).

15. *The Man of Feeling,* with an introduction by Kenneth C. Slagle (New York: W. W. Norton, 1958), p. 82.

16. On this and other Gothic fiction, see Devendra P. Varma, *The Gothic Flame* (London: Arthur Barker, 1957).

17. Clark, *The Gothic Revival* (London: Constable, 1950), pp. 115–22.

18. See *Three Gothic Novels,* ed. Peter Fairclough, with an introduction by Mario Praz (Baltimore: Penguin Books, 1968), p. 249.

19. See chapter on Eros and Psyche, pp. 78–82 and figs. 4–7.

20. Quoted in Varma, *Gothic Flame,* p. 132.

21. See Roy Pascal, *The German "Sturm und Drang"* (Manchester, Eng.: Manchester University Press, 1953), passim.

22. See Georg Brandes, *Wolfgang Goethe,* trans. Allen W. Porterfield (New York: Frank & Morris, 1925), 1:217–18.

23. George Lukács, *Goethe and His Age,* trans. Robert Anchor (New York: Grosset & Dunlap, 1969), pp. 35–49.

24. Quoted in ibid., p. 47.

25. *The Sufferings of the Young Werther,* trans. Bayard Q. Morgan (New York: Frederick Ungar, 1968), p. 151. See also Werther's long letter to Lotte, found in his desk after his suicide (pp. 135–36).

26. *Oeuvres Complètes,* 4 vols. (Paris: "Bibliothèque de la Pléiade," Editions Gallimard, 1956–69), 1:104.

27. Rousseau, *Confessions,* trans. J. M. Cohen (Harmondsworth, Eng.: Penguin Books, 1970), pp. 106–107.

28. Ibid., pp. 590–91.

29. *Goethe and His Age,* p. 37.

30. Bronson, *Johnson Agonistes & Other Essays* (Cambridge, Eng.: Cambridge University Press, 1946), pp. 1–52.

31. For the context of this phrase, see pp. 24 and 25 in the present volume.

32. Diderot, *Supplement to Bougainville's "Voyage,"* conclusion.

33. Coleridge, *Dejection: An Ode,* stanza 7.

34. Wordsworth, *Resolution and Independence,* stanza 7. For a discussion of the poet's attacks on nature, see my analysis of *Nutting* in *The Romantic Body* (Knoxville: University of Tennessee Press, 1985), pp. 95–96.

35. Introduction to *Three Gothic Novels,* esp. p. 9.

36. Alan D. McKillop, "Local Attachment and Cosmopolitanism—The Eighteenth-Century Pattern" in *From Sensibility to Romanticism,* ed. Frederick W. Hilles and Harold Bloom (New York: Oxford University Press, 1965), pp. 191–218.

37. The emphasis on Romantic regressiveness that appears in this chapter appears again at the end of this volume when I discuss Blake and respond to similar charges made against him (see pp. 242–44). I urge the reader to supplement the view of this essay and that of the immediately ensuing one on Shelley with my treatment of love and sexuality in *The Romantic Body,* which, without negating what I say here, lays more emphasis on the uxorial and long-range commitment in Romantic sensibility. But of course some may see in the patriarchal home, that nineteenth-century love nest with sanctions, simply another form of regression.

CHAPTER 4

1. See Elizabeth Hazelton Haight, *Apuleius and His Influence* (London: G. G. Harrap, 1963), p. 164, and Maxime Collignon, "Essai sur les monuments grecs et romains...," in *Bibliothèque des écoles françaises d'Athène et de Rome* (Paris, 1877), fasc. 2, pp. 285–446, esp. pp. 364, 436–38.

2. Bush, *Mythology and the Renaissance Tradition in English Poetry* (1st ed., 1932; rev., New York: W. W. Norton, 1963), p. 241.

3. Panofsky, "Blind Cupid," *Studies in Iconology* (New York: Oxford University Press, 1962), p. 101.

4. Coleridge, *The Notebooks,* ed. Kathleen Coburn (Princeton: Princeton University Press, 1973), entry no. 3561.

5. Boswell, *Life of Johnson,* ed. George B. Hill and L. F. Powell, 6 vols. (Oxford: Clarendon Press, 1934), 3:246.

6. Blake, *Jerusalem,* plate 32 [36], lines 44–47, in *The Complete Poetry and Prose,* ed. Erdman, p. 179.

7. See the sonnet quoted by Missirini and the accompanying comment in J. S. Mesmes, *Memoirs of Antonio Canova* (London, 1825), pp. 350–63. The word *angel* for woman goes back at least to the *dolce stil nuovo* and was used by novelists from Richardson to Dickens and beyond—sometimes even of virginal men. Cf. Sir Charles Grandison and Angel Claire.

8. Quoted by Mario Praz in *On Neoclassicism,* trans. Angus Davidson (Evanston: Northwestern University Press, 1969), p. 147.

9. Ibid., pp. 148–51. For a fuller discussion of this kind of delicacy, involving the verbal as well as the visual, see my *Sex and Sensibility* (Chicago: University of Chicago Press, 1980), Index, s.v. "Angélisme." See also "Notes on 'Delicacy,' " chap. 12 of C. J. Rawson, *Order from Confusion Sprung: Studies in Eighteenth-Century Literature from Swift to Cowper* (London: George Allen and Unwin, 1985), pp. 341–54.

10. Coburn, *Notebooks,* entry no. 1637.

11. Jung and Knight are quoted or referred to in Jean Perrin, *Les Structures de l'Imaginaire Shelleyen* (Grenoble: [Grenoble] Presses Universitaires, 1973), p. 644.

12. Pater, *Marius the Epicurean,* chap. 5 and beginning of chap. 6. Cf. Byron's "innocence" in a homoerotic relationship (pp. 177–79) and also the discussion of Gray in chap. 8 in the present volume.

13. Coleridge, *The Friend,* essay 1 (1818).

14. Peacock, *Rhododaphne,* canto 7 (London, 1818), p. 144.

15. In a letter to Hogg of 8 May 1817, Shelley says that "the story of Cupid & Psyche [surpasses] any imagination ever clothed in the language of men." He had been reading Apuleius, "a fictitious composition of . . . miraculous interest and beauty." Mary Shelley's fragmentary translation of Apuleius' telling of the legend is preserved in her notebook now in the Poetry Room of the Library of Congress.

16. See, e.g., Edward Carpenter and George Barnefield, *The Psychology of the Poet Shelley* (London, 1925), pp. 56–69.

17. Jean-Pierre Richard on Chateaubriand, quoted by Perrin, *Les Structures,* p. 562.

18. "Essay on Love," *Shelley's Prose,* ed. David Lee Clark (Albuquerque: University of New Mexico Press, 1954; rev. 1966), pp. 169–71.

19. A. J. L. Busst, "The Image of the Androgyne in the Nineteenth Century," in *Romantic Mythologies,* ed. Ian Fletcher (London: Routledge & Kegan Paul, 1967), pp. 3–4, 6.

20. Erich Neumann, *Amor and Psyche* (London: Routledge & Kegan Paul, 1956), p. 59.

21. *Paradise Lost,* 5:475–81. Cf. *Comus,* lines 1002–10.

22. See Carolyn G. Heilbrun, *Toward a Recognition of Androgyny* (New York: Knopf, 1973). For a view of similitude that contrasts strongly with the one presented toward the end of this chapter, see the essay on Samuel Johnson's views of friendship in the present volume (pp. 123–24, 135). Johnson is close in spirit to my earlier illustrations from Rome and the Renaissance (see fig. 4 and p. 77).

CHAPTER 5

1. See Hagstrum, *The Sister Arts,* pp. xxi, 110, 167–68.

2. *Essays of John Dryden,* 2:121.

3. John Heath Stubbs says: *Annus Mirabilis* has "verve and baroque extravagance" as well as "baroque wit" and calls Dryden's heroic ideal "baroque." See "Dryden and the Heroic Ideal" in *Dryden's Mind and Art,* ed. Bruce King (Edinburgh: Oliver & Boyd, 1969), 4:23. Robert Etheridge Moore calls Dryden's special quality in his heroic plays "baroque," and sees in *The Tempest* "a fascinating illustration of the baroque passion for piling into a single word so wide a variety of appeal as to land it straight into the lap of the grotesque" (*Henry Purcell & the Restoration Theatre* [London: Heinemann, 1961], pp. 17, 183). See also Hagstrum, *Sister Arts,* pp. 197–98. Imbrie Buffum regards 1660 as the date for the advent of the baroque into England. If so, Dryden's style in the decade under consideration was abreast of an exciting new development. See *Studies in the Baroque from Montaigne to Rotrou* (New Haven: Yale University Press, 1957), p. viii. See also Margaret Bottrall, "The Baroque Element in Milton," *English Miscellany* 1 (1950): 31–42.

4. On the importance of beginnings in poetic careers, see Lawrence Lipking, *The Life of the Poet* (Chicago: University of Chicago Press, 1981). Stephen D. Cox has said: "Nothing is more common in eighteenth-century literature and philosophy than the search for the 'true self,' ...." See *"The Stranger Within Thee": Concepts of the Self in Late Eighteenth-Century Literature* (Pittsburgh: University of Pittsburgh Press, 1980), p. 7.

5. *Works of Dryden,* ed. H. T. Swedenberg, Jr., et al. (Los Angeles: University of California Press, 1956–), 10:366 (note on *Tempest,* 3.2.38) (hereafter in this chapter cited as *Works).*

6. George Watson, ed., *John Dryden: Of Dramatic Poesy and Other Critical Essays,* 2 vols. (New York: Dutton, 1962), 2:203. Hereafter abbreviated Watson.

7. *Works,* 1:53.

8. See Margarete Baur-Heinhold, *Theater des Barock Festliches Bühnenspiel im 17. und 18. Jahrhundert* (Munich, 1966), passim. See translation by Mary Whittall (London: Thames & Hudson, 1966).

9. Any collection of baroque art will provide examples. See also Raffaelle Carrieri, *Fantasia degli Italiani* (Milan, 1930), passim.

10. The grotesque had its origins in fanciful murals, found in Roman *grotte,* combining human and animal motifs with foliage and flowers. See Arthur Clayborough, *The Grotesque in English Literature* (Oxford: Clarendon Press, 1965), p. 1.

11. "A Parallel of Painting and Poetry" and "Dedication of the *Aeneis*" (1697) in Watson, 2:189, 229.

12. "Parallel," Watson, 2:190. See Clayborough, *Grotesque,* p. 3.

13. See Neander's elaborate definition of humor, in which laughter is associated with the bizarre or fantastic and pleasure with neutral imitation. *Of Dramatic Poesy* (1668), Watson, 1:72–73.

14. See the note on Dryden's contrast between the lazar and Venus in his "Account" of *Annus Mirabilis* (1667) in *Works,* 1:56, 274–76.

15. "Defence of an Essay of Dramatic Poesy" (1668), Watson, 1:114–15.

16. *Works,* 10:110. It must have cost Dryden something to admit the grotesque to his critical system, so committed was he to natural and ideal imitation. Robert D. Hume rightly says that imitation was Dryden's "critical keystone" and that growing realism did not obviate his requirement that art imitate the idea of perfect nature. *Dryden's Criticism* (Ithaca: Cornell University Press, 1970), p. 217.

17. "Upon the Death of Lord Hastings" (1649), lines 82–83.

18. For the references in this paragraph, see "Dedication of Plutarch's Lives," *Works of John Dryden,* ed. Walter Scott and George Saintsbury, 18 vols. (Edinburgh, 1888–92), 17:16–17; "A Short Account of Virgil's Persons, Manners, and Fortune," ibid., 13:311; *Astraea Redux,* lines 45–48; *Annus Mirabilis,* stanza 223; Dedication of *Examen Poeticum,* Watson, 2:167; Second Prologue of *Secret Love,* lines 47–48.

19. Earl Miner's phrase in *Works,* 3:445.

20. These lines and phrases come from the Hind's fable of the Pigeons in *The Hind and the Panther,* part 3, lines 1042–57.

21. Louis I. Bredvold notes Dryden's "delight in testing certain arguments by throwing them into the arena with their opposites. Such a debate is more than a rhetorical exercise; ... it is the vigorous play of the intelligence." *Intellectual Milieu of John Dryden* (Ann Arbor: University of Michigan Press, 1934; reprinted 1966), p. 110.

22. The phrase is quoted by Arthur C. Kirsch in *Dryden's Heroic Drama* (Princeton: Princeton University Press, 1965), p. 58.

23. Preface to *The Rival Ladies* in *Works,* 8:101.

24. For facts of production and publication and for other circumstances relative to these and other plays discussed in this chapter, often with critical commentary, particularly on the music of the poetry, see John Anderson Winn,

John Dryden and His World (New Haven: Yale University Press, 1987), pp. 145–57, 165–68, 178–91, 200–207.

25. *Works,* 9:352. John Loftis concludes, regarding the Dryden-Newcastle collaboration, that the dramatic superiority of the play is owing to Dryden but that much of the comedy may have originated with Newcastle. See *Works,* 9:355–56 and n. 30. F. H. Moore believes that Newcastle wrote the first three acts, Dryden the last two, and that then Dryden went over the whole play, putting it in its final form. But he credits Dryden with the success of the play. See "The Composition of *Sir Martin Mar-All,*" *Essays in English Literature of the Classical Period Presented to Dougald MacMillan,* ed. Donald W. Patterson and Albrecht B. Strauss, *Studies in Philology,* Extra Series No. 4, Jan. 1967, pp. 27–38. Reviewing the evidence, I cannot be absolutely certain that the Warner speeches are peculiarly Dryden's, and my suggestion that he is a Neander especially close to Dryden will have to be regarded as speculation.

26. "To My Honored Friend, Dr. Charleton" (1662), lines 13–14.

27. Jeffrey Spencer has called my attention to a striking parallel to this passage in the essay "Of Canniballs" by "honest *Montaigne*" (as Dryden called him): *Essays,* trans. Charles Cotton, 3 vols. (1685–86), 1:xxx, 366–68. It reads:

I find, that there is nothing Barbarous and Savage in this Nation, by any thing that I can gather, excepting, That every one gives the Title of Barbarity to every thing that is not in use in his own Country: As indeed we have no other level of Truth and Reason, than the Example and Idea of the Opinions and Customs of the place wherein we Live. There is always the true Religion, there the perfect Government, and the most accomplish'd Usance of all things. They are Savages at the same rate, that we say Fruits are wild, which Nature produces of her self, and by her own ordinary progress; whereas in truth, we ought rather to call those wild, whose Natures we have chang'd by our Artifice, and diverted from the common Order. ... neither is it reasonable, that Art should gain the Preheminence of our great and powerful Mother Nature. We have so [oppress'd] her with the additional Ornaments and Graces, we have added to the Beauty and Riches of her own Works, by our Inventions, that we have almost smother'd and Choak'd her; and yet in other places, where she shines in her own purity, and proper lustre, she strangely baffles and disgraces all our vain and frivolous Attempts. ... These Nations then seem to me to be so far Barbarous; as having receiv'd but very little form and fashion from Art and Humane Invention, and consequently, not much remote from their Original Simplicity. The Laws of Nature however govern them still, not as yet much vitiated with any mixture of ours.

28. *Works,* 8:283. This play was written in collaboration with Sir Robert Howard, but the California editors conclude that Dryden is "essentially its creator" and speak of the play as his. Ibid., 7:23.

29. Arthur Kirsch argues that the "real hero" of this play is Cortez (*Dryden's Heroic Drama*, p. 89). There is little doubt that Kirsch is right about Dryden's intention, but the effect of the concluding act is to elevate Montezuma and the philosophy that he expresses.

30. 5.1.43–48. These lines anticipate the majestic opening of *Religio Laici*, where the sun no longer stands for natural religion but for supernatural revelation.

31. This powerful and satirical oxymoron is uttered to the Christian priest by the grieving and embarrassed Cortez, who runs to take Montezuma off the rack: "how now, Religion, do you Frown? / Haste Avarice, and help him down" (5.2.115–16). Whatever may be said about Dryden on English imperialism, his understanding of Spanish behavior in the New World cannot be faulted.

32. "Preface to Troilus and Cressida" (1679), Watson, 1:253.

33. 2.3.160. Maximillian E. Novak concludes that Dryden is essentially right about the nature of his collaboration with Davenant—"that Davenant's role was limited to suggestions for a character like Hippolito, to the writing of some sections concerned with the sailors, and to a general supervision." See *Works*, 10:321. It may be, therefore, that some of the materials we are considering as part of Dryden's vision of the grotesque may be less his than Davenant's. Yet surely, as an intimate collaborator, he was close enough to these scenes to allow us to regard them as a part of his vision of social evil at this time, particularly since they fit Dryden's values so snugly.

34. Compare Horace's monster, with a human head, a horse's neck, feathered limbs, and a fish's tail (*Ars Poetica*, lines 1–5), which Dryden frequently used to exemplify the grotesque. See, e.g., "Dedication of the *Aeneis*," Watson, 2:229; and "A Parallel of Painting and Poetry," Watson, 2:189.

35. *Tempest*, 3.5.121, 154, 155–62.

36. On Mary Magdalenes and Cleopatras that resemble each other in baroque art and on the *madonna voluttà*, see Hagstrum, *Sister Arts*, pp. 119–20, 195–96.

37. Bruce King, *Dryden's Major Plays* (Edinburgh: Oliver & Boyd, 1966), pp. 50–58; see also Louis Teeter, "The Dramatic Use of Hobbes's Political Ideas," *ELH* 3 (June 1936): 161–62.

38. Preface to *Tyrannick Love* in *Works*, 10:112. Novak, who notices the grotesque quality in Maximin, relates it in part to the Emperor's plebeian and boorish qualities (ibid., p. 389).

39. Preface to *Tyrannick Love*, *Works*, 10:109.

40. Note on lines 1121–24 in *Works*, 1:317.

41. See Preface and esp. the following scenes in *The Wild Gallant*: 2.1; 2.2; 3.2; 4.2; 5.2, 3, 4.

42. See Alan C. Dessen, *Jonson's Moral Comedy* (Evanston: Northwestern University Press, 1971), pp. 221–35.

43. Quoted by Kirsch, *Dryden's Heroic Drama*, p. 39.

44. *A Short View of the Immorality and Profaneness of the English Stage,* pp. 61, 191, 193, in a facsimile of 3rd ed., 1698 (Munich, 1967), with a *Nachwort* by Ulrich Broich.

45. "But *Shakespeare's* Magick could not copy'd be, / Within that Circle none durst walk but he" (Prologue to *Tempest,* lines 19–20). For a somewhat different view of the grotesques in Dryden's *Tempest,* see Willard Farnham, *The Shakespearean Grotesque* (Oxford: Clarendon Press, 1971), pp. 156–59, which studies Caliban's transformation "from a monstrous underling capable of strange nobilities of spirit into a monstrous underling pure and simple" (p. 159).

46. *The Secular Masque* (1700), line 93.

47. I borrow this term (used in connection with literature and art) from my own *Samuel Johnson's Literary Criticism* (Chicago: University of Chicago Press, 1967), chap. 1 ("Experience and Reason"), and from Donald Greene's article "Augustinianism and Empiricism: A Note on Eighteenth-Century Intellectual History" in *Eighteenth-Century Studies* 1 (Sept. 1967): 33–68, esp. 34–36. See also Robert D. Hume's discussion in chap. 5 (on neoclassicism) of his *Dryden's Criticism.* For a defense of the use of the term *neoclassicism,* see James William Johnson, *The Formation of English Neo-Classical Thought* (Princeton: Princeton University Press, 1967), chap. 1. I agree with this last work only up to a point, and I myself use the term only in extremely limited contexts and do not apply it to an entire period.

48. The French phrase comes from Irving Babbitt, who used it years ago to attack what he regarded as the Romantics' lack of vital control. It became an important term in his kind of secular humanism.

CHAPTER 6

1. Johnson, Preface to Shakespeare (1765) in *Johnson on Shakespeare,* ed. Arthur Sherbo, vols. 7–8 (1968) of *The Yale Edition of the Works of Samuel Johnson* (New Haven: Yale University Press, 1958–), 7:66 (hereafter cited as *Yale Works*).

2. Ibid.

3. Johnson, *The Rambler,* ed. W. J. Bate and Albrecht B. Strauss, vols. 3–5 (1969) of *Yale Works, Rambler* no. 6 (3:34–35).

4. Johnson, *Poems,* ed. E. L. McAdam, Jr., with George Milne, vol. 6 (1964) of *Yale Works,* pp. 3, 37, 38, 71, 78.

5. Ibid., p. 78.

6. M. Manilius, *Astronomica,* line 142. The idea that the elements are propelled by love and hate and form unity out of discord goes back at least to Empedocles (Fragments 220 [B53]). Other ancients who discuss the cosmology of elemental strife and union, with varying degrees of belief and disbelief, are Plato (*Sophist* 242 D), Aristotle (*Metaphysics* 984b–985a; *De Generatione et Corruptione* 315a:15–20), Horace (*Epistles* 1.12.19, where the phrase *concordia discors* appears), Seneca (*Naturalium Questionum,* 7.27.4, where the phrase *concordia ex discordibus* appears), and Cicero (*Laelius: De Amicitia* 7.24). By the time of the Renaissance, the extension of the idea to *musica humana* from the *musica mundana* had become commonplace. See Spenser, *Faerie Queene* 3.2.15.9. John Denham's *Cooper's Hill* also expresses the idea (lines 203–206).

7. Boswell's *Life of Johnson, Together with Boswell's Journal of a Tour to the Hebrides and Johnson's Diary of a Journey into North Wales,* 6 vols., ed. George B. Hill and L. F. Powell (Oxford: Clarendon Press, 1934–64), 2:101, 4:210 (hereafter cited as *Life).*

8. Johnson, *The Idler* and *Adventurer,* ed. W. J. Bate, John M. Bullitt, L. F. Powell, vol. 2 (1963) of *Yale Works,* pp. 305–306.

9. See pp. 37–48 and 251 n. 41 in the present volume.

10. Hagstrum, *Samuel Johnson's Literary Criticism,* Index, s.v. "Mean, golden."

11. Johnson, *Sermons,* ed. Jean H. Hagstrum and James Gray, vol. 14 (1978) of *Yale Works,* pp. 9, 13–14.

12. Samuel Richardson, *Clarissa,* 4 vols. (Everyman's Library, 1932; rpt. New York: E. P. Dutton, 1967–68), 2:192–93.

13. Johnson to Mrs. Thrale, *The Letters of Samuel Johnson, with Mrs. Thrale's Genuine Letters to Him,* 3 vols., ed. R. W. Chapman (Oxford: Clarendon Press, 1952), 1:325, no. 308.

14. See my comments on Eros and Psyche, pp. 78–92 in the present volume.

15. Johnson to Mrs. Thrale, *Letters,* 2:449–50, no. 749.

16. Thus *contrary* used as a noun is defined as "A thing of opposite qualities," and lines from Southerne's *Oroonoko* point to a valuable contrary in medicine:

> What is not to be cured by *contraries,*
> As bodies are, whose health is often drawn
> From rankest poisons.

Similarly, the second meaning of *discord* ("Difference or contrariety of qualities") is illustrated by lines of Dryden that point to a potential good:

> *Discord,* like that of music's various parts
> *Discord* that makes the harmony of hearts;
> *Discord* that only this dispute shall bring,
> Who best shall love the duke and serve the king.

Johnson also illustrates this meaning with the famous phrase of Pope that all discord is "harmony not understood."

17. Johnson to Boswell and to Mrs. Thrale, *Letters,* 2:326–28, nos. 646, 647.

18. Johnson calls his imaginations "tumultuous," "vain," "depraved," and regards them as being in need of reclamation. Sexual fantasies seem to arise with particular force at the time of his wife's death and recurringly on its painfully remembered anniversaries. But sensual thoughts were not confined to recollections of Tetty. Long after her death and quite apart from its commemoration, Johnson continues to resolve "to reclaim imaginations," to "purify my thoughts from pollution," "to repel sinful thoughts." He confesses that his thoughts "have been clouded with sensuality," and he prays for help "against the incursion of wicked thoughts" and asks God to "give him good desires." See *Diaries, Prayers, and Annals,* ed. E. L. McAdam, with Donald and Mary Hyde, vol. 1 (1958) of *Yale Works,* pp. 46, 47, 51, 53, 64, 69, 70, 71, 79, 92, 276.

19. Hagstrum, *Sex and Sensibility,* p. 270 and n. 53.

20. Johnson, *Irene,* in *Poems (Yale Works,* p. 111). In this chapter, *Irene* citations will be referred to by act, scene, and line in the text.

21. Johnson, Life of Cowley in *Works of Samuel Johnson,* 9 vols. (Oxford, 1825), 7:15–16.

22. Life of Pope, ibid., 8:343.

23. Life of Cowley, ibid., 7:16.

24. For sexuality present even in Wordsworth's criticism, see Hagstrum, *The Romantic Body,* pp. 74–77.

CHAPTER 7

1. Bloom, *The Anxiety of Influence* (New York: Oxford University Press, 1973), p. 28.

2. *Deconstruction and Criticism,* ed. Geoffrey Hartman et al. (New York: Seabury Press, 1979), p. ix.

3. Boswell, *Life of Johnson,* 2:173–74, 449.

4. Quoted by Jonathan Culler, *On Deconstruction: Theory and Criticism after Structuralism* (Ithaca: Cornell University Press, 1982), p. 182.

5. Derrida, *Of Grammatology,* trans. Gayatri Spivak (Baltimore: Johns Hopkins University Press, 1974), p. 165.

6. I owe this and the preceding example to Wendell V. Harris's witty, ironic, but instructive "glossary" in "Contemporary Literary Criticism Made Easy," *The Western Humanities Review,* Summer 1983, pp. 147–53.

7. *Rambler* no. 76, par. 1 in *Yale Works,* 4:34.

8. For these views of Johnson, see my *Samuel Johnson's Literary Criticism* (rev. ed., 1967), pp. xi, 195, n. 31.

9. Frank Lentricchia, *After the New Criticism* (London: Athlone Press, 1986), pp. 148, 267.

10. Miller is quoted in Culler, *On Deconstruction,* p. 23; Miller is applying the language of Nietzsche to his canny critics.

11. These comments come from Johnson's famous attack on the concept of the Great Chain of Being in his review of Soame Jenyns's "Free Enquiry" (*Works of Samuel Johnson* [Oxford, 1825], 6:52, 64).

12. Valéry is quoted by Hartman in *Saving the Text* (Baltimore: Johns Hopkins University Press, 1981), p. xvi.

13. Life of Butler, *Works* (1825), 7:152.

14. René Wellek, "Destroying Literary Studies," *The New Criterion* 2 (Dec. 1983): 3.

15. Boswell, *Life of Johnson,* 1:444.

16. *Rambler* no. 125 (*Yale Works,* 4:300).

17. See W. J. T. Mitchell, *Iconology: Image, Text, Ideology* (Chicago: University of Chicago Press, 1986), p. 97.

18. Searle, "The World Turned Upside Down" (a review of Culler, *On Deconstruction*), *New York Review of Books,* 27 Oct. 1983, p. 79.

19. Rockwell Gray, Harry White, and Gerald Nemanic, "Interview with Saul Bellow," *TriQuarterly* 60, "Chicago" (Spring/Summer 1984): 17.

20. *Dictionary,* 1755, s.v. "lexicographer;" Life of Milton, *Works* (1825), 7:85; Preface to Shakespeare (*Yale Works,* 7:102); *Idler* no. 60, *Yale Works,* 2:185.

21. Life of Cowley, *Works* (1825), 7:1; Boswell, *Life of Johnson,* 3:7; *Rambler* no. 154 (*Yale Works,* 5:59).

22. *Deconstruction and Criticism,* p. vii.

23. *Rambler* no. 25 (*Yale Works,* 3:136–38); *Rambler* no. 129 (*Yale Works,* 4:322).

24. Hartman, *Criticism in the Wilderness* (New Haven: Yale University Press, 1980), pp. 2–4, 196, 204.

25. *Idler* no. 36 (*Yale Works,* 113). All these are in fact subdivisions of the same style.

26. *Idler* nos. 23, 61 (*Yale Works,* 3:127, 192, 217, 219).

27. *Rambler* no. 173 (*Yale Works,* 5:151); *The Plan for an English Dictionary, Works* (1825), 5:31. Emphasis added.

28. *Plan, Works* (1825), 5:31.

29. Ibid., p. 27.

30. Life of Cowley, *Works* (1825), 7:17.

31. Ibid., p. 16.

32. Ibid., p. 17.

33. John Cleveland (1613–58), a royalist poet who was much admired in his lifetime and whom Johnson lists among the immediate "metaphysical" successors of Marino, Jonson, and Donne, caused Dryden to create the term *cleve-landism* for the "wresting and torturing" of a word into another meaning and to say: "we cannot read a verse of Cleveland without making a face at it, as if every word were a pill to swallow...." *Essays of John Dryden,* ed. W. P. Ker, 1:31, 52.

34. Life of Butler, *Works* (1825), 7:152.

CHAPTER 8

1. "Ode on a Distant Prospect of Eton College," lines 91–94. The poetry of Gray is quoted from *The Poems of Thomas Gray, William Collins, Oliver Goldsmith,* ed. Roger Lonsdale (London, 1969) (hereafter in this chapter cited as *Poems*).

2. *The Correspondence of Thomas Gray,* ed. Paget Toynbee and Leonard Whibley, 3 vols. (Oxford: Clarendon Press, 1971), 1:209 (hereafter in this chap. cited as *Corresp.*).

3. "Mourning and Melancholia" (1917) in *Sigmund Freud: Collected Papers,* 5 vols (New York: Basic Books, 1959), 4:152–70.

4. *The Bard,* line 142. Gray's identification with the Bard is quoted in R. W. Ketton-Cremer, *Thomas Gray: a Biography* (Cambridge, Eng.: Cambridge University Press, 1955), p. 134 (hereafter in this chap. cited as *Gray*).

5. Marianne Dashwood says of her recent almost fatal seizure of sensibility: "Had I died,—it would have been self-destruction" (chap. 46).

6. End of chap. 7.

7. See 1st ed. (1794), 4 vols. (1:13–14). The father worries about Emily's "susceptibility" which is "too exquisite to admit of lasting peace." On this novel, see my discussion (pp. 169–75) and also my discussion of Byron (pp. 177–91), for still another version of sensibility.

8. For a fuller discussion of sincerity, see Hagstrum, *Samuel Johnson's Literary Criticism,* pp. 45–46. See also pp. 189–91 in the present volume (on Byron's simplicity).

9. Ian Jack, "Gray's *Elegy* Reconsidered," in *From Sensibility to Romanticism,* ed. F. W. Hilles and Harold Bloom (New York: Oxford University Press, 1965), esp. pp. 145–46.

10. For a sensitive interpretation that links Gray's sensibility to the need for contact with younger writers (but without homoerotic implications), see Morris Golden, *Thomas Gray* (Boston: Twayne, 1988 ["Updated Edition"]), p. 12.

11. See *Gray,* p. 253 and Roger Martin, *Essai sur Thomas Gray* (London: Oxford University Press, 1934), p. 119. Despite my slight disagreement on this point, I admire Martin's study; it remains the profoundest analysis of Gray's character and poetry.

12. Cecil, *Two Quiet Lives* (New York: Bobbs-Merrill, 1948), pp. 184–85. Although less penetrating than Martin, Cecil does acknowledge that Gray was passionate.

13. See *Corresp.,* Appendix A.

14. See *The Autobiography, Times, Opinions, and Contemporaries of Sir Egerton Brydges,* 2 vols (London, 1834), 2:395. Brydges knew Bonstetten, to whom apparently he had talked about Gray.

15. See *Correspondence of Gray and Nicholls,* ed. John Mitford (London, 1843), p. 15, where a letter by T. J. Mathias on the death of Norton Nicholls is quoted.

16. *Corresp.,* 3:926. William Powell Jones has written, "Gray never loved any woman except his mother. . . . He was intimate only with men." *Thomas Gray, Scholar* (Cambridge, Mass.: Harvard University Press, 1937), p. 27.

17. *De Principiis Cogitandi,* Liber Primus, lines 64–84. For a discussion of date, see *Poems,* pp. 321–22.

18. Stephen D. Cox puts matters this way: "His frustrated and repressed homosexuality distanced him permanently from full intimacy with other people." *"The Stranger within Thee,"* p. 88. "Full intimacy" needs definition; if Gray is being denied passionate though not sexually overt relationships with men, the comment is not in the spirit of this analysis.

19. I derived this view from Frank Ellis and expressed it in *The Sister Arts,* p. 295 and n. 12.

20. "Eton," line 40; "Sonnet on the Death of Mr. Richard West," line 8.

21. Wordsworth, "Resolution and Independence," lines 48–49. See also lines 24–28.

22. Emphasis added. I have reversed the order of lines 120 and 124 of the *Elegy.*

23. Duncan C. Tovey, ed. *Letters of Gray,* 3 vols. (London: Bohn's Standard Library, 1900–12), 3:64, n. 3, where Mason is quoted.

24. I owe the Milton example to Roger Martin, *Essai,* pp. 364–65; he quotes it from Mason.

25. *Rambler* no. 28, par. 9.

26. On Mason's excisions, see *Corresp.,* 1:xiii–xvi and editors' notes to several letters from one to 52, and also Roger Martin, *Chronologie de la Vie et de l'Oeuvre de Thomas Gray* (London: Oxford University Press, 1931), pp. 16–17.

CHAPTER 9

1. Auerbach, *Mimesis* (Princeton: Princeton University Press, 1968), pp. 26, 27, 46.

2. See Hagstrum, *The Sister Arts,* Index, s.v. *Enargeia.*

3. See Hagstrum, _The Sister Arts,_ in general.

4. Ibid., pp. 33–34.

5. See Preface to anon. trans. (London, 1719).

6. _Tristram Shandy,_ 4.7. See William V. Holtz, _Image and Immortality_ (Providence: Brown University Press, 1970), a study of Sterne and painting.

7. See p. 119 in the present volume and Judith Kaufman Budz, "Nathaniel Hawthorne and the Visual Arts," Diss., Northwestern University, 1973.

8. Hugh Witemeyer, _George Eliot and the Visual Arts_ (New Haven: Yale University Press, 1979) and my review of Witemeyer in _Nineteenth-Century Fiction_ 34 (1979): 217–20.

9. Viola Hopkins Winner, _Henry James and the Visual Arts_ (Charlottesville: University Press of Virginia, 1970), pp. 74–77.

10. Donald T. Torchiana, _"The Day of the Locust:_ The Painter's Eye" in _Nathanael West: The Cheaters and the Cheated,_ ed. David Madden (De Land, Fla.: 1973), pp. 249–82.

11. James R. Foster, _History of the Pre-Romantic Novel in England_ (New York: Modern Language Association of America, 1949), p. 263.

12. Christopher Hussey, _The Picturesque_ (London: G. P. Putnam's Sons, 1927).

13. Foster, p. 262.

14. Quoted by Devendra P. Varma, _The Gothic Flame_ (London: Arthur Barker, 1957), p. 94.

15. De Quincey's word, quoted by Bonamy Dobrée, ed. _The Mysteries of Udolpho_ (London: Oxford University Press, 1966), p. x.

16. Émile Legouis and Louis Cazamian, _A History of English Literature_ (New York: Macmillan, 1935), p. 970.

17. Foster, p. 265; Varma, p. 86.

18. Dobrée, p. xi.

19. Quoted by Varma, p. 128.

20. See _New Arcadia,_ vol. 1, book 2, passim.

21. Varma, p. 21.

22. Malcolm Ware, _Sublimity in the Novels of Ann Radcliffe_ (Upsala: Lundequistska Bokhandeln, 1963). See also Samuel H. Monk, _The Sublime_ (Ann Arbor: University of Michigan Press, 1960), pp. 217–20.

23. See Elizabeth Manwaring, _Italian Landscape in Eighteenth-Century England_ (New York: Oxford University Press, 1925), pp. 212–18. Manwaring perceives that Mrs. Radcliffe's "most characteristic scenes are composed of a union of the savage and the soft, Salvator and Claude" (p. 217).

24. Catherine Morland "had reached the age of seventeen without having seen one amiable youth who could call forth her sensibility; without having inspired one real passion" (_Northanger Abbey,_ chap. 1). See also my _Sex and Sensibility,_ pp. 268–74.

25. *Mysteries* (London, 1794), 2:170–71. The passages most clearly illustrating the union of expectant love with picture or landscape occur on the following pages of the 1st ed., cited here: 1:26, 89, 277; 2:10 (love is banished by mountains here), 170, 189f., 210, 212, 220, 230; 3:101–102, 336–38, 350, 358; 4: passim, but esp. 189ff., 226ff., 409ff.

26. Donald Greene, "Pictures to the Mind" in *Johnson, Boswell, and Their Circle: Essays Presented to L.F. Powell* (Oxford: Clarendon Press, 1965), pp. 137–39.

27. For other views, not necessarily inconsistent with those presented in this chapter, see Leslie Fiedler, *Love and Death in the American Novel,* rev. ed. (New York: Stein and Day, 1966 [the classic statement of Gothic fiction as a substitute of terror for sexual love]); Robert D. Hume, "Gothic versus Romantic: A Revaluation of the Gothic Novel," *Publications of the Modern Language Association of America* 84 (March 1969): 282–90 (places the novel historically and perceives that a psychological interest is present and that it lies in moral ambiguity); Mary Poovey, "Ideology and *The Mysteries of Udolpho*," *Criticism* 21 (Fall 1979): 307–30 (argues that the novel is escapist only on the surface, that its sentimentality is upper middle class, and that its end restores patriarchy); Donald S. Durant, "Aesthetic Heroism in *The Mysteries of Udolpho*" in *The Eighteenth Century: Theory and Interpretation* 22 (Spring 1981): 175–88 (argues that the author's pictorial style creates a "distinctive philosophy of the mind," expressing her "theory of the visual mind," so dramatizing the experiences of her contemporaries); Mary Laughlin Fawcett, "*Udolpho's* Primal Mystery" in *Studies in English Literature 1500–1900* 23 (Summer 1983): 481–94 (regards Radcliffe's seeing as "primal," in which she views "the place of her own engendering").

CHAPTER 10

1. For a list of poems Leslie Marchand regards as belonging to this series, see *Byron: A Biography,* 3 vols. (New York: Knopf, 1957), 1:108, n. 6; 308, n. 5 (hereafter cited as Marchand). My list is somewhat longer, adding poems from 1816 in which I hear echoes of the Edleston relationship. The poems are quoted from *Lord Byron: The Complete Poetical Works,* vols. 1–5, ed. Jerome J. McGann (Oxford: Clarendon Press, 1980–86). Poems are cited by title and beginning words; for longer poems canto and stanza are given.

After writing this chapter, I came across Bernard Blackstone's brief but sensitive discussion of the Thyrza poems in *Byron: A Survey* (London: Longman, 1975), esp. pp. 74–76, 97–98, 104–105. Professor Blackstone believes that "Dear object of defeated care!" (*Complete Poetical Works,* 1:287–88 and notes) belongs to the Thyrza sequence. Perhaps; but not unmistakably so, and its two short stanzas do not contribute much to the mood and imagery of this poetry. My chief disagreement with Blackstone is that he finds that Edleston takes many different shapes and enters a whole series of "nostalgic-erotic-mystic-guilty-exultant experiences" (p. 76). But I find "Thyrza" to be kept individual, distinct, and set apart, an oasis of ideality and innocence, as it were. As my discussion will show, I do not discover evidence of guilty or ambivalent feelings in Byron about this relationship, though of course Hobhouse may have had them on Byron's behalf.

Recently I have encountered two important studies germane to my topic. See Cecil Y. Lang, "Narcissus Jilted: Byron, *Don Juan,* and the Biographical Imperative" in Jerome J. McGann, ed., *Historical Essays and Literary Criticism* (Madison: University of Wisconsin Press, 1985), pp. 143–79. Lang brilliantly interprets Byron's encounter with the Ali Pacha of Albania as homosexual. His most subtle interpretive strokes are applied to the encounter with Catherine of Russia (*Don Juan,* Canto 9), where, in the bawdiest verse Byron ever wrote, Juan stands for the poet and the queen for Ali Pacha. The article is also a telling defense of the view that biographical facts can alter and influence critical interpretation.

See also Louis Crompton, *Byron and Greek Love: Homophobia in 19th-Century England* (Berkeley: University of California Press, 1985). Crompton believes that Byron was bisexual and that his homoerotic side was characterized by the concealment of desire, alienation, paranoia, and sense of solidarity with others of like orientation that gay men feel in a Christian society (p. 237). Though he calls Byron's love of Edleston "chaste and clandestine" (p. 104), he thinks that the poet's gay orientation came out as he "spoke through the mask of the Thyrza lyrics" (p. 237).

2. "I took the name of Thyrza from Gesner. She was Abel's wife." Quoted in *The Works of Lord Byron. Poetry,* ed. Ernest Hartley Coleridge (London, 1898–1904), 3:30, n. 2. There is nothing in Solomon Gessner's *Death of Abel* (1781, trans. Mrs. Mary Collyer in 1818) that is relevant to this series but much that would interest the reader of *Cain* or *Manfred.*

3. Quoted in Marchand, 1:296, n. 3.

4. For the facts and the quotations in this paragraph, see Marchand, 1:107–108; *Byron's Letters and Journals,* ed. Marchand, Vol. 1: *In My Hot Youth* (Cambridge, Mass.: Harvard University Press, 1973), 88, 110, 122–25. This distinguished scholarly work appeared between 1973 and 1982 in 12 vols.

5. *Letters and Journals,* Vol. 2: *Famous in My Time* (1973), 110, 114, 117, 119–20, 163–64.

6. Marchand, *Byron's Poetry* (Cambridge, Mass.: Harvard University Press, 1968), p. 118.

7. Ibid.

8. *Letters and Journals,* Vol. 3: *Alas! the Love of Women!* (London, 1974), 67.

9. See my discussion of Shelley in the chapter on Eros and Psyche (pp. 85–91).

10. Marchand, 1:57–58, 62, 78, 90 and n. 2, 118 and n. 5, 122; *Letters and Journals,* 1:103ff., 165.

11. *Letters and Journals,* 1:241.

12. See the Latin poem, "Edlestone," beginning "Te, te, care puer." Mourning his dearest friend, recalling their embraces, longing for his own death, he says that remembering his friend means much more to him now than seeking garlands, perfumes, and girls:

> Heu quanto minus est iam serta, unguenta, puellas
> Carpere cum reliquis quam meminisse tui?
>
> > (*Complete Poetical Works,* 1:354, 459)

13. *Don Juan,* 5.158.

14. Knight, *Lord Byron's Marriage* (New York: Macmillan, 1951), p. 14.

15. 2.9, 95–98.

16. Byron: On thee shall press no ponderous tomb;
>   But on thy turf shall roses rear
>   Their leaves . . .

Tibullus: Et 'bene' dicedens dicet 'placideque quiescas,
>   Terraque securae sit super ossa levis.'
>
> > (*Elegia,* 2.4.49–50)

Dryden: The Sacred Poets first shall hear the Sound,
>   And foremost from the Tomb shall bound:
>   For they are cover'd with the lightest Ground.
> ("To the pious Memory of . . . Anne Killigrew," lines 188–90)

On a possible relation between the *Hebrew Melodies* and the Thyrza series, Thomas L. Ashton, editor of *Byron's Hebrew Melodies* (London: Routledge & Kegan Paul, 1972), comments: "Edlestone's voice had made a particularly lasting impression on Byron. Hearing Nathan rehearse his sacred songs perhaps awakened feelings in Byron that made his collaboration with the musician possible" (p. 18).

17. Frye, *Fables of Identity* (New York: Harcourt, Brace and World, 1963), p. 174.

18. For a discussion of sincerity in love poetry, see Hagstrum, *Samuel Johnson's Literary Criticism,* pp. 45–46, and p. 156 in the present volume (on Gray). For a discussion of Byron's ideal of sincerity in *Hours of Idleness* and its immediate antecedents, see Jerome J. McGann's discussion in *Fiery Dust: Byron's Poetic Development* (Chicago: University of Chicago Press, 1968), pp. 10–27. McGann's point—that it is not sincerity so much as an illusion of sincerity that governs and that illusion is related to poetry as a "self-dramatizing vehicle" (p. 26)—seems applicable to the *Hours* as a whole and to Byron in

general. In my view the less sophisticated neoclassical ideal of direct sincerity is more applicable to the Thyrza poems, which tend to lack variety, self-dramatization, wit, extravagance, and posturing.

19. Eliot, *On Poetry and Poets* (1937), quoted in M. H. Abrams, *English Romantic Poets* (New York: Oxford University Press, 1960), p. 197.

20. See McGann, *Fiery Dust,* pp. 9–12, for a description of Moore's poetry and for an appreciation of how the young Byron absorbed it.

21. Cited in *The Oxford Anthology of English Literature (Romantic Poetry and Prose),* ed. Harold Bloom and Lionel Trilling, 3 vols. (New York: Oxford University Press, 1973), 2:310 n.

CHAPTER 11

1. Annotations to An Apology for the Bible (1798), *The Complete Poetry and Prose of William Blake,* ed. Erdman, p. 614 (hereafter cited as E.).

2. See Ellis K. Waterhouse, *Painting in Britain 1530–1790* (London: Penguin Books, 1953), whose 192 plates contain not a single Christ; Eric Mercier, *English Art 1553–1625* (Oxford: Clarendon Press, 1962), whose 96 plates contain only one Christ; and chap. 8 ("Le Renouveau de l'Art Religieux") in Marcel Brion, *Peinture Romantique* (Paris: Editions Albin Michel, 1967), esp. p. 231.

3. See Robert Rosenblum, *Transformations in Late Eighteenth-Century Art* (Princeton: Princeton University Press, 1967), pp. 28–29.

4. See the dozen or so paintings that portray Christ in Pierre Gassier and Juliet Wilson, *Life and Complete Works of Francisco Goya* (New York: Reynal & Co., 1971).

5. For the biblical passages quoted or alluded to in this paragraph, see John 2:21, 1 Cor. 6:19, Eph. 5:21, 1 Peter 2:24, Col. 1:14, 1 Cor. 12:12, 15:44.

6. For a reproduction, see E., pl. 2; for text, E., pp. 273–75.

7. See Annotations to An Apology for the Bible, passim, but esp. E., p. 620.

8. This phrase Paine coined in *The Crisis,* vol. 7 (1778); it is quoted by Moncure Daniel Conway, ed., *The Writings of Thomas Paine* (New York: G. P. Putnam's Sons, 1899), 4:6.

9. Frederick Tatham's manuscript Life of Blake (*c.* 1832) in G. E. Bentley, Jr., *Blake Records* (Oxford: Clarendon Press, 1969), p. 531. The phrases quoted are not marked as direct quotations from either Paine or Blake; the language may therefore be Tatham's.

10. The quotations from Paine in this paragraph come from Conway, *Writings,* 4:25, 26, 423. For other comments on Jesus and the Bible, see pp. 32, 34, 39, 45, 165, 169, 293. For Paine the resurrection was the story of an apparition created by timid minds (p. 169), and he confesses to knowing Job and the Psalms poorly (p. 48).

11. Kathleen Raine, *Blake and Tradition* (Princeton: Princeton University Press, 1968), 2:15.

12. The quotations from Priestley in this paragraph are drawn from the following: *An History of Early Opinions concerning Jesus Christ* (1786), 1:61, 179; 4:[1]; *The History of the Corruptions of Christianity* in *Theological and Miscellaneous Works of Priestley* (1818), 5:92; *A General History of the Christian Church* (1790) 1:iv. For the ideas attributed to Priestley in this paragraph, see also ibid., 1:12 (on the resurrection and immortality); *The Doctrines of Heathen Philosophy* (1804), dedication and p. v (on his profession of Christianity and on Socrates and Jesus); *General History*, 1:xxii (on medieval Christianity); *Institutes of Natural and Revealed Religion* in *Works*, ed. Joseph Rutt (1817), 2:84 (on depraved religions, including the burning of wicker-works filled with men); and *Autobiography*, ed. Jack Lindsay (Teaneck, N.J.: Fairleigh Dickinson University Press, 1970), p. 111 (Priestley's profession of faith while in Paris).

13. See Jean H. Hagstrum, *William Blake: Poet and Painter* (Chicago: University of Chicago Press, 1964), p. 126.

14. I refer to the Huntington Library series; the illustrations in the Museum of Fine Arts, Boston, contain only four designs in which Christ appears. For a reproduction of all the *Paradise Regained* illustrations, see Joseph A. Wittreich, Jr., ed., *Calm of Mind: Tercentenary Essays . . . in Honor of John S. Diekhoff* (Cleveland: Case Western Reserve University Press, 1971), plates 1–12. For an interpretation, see Wittreich's article, "William Blake: Illustrator-Interpreter of *Paradise Regained,*" ibid., pp. 93–132.

15. Department of Prints and Drawings, 1860–6–16–133. Reproductions of the other works by Michelangelo referred to appear as follows: Paolo D'Ancona and others, *Michelangelo* (Milan, Bramante, 1964), pl. 1, illustrations 29, 41, 213; Ludwig Goldscheider, *Michelangelo* (London, Phaidon Press, n.d.), plates 155–57, 229; Frederick Hartt, *Michelangelo Drawings* (New York, Harry N. Abrams, n.d.), illustrations 180–85, 350, 408–30.

16. The paintings referred to so far in this paragraph are reproduced in Geoffrey Keynes, *William Blake's Illustrations to the Bible* (London, 1957), under the following titles: *The Virgin Hushing the Young Baptist,* pl. 99, and *Christ in the House of the Carpenter,* pl. 108.

17. Blake here illustrates *Paradise Lost,* 8:452–90. The Young illustrations in this paragraph are the following, referred to by the number pencilled on the original in the British Museum: 68 (Night II, p. 35: the Good Samaritan); 512 (Night IX, p. 94: Christ as the vine); 534 (Night IX, p. 116: Christ reclining at table).

18. Keynes, *Bible,* pl. 111 (*Christ Baptizing*).

19. Frontispiece (in color) to Keynes, *Bible.*

20. Kerrison Preston, *The Blake Collection of W. Graham Robertson* (London: Faber & Faber, 1952), pl. 14.

21. *Four Zoas*, deleted marginal lines from Night the First (E., p. 825); *Jerusalem*, 90:34–38 (E., p. 250).

22. *Four Zoas*, Night the Eighth, p. 104, 2nd portion (E., p. 378); *Jerusalem*, 9:9–19 (E., p. 152); *Milton*, 42 [49]:12 (E., p. 143). I recognize—and have studied in "Babylon Revisited, or the Story of Luvah and Vala"—many other meanings of the mantle, or robe, of Luvah and the body of Vala, meanings that refer to the corrupt Church and the warlike State. But here I urge that the primary and literal meaning of physical passion be retained. See Joseph Wittreich and Stuart Curran, ed., *Blake's Sublime Allegory* (Madison, University of Wisconsin Press, 1972).

23. Annotations to Reynolds (E., p. 660); A Vision of the Last Judgment (E., p. 555); *Jerusalem*, pl. 77 (E., p. 231); letter to Cumberland, 12 Apr. 1827 (E., p. 783–84).

24. See Young illustrations frontispiece to whole work (fig. 14); 127 (*Night* 4, p. 18); 121 (Ibid., p. 12); "The Little Girl Lost" (E., pp. 20–21); "Ah! Sun-Flower" (E., p. 25); *America*, 6:2, 5 (E., p. 53). See also the following representations of the risen Christ: *Christ Appearing to the Apostles* in Martin Butlin, *The Paintings and Drawings of William Blake* (New Haven: Yale University Press, 1981), cat. nos. 326, 327, pls. 417, 418; *The Conversion of Saul* in Butlin, cat. no. 506, pl. 575.

25. Bentley, *Records*, pp. 42, n. 1; 283.

26. Germain Bazin, *Fra Angelico* (London: Hyperion Press, 1949), passim and esp. pp. 56, 78–79, 89–91, 116, 141; John Pope-Hennessy, *Fra Angelico* (London: Phaidon Press), pl. 55 and passim.

27. See Butlin, cat. nos. 401, 402, pls. 502, 503 (*The Nativity, The Adoration*); Keynes, *Bible (Child Praying)*. Milton in his *Nativity Ode*, where Christ is referred to as "That glowing Form, that Light unsufferable/And that far-beaming blaze of Majesty" (stanza 2), and some of Fra Angelico's paintings may have influenced Blake's portrayals of Christ in mysterious light. See the *Transfiguration* in Florence (Pope-Hennessy, pls. 93–94) and *The Harrowing of Hell* in Wilhelm Hausenstein, *Fra Angelico* (Munich: Kurt Wolff, 1923), pl. 23.

28. Butlin, cat. nos. 429, 463, 464, pls. 497, 551, 553 (*Christ the Mediator, Christ Girding Himself with Strength, Mercy and Truth are Met Together*).

29. *Vision of the Last Judgment* (E., p. 554). For Blake's *Epitome of James Hervey's "Meditations among the Tombs,"* see Butlin, cat. no. 770, pl. 967.

30. *Vision of the Last Judgment* (E., p. 560).

31. Samuel Palmer said that Blake "was fond of the works of Saint Theresa, and often quoted them with other writers on the interior life" (Bentley, *Rec-*

ords, p. 41). See *Jerusalem,* 72:50–51 (E., p. 227) and *Milton,* 22 [24]: 54–61 (E., p. 118).

32. See Jean H. Hagstrum, "The Wrath of the Lamb: A Study of William Blake's Conversions" in F. W. Hilles and Harold Bloom, eds., *From Sensibility to Romanticism* (New York: Oxford University Press, 1965), pp. 311–30.

33. Anna Brownell Jameson, *Sacred and Legendary Art* (reprinted from ed. of 1896; New York: AMS Press, 1970), 2:444.

34. Memling's altarpiece bears the full title, *Virgin Enthroned with Saints, Angels and the Donor Sir John Donne of Kidwelly and his Family.* Now at the National Gallery, London, it was formerly in the Duke of Devonshire's collection at Chatsworth. Blake, who loved early Christian art, undoubtedly had seen Memling originals and engravings. His friends, Charles and Elizabeth Aders, owned several Memlings, but apparently no Saint Christopher. See J. D. Passavant, *Kunstreise durch England und Belgien* (Frankfurt am Main, 1833), pp. 92–98 and Bentley, *Records,* p. 310, n. 1. I am not arguing a direct influence but saying that Blake knew the Christopher legend and found its expression in early (fifteenth century) art congenial to his imagination.

35. 513 (Night 9, p. 95), 527 (ibid, p. 109), 528 (ibid., p. 110).

36. 148 (Night 4, p. 39), 485 (Night 9, p. 67), 513 (ibid., p. 95), 531 (ibid., p. 113); and possibly also 518 (ibid., p. 100) and 529 (ibid., p. 111).

37. 261 and 263 (Night 6, pp. 40, 42); 264 (an illustration with no text); 265 (a title-page illustration).

38. Pp. 114, 115, and 116 in the manuscript of *Vala, or the Four Zoaz.* See the facsimile ed. by G. E. Bentley, Jr. (Oxford: Clarendon Press, 1963). For the Christian revisions of *Vala,* see ibid., pp. 174ff.

39. See Hagstrum, *Blake: Poet and Painter,* plates 20–24 and p. 43.

40. Bentley, *Vala,* p. 122.

41. E., p. 722. Emphasis added. Albert S. Roe in his *Blake's Illustrations to the Divine Comedy* (Princeton: Princeton University Press, 1953) rightly believes that this epistolary poem is parallel to Dante's vision of Christ (which he reproduces as his plate 90); he also finds *Jerusalem,* 4:1–5 (E., p. 147) and Blake's *Crucifixion* (see fig. 76) to be parallels (p. 176).

42. *Jerusalem,* 96: 7 (E., p. 255). Emphasis added.

43. Ibid., 38 [43]: 20–21 (E., p. 185) and pl. 3 (E., p. 145).

44. For the passages quoted in this paragraph and for the conception of form as manly and familial, the crucial passages are: *Jerusalem,* 38 [43]: 10–28 (E., pp. 184–85) and ibid., 33 [37]: 14–26 (E., p. 180).

45. For the quotations and allusions in this and the preceding paragraph, see *Jerusalem,* 38 [43]:19 (E., p. 185); ibid., pl. 52 (E., p. 201); Annotations to Lavater (E., pp. 583–601); A Descriptive Catalogue, section 5, comment on p. 47 (E., p. 544); Apostrophe to Nature from Shaftesbury, *The Moralists*; Pope, *An Essay on Man,* 4:361–66.

CHAPTER 12

1. *Four Zoas,* 5:29 in E., p. 303; ibid., 99:1 in E., p. 371.

2. The phrase comes from *America,* 16:14 (E., p. 57), but is fully applicable to the *Marriage.*

3. For the quotations from and references to Blake in this paragraph, see *The Book of Urizen,* pls. 15, 18 (E., p. 78); *Four Zoas,* 21:1–6 (E., pp. 310–11); 21:4 (E., p. 306); 39:10 (E., p. 327); 71a:5 (E., p. 348); 133:26 (E., p. 402); *Milton,* 14:33, 35 (E., p. 108); *Jerusalem,* 34:8, 21 (E., pp. 179–80).

4. *Four Zoas,* 20:12–13 (E., p. 313); 105:16–17 (E., p. 378); *Milton,* 20:44 (E., p. 114); 35:1 (E., p. 135): *Jer.,* 15:18–20 (E., p. 159); 55:3 (E., p. 204).

5. See later, p. 278 n. 16, for a different mood as death approached.

6. *Jer.,* 55.1 (E., p. 204); 68:65 (E., p. 222); Blake's letter to George Cumberland, 12 Apr. 1827 (E., p. 784). The unfortunate absence of women in Great Eternity cannot be discussed here, but on the subject of women in Blake, see my *Romantic Body* pp. 136–40. It should be remembered that Great Eternity, as distinct from Eden, technically represents, at least in part, the great of the Western tradition, and not possibilities open to men and women now.

7. *Jer.,* 55:16–17 (E., p. 204). See also *Urizen,* 19:2–9 (E., p. 78); *Four Zoas,* 22:39 (E., p. 312); 115:42–50 (E., p. 38); *Jer.,* 55:1–35 (E., pp. 204–205).

8. S. Foster Damon, *A Blake Dictionary* (Providence: Brown University Press, 1965), s.v. "Eyes of God"; *Four Zoas,* 115:49 (E., p. 381); 108:14 (E., p. 383). For a discussion of Urizen, see John Sutherland, "Blake and Urizen," in *Blake's Visionary Forms Dramatic,* ed. David V. Erdman and John E. Grant (Princeton: Princeton University Press, 1970), pp. 244–62. This chapter is intended to resist Sutherland's belief that "Blake was never in any danger of being dominated by Urizen" (p. 259).

9. *Four Zoas,* 12:8 (E., p. 307); 79:23–24 (E., p. 355); 119:21, 23 (E., p. 389); Annotations to Bacon for p. 67 (E., p. 625). Compare the phrase that Blake applies to Urizen, "Schoolmaster of souls," with Galatians 3:24: "Wherefore the law was our schoolmaster."

10. Bentley, *Blake Records,* p. 316.

11. See p. 200 in the present volume for other aspects of Michelangelo.

12. Urizen is anticipated frequently in Blake's first work, *Poetical Sketches,* published in 1783 (see esp. "Winter" and the several warlike tyrants, human and divine, of the dramas); in *Tiriel,* a searing portrait of a political and domestic tyrant; in *The French Revolution,* with its visions of aged terror, full of imagery intimately associated with Urizen. Urizen is of course a presence in both the words and designs of *The Songs of Experience* and of the Lambeth prophecies. It should be noted that he appears as a tyrant before he appears as Reason, and there is little doubt that his tyranny is a more basic and important quality than his rationality. In other words, he fits the patriarchy, religious and political, more closely than he fits the Enlightenment and Deism.

13. See Leopold Damrosch, *Symbol and Truth in Blake's Myth* (Princeton: Princeton University Press, 1980), pp. 153–55.

14. *Milton,* 10:1 (E., p. 104), emphasis added; 38:51, 56 (E., pp. 139–40).

15. Harold Bloom, *Poetry and Repression: Revisionism from Blake to Stevens* (New Haven: Yale University Press, 1976), p. 2.

16. Letter to John Flaxman, 12 Sept. 1800 (E., p. 708); letter to Thomas Butts, 22 Nov. 1802 (E., p. 720). Blake's own fear of emptiness must have been lifelong. In an amazing letter written to John Linnell in the year of his death, he confesses to a "terrible fear" at the thought of moving (Blake's term is "removal," which must refer to changing of abode), an "Intellectual Peculiarity," as he called his fear, that left him only these alternatives—to be "shut up in Myself" or to be "Reduced to Nothing" (Feb. 1827; E., p. 782).

17. Quoted in a review by Stephen Spender in *New York Review of Books,* 30 June 1983, p. 26.

18. Harold Bloom, *A Map of Misreading* (New York: Oxford University Press, 1975), pp. 10, 78–80. See also *Figures of a Capable Imagination* (New York: Seabury Press, 1976), p. xii.

19. Joseph A. Wittreich, Jr., *The Romantics on Milton: Formal Essays and Critical Asides* (Cleveland: The Press of Case Western Reserve University, 1970), pp. 113, 119, 276.

20. For Bloom's brilliant analysis of the Merkabah image, see *Poetry and Repression,* pp. 83–95.

21. "Preface to *The Excursion,*" lines 62–68 in *Poetical Works of William Wordsworth* (Oxford: Clarendon Press, 1949–72), 5:5.

22. *Milton,* 13:20–21 (E., p. 107); 23:51 (E., p. 119); *Four Zoas,* 9:17 (E., p. 305); 56:19–27 and 55b:21–22 (E., p. 338). The cosmic law is what Blake calls "the Universal Dictate"; it is, as articulated by Blake's Milton, to "despise death, not to fear it, and to annihilate the self in mutual love." *Milton,* 21:53 (E., p. 116); 38:34–41 (E., p. 139). From such Christlike incarnation, resurrection results. Blake is never more Christian than in his expression of this universal law of sacrificial, incarnational love.

23. In connection with this belief in form, it is interesting to note that Blake felt the need to redefine the term "infinity" in his late works. The word could be a virtual synonym for God. But in *Jerusalem* it is said, "The Infinite alone resides in Definite & Determinate Identity" (55:64 [E., p. 205]), and in *Milton* the sons of Los create forms "with bounds to the Infinite putting off the Indefinite" (28:4 [E., p. 125]). David E. James sees Blake's *Laocoön* (a representation of "Jah & his two Sons Satan and Adam") as portraying a reversal of the fall, beginning the process of regeneration through the assumption of spatial and temporal form. If so, *Laocoön* can be regarded as a manifestation of the Divine Hand at work. See *Publications of the Modern Language Association of America* 98 (March 1983): 226–36. The idea that ultimate reality embraces the principle of limit and form may distress those who dwell too much on Blakean exuberance and who confine measure and boundary to Urizen alone. But neither he nor God can be understood without the idea of the Divine Hand, nor indeed can the idea of contraries, which include both Reason and Energy.

24. See Thomas McFarland, *Romanticism and the Forms of Ruin* (Princeton: Princeton University Press, 1981), p. 201.

25. *Jer.,* 25:9 (E., p. 170). Leslie Tannenbaum, in *Biblical Tradition in Blake's Early Prophecies* (Princeton: Princeton University Press, 1982), pp. 202–208, believes Blake derives a sharp separation between Jehovah and Elohim from the two distinct narrative accounts in Genesis, Elohim being evil and associated with Urizen, Jehovah being good and associated with Los. The argument is not compelling even for the earlier prophecies; for Blake as a whole it tends to ignore or deemphasize the powerful association Blake establishes between Urizen and Jehovah in their fallen state: both are leprous and Sinaitic; both are thunder-gods and associated with stars; both are patriarchal and accept worship from their suffering victims.

26. See Ronald Paulson, *Representations of Revolution (1789–1820)* (New Haven: Yale University Press, 1983), pp. 31, 363.

27. Sigmund Freud, *Standard Edition of the Complete Psychological Works* (London: The Hogarth Press, 1955–), 18:105. See also 11:172–73; 17:27–28; 21:183.

28. C. G. Jung, *Collected Works,* ed. Sir Herbert Read et al. (New York: Pantheon Books, 1955–), 5:333, 391; 7:109–110; 9:1, 215–16; 12:123.

29. Poem in a letter to Thomas Butts, 2 Oct. 1800, lines 72–74 (E., p. 713).

30. See my *Romantic Body,* pp. 122–30.

31. A descriptive Catalogue, Number V (E., p. 545).

32. Letter to Dr. Trusler, 23 Aug. 1799 (E., p. 703).

33. See especially sermons 3, 4, and 16 in *Samuel Johnson: Sermons* (Yale Works, 14:29, 39, 176). I do not wish to suggest that the supreme being for Johnson was not also a gracious and benevolent father, but to emphasize the dominant qualities.

34. *Jer.,* 92:17–19 (E., p. 252).

Index

Index